Nigeria in the Fourth Republic

Nigeria in the Fourth Republic

Confronting the Contemporary Political, Economic, and Social Dilemmas

Edited by
E. Ike Udogu

LEXINGTON BOOKS
Lanham • Boulder • New York • London

Published by Lexington Books
An imprint of The Rowman & Littlefield Publishing Group, Inc.
4501 Forbes Boulevard, Suite 200, Lanham, Maryland 20706
www.rowman.com

86-90 Paul Street, London EC2A 4NE, United Kingdom

British Library Cataloguing in Publication Information Available

Library of Congress Cataloging-in-Publication Data available

ISBN 978-1-66690-049-1 (cloth)
ISBN 978-1-66690-050-7 (electronic)

Contents

Foreword

A Salute to Honorable Professor Julius O. Ihonvbere: An Intellectual Giant in Nigeria's Currently Challenged Political Tunnel

A. B. Assensoh and Yvette M. Alex-Assensoh

Indeed, all the contributors to this book, as a very special volume, have provided their respective chapters as a tribute to the Honorable Professor Julius O. Ihonvbere, as one of the founding members of the US-based African Studies and Research Forum (ASRF).[1] The volume certainly represents the unrelented efforts of the editor and contributors to convey to the readers the essence as well as the measure of what it takes for Julius to be appreciated, especially as he currently is a valuable member of the Federal House of Representatives for Edo State's Owan Federal Constituency in Nigeria.

As an active founding member of the ASRF, Professor Ihonvbere, in a variety of ways, collaborated enthusiastically with and keenly supported many members of this esteemed research-oriented forum. The end-results included the production of very remarkable scholarship as well as the exhibition of high-quality administrative endeavors on the part of the various bona fide members of the group.

Dr. E. Ike Udogu, a former director of Research and Publications of the ASRF and professor of Political Science, took the initiative to assemble several distinguished Pan-African scholars of the highest caliber to produce chapters that constitute this volume, which is appropriately titled *Nigeria in the Fourth Republic: Confronting the Contemporary Political, Economic, and Social Dilemmas*.

The participating scholars of this project are Professors George Klay Kieh, Jr., dean of the School of Public Affairs at Texas Southern University and president, ASRF; Olufemi Vaughan, an endowed professor of Amherst College; Kelechi A. Kalu, an international affairs professor and ex-vice provost at University of California-Riverside; Bennett A. Odunsi a 2012 Topp's

African-centered scholar of the Decade award recipient at Jackson State University in Mississippi; A. B. Assensoh and Yvette M. Alex-Assensoh of Indiana University and University of Oregon; Philip C. Aka, former dean of the Faculty of Law of International University of Sarajevo in Bosnia and Herzegovina; Joseph A. Balogun, a distinguished professor in the College of Health Sciences at Chicago State University; and Samuel Zalanga, professor of Sociology at Bethel University (and current director of Research and Publications for the ASRF).

The Honorable Professor Ihonvbere earned his Bachelor of Arts (BA) degree in History and Political Science from University of Ife (now Obafemi Awolowo University, OAU), Nigeria; received his Master of Arts (MA) degree in International Relations from the Norman Paterson School of International Affairs of Carleton University in Ottawa, Canada, and, in 1984, he capped it all by earning his Doctor of Philosophy (PhD) degree in Political Science from Canada's University of Toronto.

With a very strong belief in the axiom that charity begins at home, the young Political Science scholar returned to Nigeria to serve his alma mater (OAU) as an assistant lecturer in International Relations. Subsequently, he joined the faculty of University of Port Harcourt to lecture in Political Science before accepting a position at one of his Canadian alma maters (University of Toronto) as a visiting professor. Then, in 1993, upon being appointed as an associate professor of Political Science at Houston-Tillotson College of University of Texas, in Austin, he moved from Toronto; after attaining the rank of professor of government, Dr. Ihonvbere left to join the staff of New York-based Ford Foundation. In his new Ford Foundation position, he was generously supportive of the ASRF and several of its members through his grantsmanship largesse on research and conferences. These were backings and measures which aimed at advancing democracy, good governance, and development on the African continent.

AN INTELLECTUAL WORTHY OF EMULATION

Our revered colleague is both a scholar and a political activist. Indeed, as an academic, he published in numerous national and international journals, including *Journal of Third World Studies* (now re-named as *Journal of Global South Studies*); *Africa Today*, published by Indiana University Press; *The Journal of Modern African Studies*; *International Politics*; *Third World Quarterly*; *World Development*; *African Development Magazine*; former *West Africa Magazine* of London, UK; *The Journal of Political and Military Sociology*, among several others.

Additionally, in the scholarly realm, Professor Ihonvbere has authored/co-authored as well as edited and co-edited many mainstream books with academic precision; coupled with as many as nine full monographs; about eighty refereed academic papers; as many as fifty book chapters; and numerous commentaries and, indeed, varied invited researched-*cum*-conference papers. Below are several of his impressive volumes:

- *Political Liberalization and Democratization in Africa: Lessons from Country Experiences* (co-edited with John Mbaku)
- *Africa and the New World Order*
- *Towards a New Constitutionalism in Africa*
- *Labor, State and Capital in Nigeria's Oil Industry*
- *The Illusions of Power: Nigeria in Transition* (with Timothy Shaw)
- *Multiparty Democracy and Political Change: Constraints to Democratization in Africa* (co-edited with John Mbaku)
- *Nigeria: The Politics of Adjustment and Democracy*
- *Economic Crisis, Civil Society and Democratization: The Case of Zambia*
- *The Rise and Fall of Nigeria's Second Republic, 1979–1984* (with Toyin Falola)
- *The Political Economy of Crisis and Underdevelopment in Africa: Selected Works of Claude Ake*
- *Towards a Political Economy of Nigeria: Petroleum and Politics at the (Semi-) Periphery* (co-authored with Timothy Shaw)
- *Nigeria and the International Capitalist System* (co-edited with Toyin Falola)

AN INTELLECTUAL GIANT IN NIGERIA'S CHALLENGED POLITICAL TUNNEL

As noted previously Professor O. Ihonvbere is both a very serious academic and a "benevolent" political activist. It is, therefore, certainly neither an exaggeration nor gainsaying to assert unequivocally that Nigeria, although very much oil rich and an OPEC member, has faced various teething political challenges, just like almost all other postcolonial African nation-states. Yet, very dedicated citizens like the Honorable Professor O. Ihonvbere have, in the face of the well-known challenges, returned home from their self-imposed exiles to confront national politics squarely in the face.

Consequently, he served as a special adviser to former president Olusegun Obasanjo on Program and Policy Monitoring as well as later becoming the secretary of state of Edo State. Currently, he represents an important constituency (Owan) of Edo State in Nigeria's Federal House of Representatives. According to the available legislative records, he has, very impressively, been serving actively in varied positions of the Federal House of Representatives, which include, but are not limited to, those of the deputy chairman, Ad-hoc Committee on Media and Public Affairs; chairman of Ad-hoc Committee on Rules and Business; as chairman, Ad-hoc committee on the Legislative Agenda that designed the Legislative framework of the ninth Assembly known as the Legislative Agenda of the House of Representatives, Federal Republic of Nigeria, 2019–2023; and, also, he was selected to chair a committee to work on a background for the establishment of a National Assembly Archives. Accordingly, we today count the intellectual giant among the actively serving members in the Federal House of Representatives, where he is squarely rubbing shoulders with the fellow elected House Members.

The ASRF and its entire membership, indeed, admire their intellectual colleague's tenacity to serve and his zeal to succeed in Nigeria's very challenging political tunnel. In fact, he has been described by the civil society organization (AFRIGOV) as one of the most widely published politicos in the nation's political history and who also is among the selfless as well as influential political actors in Nigeria today.

Having served with distinction, his fellow human beings and society in general, this Member of the House of Representatives has been honored with numerous traditional titles from various geographic areas of Nigeria, and they include the following: *Irialugie* of Auchi Kingdom, *Ogieanor* of Uzuaire, and the *Iyase* (traditional Prime Minister) of Luleha in Owan West Local Government Area of his beloved Edo State of Nigeria.

WINNING TRUST AND APPLAUSE OF INTELLECTUAL COLLEAGUES

In view of the foregoing transparent and impressive achievements of Professor Ihonvbere, his US-based intellectual colleagues of the ASRF approved the publication of this volume in appreciation of his services to the group, academia, and his beloved country—Nigeria.

We end our foreword to this comprehensive and admirable volume with a salute to our Honorable Professor Julius O. Ihonvbere for his impressive as well as wide-ranging contributions to scholarship and his contemporary serious efforts geared toward good governance in the oil-rich Federal Republic of Nigeria, affectionately dubbed as the "Giant of Africa."

A.B. Assensoh is an Emeritus Professor of Indiana University and Courtesy Emeritus Professor of University of Oregon. He earned his Ph.D. in history from New York University, and his Master of Law (LL.M.) degree is from University of Oregon School of Law. Yvette M. Alex-Assensoh serves as Professor of Political Science and Vice President of Equity and Inclusion at University of Oregon. She received her M.A. and Ph.D.degrees in Political Science from The Ohio State University, and her Juris Doctorate (J.D.) degree with honors from the Maurer School of Law at Indiana University

NOTE

1. Professors A. B. Assensoh and Yvette M. Alex-Assensoh are an intellectual duo, who have co-authored extensively. Their published books include *African Military History and Politics: Ideological Coups and Incursions, 1900-Present* (Palgrave-Macmillan, 2003). *African Political Leadership: Jomo Kenyatta, Kwame Nkrumah, and Julius Nyerere* (Krieger Publishing, 1998); *Malcolm X: A Biography* (Greenwood/ABC-CLIO, 2014); *Malcolm X and Africa* (Cambria Press, 2016); *Kwame Nkrumah's Political Kingdom and Pan-Africanism Re-interpreted, 1909–1972* (Lexington Books, 2022); *Kofi Annan, Biography* (African Histories' Series, 2022).

Preface

Nigeria is a troubled country and at the crossroads not because of lack of resources, human capital, population, ethnic, and religious composition per se. The country has been in turmoil since she gained home rule in 1960, in part because of the authoritarian governance technique of the political actors who inherited power from the departing colonial overseers and military interregnums that frequently meddled in politics. The problem of uniting the interests of a society with deep ethno-religious and social divisions from the start was and is difficult partly because the colonial administration arguably wanted it to be that way to be able to control the vast territory called Nigeria.

My contention is that the genre of governorship inherited by Nigeria's political captains at the end of colonial rule has endured in postcolonial Nigeria, principally by way of education and political socialization. In other words, it was difficult for Nigerian nationalists carefully schooled and socialized in the governance methods of the colonial administrators to suddenly peel off the authoritarian character imbibed during colonial rule. In short, the imperial power in London governed autocratically but imposed on its successors a liberal democratic constitution and form of government; it was and is an impossible mission, some academics have argued, for Nigeria's new leaders who mimicked the colonial officers' governance genre and technique to adopt liberal democracy. They loved their inherited power and displayed it on Nigerian compatriots who were and are expected to treat them with the same quality of respect as they did to the colonial supervisors. The problems that arose, and that still exist in Nigeria, after the granting of self-rule to the polity were, and are, how to free Nigerian leaders from their authoritarian ways: a situation that was exacerbated by military despotism.

Today, the issue is how to superimpose autocratic rule with the principles of liberal democracy. Liberal democracy presupposes conducting free and fair elections, adhering to the rule of law, protection of minority rights, separation of powers, respecting the due process of law, promoting the existence of more than one political party, implementing an efficacious constitutional document, insisting on government accountability, respecting freedom of the press, and instituting an independent judiciary. The problem that Nigeria's custodians of the state confront in adopting the dogmas of liberal democracy proficiently has led in part to the current political, social, economic, and religious quandaries and disarticulations in Nigeria.

Nigeria is in its Fourth Republic after sixty years as a sovereign state; she is currently wrestling with the question of its existence as a corporate state with deep and serious ethno-religious conflicts and economic instability that are about to tear the country asunder. Solutions to resolve the political nightmares in the country exist in the constitutions and in the works of numerous academics, experts, and journalists—not least in the book, *Nigeria in the Twenty-First Century: Strategies for Political Stability and Peaceful Coexistence*. In this volume, the chapters "The Need for an Effective Policy of Ethnic Reconciliation" and "Building a Sustainable Democracy and Political Stability in the New Millennium" are tackled by Philip C. Aka and E. Ike Udogu. In sum, in view of the country's perennial crisis that has tended to stultify its great development, I appreciate the collaboration of these seasoned scholars to this illuminating volume, *Nigeria in the Fourth Republic: Confronting the Contemporary Political, Economic, and Social Dilemmas*.

Acknowledgments

I am highly indebted to members of the ASRF for their support of scholarship on Africa since its founding in the 1990s. Indeed, it is refreshing that the ASRF will be celebrating its Silver Jubilee in 2021. This celebration will in part highlight the troupe's prodigious publications that can fill many bookshelves with weighty volumes. This achievement has been possible because of the indefatigable hard work of its members. I salute the ASRF for its scholarly contributions to academia in the last twenty-five years.

In putting together this timely book, I would like to thank the contributors who in the face of the devastating COVID-19 pandemic accepted my invitation to submit a chapter for this volume—one dedicated to Professor Julius O. Ihonvbere, a founding member of the ASRF and once its benefactor. These are Professors George Klay Kieh, Jr., Kelechi A. Kalu, Philip C. Aka, Joseph A. Balogun, Bennett A. Odunsi, Olufemi Vaughan, Samuel Zalanga, A. B. Assensoh, and Yvette M. Alex-Assensoh. I extend my special thanks to these Africanists and their institutions whose continued support has in part made it possible to contribute to this volume. Suffice it to say, however, that the views expressed in this book are those of these scholars and not those of the academies that they are associated with. I appreciate your patience with my constant and sometimes irritating memos badgering you on the deadline to submit your chapter.

I thank my colleagues in the Department of Government and Justice Studies, Appalachian State University, Boone, North Carolina, USA, for their unflinching support of my research endeavors as a faculty fellow. They made my experience as an academic very rewarding. Many thanks to my graduate assistants—some of whom I co-authored books, book chapters, articles, and book reviews.

I am grateful to my immediate family for putting up with my stress and frustration when I am overwhelmed with work and when my writing seems to have come to a cul-de-sac. I thank you for understanding my predicament and your unwavering support. Thank you for your opinions and counsels Emmanuel O. George and Akpaego I. Emmanuel. You are greatly appreciated for your input.

It is hoped that Nigerians, including Nigerian academics specializing in Nigerian politics, would find this important volume useful as we collectively seek ways to promote political stability and peaceful coexistence in the republic. In other words, this is a propitious moment in Nigerian history for scholars, politicians, entrepreneurs, and ordinary citizens to join hands together in making this potentially great country even greater in the continent and globally. This was the inspiration and aspiration that informed the contributors to this significant volume, *Nigeria in the Fourth Republic: Confronting the Contemporary Political, Economic, and Social Dilemmas*.

List of Abbreviations and Acronyms

ASRF	African Studies and Research Forum
CAN	Christian Association of Nigeria
CEDAW	Convention on the Elimination of All Forms of Discrimination Against Women
DC	District of Columbia
ECOWAS	Economic Community of West African States
EFCC	Economic and Financial Crimes Commission
FMH	Federal Ministry of Health
GDP	Gross Domestic Product
HDI	Human Development Index
FDI	Foreign Direct Investment
FSCA	Federal Sharia Court of Appeal
HCW	Health Care Workers
HIV	Human Immunodeficiency Virus
IGP	Inspector General of Police
IPOB	Indigenous People of Biafra
MASSOB	Movement for the Actualization of the Sovereign State of Biafra
MDGs	Millennium Development Goals
NAFDAC	National Agency for Food and Drug Administration and Control
NAPPPHRN	National Action Plan for the Promotion and Protection of Human Rights in Nigeria
NBC	Nigerian Broadcasting Commission
NHA	National Health Act
NHIS	National Health Insurance Scheme
NHMIS	National Health Management Information System

NNPC	Nigerian National Petroleum Corporation
NPC	Northern People's Congress
NPN	National Party of Nigeria
NSCIA	Nigerian Supreme Council for Islamic Affairs
NUC	National Universities Commission
NYSC	National Youth Service Corps
OAU	Organization of African Unity
OIC	Organization of Islamic Conference
OOP	Out-of-Pocket
PDP	People's Democratic Party
PLWDs	People Living with Disabilities
R&D	Research and Development
SAP	Structural Adjustment Program
SARS	Special Anti-Robbery Squad
SDGs	Sustainable Development Goals
SNC	Sovereign National Conference
TB	Tuberculosis
UHC	Universal Healthcare
UK	United Kingdom
UN	United Nations
UPN	Unity Party of Nigeria
US	United States
VAPP	Violence Against Persons Prohibition
WHO	World Health Organization

Chapter 1

General Introduction

E. Ike Udogu

Nigeria's Fourth Republic commenced in 1999 after she gained independence in 1960 from Britain. However, since attaining self-rule, the country has been progressing from pillar to post politically. This experience suggests that it was one thing to gain home rule and quite another to govern the society effectively. It is true that the glue theory that agglutinated the various ethnic cleavages in the fight for emancipation became unglued as soon as politics, or the struggle for power, commenced within the nation-state. Regrettably, the politics of ethnonationalism soon superseded the politics of nationalism in the competition for the control of the national cake with the marginalization of the minority ethnic groups who lacked the numerical strength and resources to compete successfully in the political contests.

Initially, the assumption was that the proverbial elephant had been slaughtered, and there was enough "meat" for everyone. Propitiously, the three titanic ethnic groups in the polity were so powerful and selfish that they wanted the whole elephant to themselves in the politics of who gets what, when, and how. The result of this political approach to governance was political volatility for as the saying goes a "hungry man is an angry man." Accordingly, the country was faced with political malaise with military interventions and the fall of one regime after another and coups and countercoups. Little wonder, then, that Nigeria is now in its Fourth Republic—with the probability of a Fifth Republic. This historic reality urgently calls upon the business, military, political, intellectual, and religious elites, among others, to intervene collaboratively to avert the current political, economic, and social abyss in which the republic finds itself.

The concern today is on how to tackle the issue that some scholars called the "National Question." Academics concerned with the national question allude to, or draw attention to, the problematic structure of the pseudo federal system in Nigeria. This is so because although the country is said to be a federation, it is administered like a unitary system of government. The truth of the matter is that the leadership is aware of the shortcomings in the way the state is run. For example, the president Olusegun Obasanjo and Goodluck Jonathan administrations setup the Political Reform Conference of 2005/2006, and the National Conference of 2014, to wrestle with the structural defects in the political system. In the end, however, the recommendations and outcomes of these meetings came to naught because they were not implemented.[1] In short, the preceding developments highlight the political trepidations caused by the worthy, but futile attempts made by regimes, statespersons, and members of the informed public to resolve the present politico-economic and socio-religious dilemmas confronting the Nigerian state.

Arguably, the situation in Nigeria, as in other African countries, has never been the deficiency of templates for solving the vexing issue of political instability in the country; the problem is that, lamentably, lawmakers have failed to apply the models sophisticatedly crafted by academics and other experts with the interest of the republic at heart for resolving the country's political, economic, and social glitches. This quandary has been so either because the actors lack the political courage to do so or because of the theory of privilege. Moreover, political actors lack the audacity to fix the system because of the influence of their benefactors and business oligarchs; they exert pressure on politicos not to enforce "positive" laws because such rules work against their interests. The theory of privilege asserts that those in a position of privilege would not give it up simply for the sake of promoting harmony or political stability. In short, they have enjoyed the prestige that flows from their position of privilege so much so that they are unwilling to "sacrifice" it just for the sake of advancing political stability in a political system that has been so beneficial to their group or class interest(s).[2]

Despite the foregoing conditions and postulations, it would be foolhardy to throw in the towel on a country that is a bellwether in the African continent due to its abundant natural resources and human capital. This is especially so at a combustible moment when the clamor by centrifugal forces—religious, ethnic, and other troupes—for disintegration has reached its crescendo. For nationalists their answer to Nigeria's present condition, or what has been referred to in Nigerian parlance as the "National Question," is the ambiguous and much debated current political concept known as "restructuring." What are some of the motives for demanding that the Nigerian polity should be restructured to further political stability and peaceful coexistence? Attahiru M. Jega provides the following brief list: (1) Heightened mobilization and politicization of ethnic, regional, and religious identities; (2) deep-rooted perceptions of marginalization (by certain minority and majority collectivities); (3) bad governance (by political actors who are not nationalists and see the state as their private fiefdom); (4) crisis of rising expectations (and frustrations by citizens who see the vast natural resources being squandered by a few); (5) increasing devastating poverty, joblessness, and deteriorating socioeconomic conditions of the citizens (in the midst of plenty); (6) brinkmanship (of political actors/war lords who must recoup, at whatever cost, their investments in electoral contestations).[3] A contemporary emphasized solution that tends to subsume other solutions for confronting the political problem is "true federalism." Those who advocate the practice of this form of governance have been very vocal and presumptuous of its efficacy in a system that has been run in a unitary modus operandi or technique since the problematic incursion and institution of a military rule in 1966.

Nevertheless, some of its ardent supporters continue to agitate for a return to Federal Constitutional Governance structure akin to that of 1960 and 1963 independence and republican constitutions. These observers have adamantly and consistently argued that it is superior to the current constitution that on paper asserts that the country is a federal republic but administered in a unitary method. Given the national character of the country's ethnic mosaic and power distribution, ethnic minorities have been vociferous in calling for true federalism. In this scheme, the states will, inter alia, govern their societies and manage their generated resources and the federal government would manage defense and foreign affairs mainly.

Indeed, the youths of the South and the Middle Belt have been marching, rallying, and protesting on the streets in favor of moving the country toward the practice of true federalism. These visible demonstrations have exacerbated political angst and instability in the republic. These agitations, moreover, have promoted mutual distrust among its citizens that is emblematic and reminiscent of the inflammable political milieu before the advent of the Nigerian Civil War of 1967–1970 that claimed so many lives.[4] It is critical for scholars and others interested in Nigerian unity to constantly act to resolve the political, economic, and social quandaries currently inherent in the polity.

This volume, *Nigeria in the Fourth Republic: Confronting the Contemporary Political, Economic, and Social Dilemmas*, is a tribute to Professor Julius O. Ihonvbere. He was a founding member of the African Studies and Research Forum. Our impetus to write on this topic is related to his membership in the Nigerian House of Representatives and our concerns on the preceding issues and how to solve them. We believe that Nigeria has the potential for greatness and that her best years are yet to come if politicos would promote a spirit of nationalism among its diverse nationalities. Most importantly, her leaders would have to cultivate the political pluck to implement the splendid reports of national conferences, and templates suggested by scholars and experts on how to advance political stability and peaceful coexistence in the nation-state. In this way, Nigeria would not squander its golden opportunity to develop substantially and shine in the continent and globally. To resolve the perennial problem of instability in the society will require a dedication by all Nigerians, and supporters of Nigeria, to the struggle of confronting the daunting challenges in the Fourth Republic.

It was against the backdrop of the foregoing political angst in the country that the African Studies and Research Forum undertook the intimidating task of writing this book. It is intended to be a small step, but a significant one, in the group's move to contribute toward the process of solving the society's political, economic, and social quagmires. Accordingly, the seasoned scholar, George Klay Kieh, Jr., wrote chapter 2 titled "'False Starts' and Missed Opportunities in Nigerian Politics." Just as he has done in his other edifying works on democracy, state failure, and collapse,[5] he brought his expertise to bear on this topic. Using "false starts and missed opportunities analytical paradigm," Kieh, Jr., examined the nature and dynamics of the "false starts" and missed opportunities during critical historical junctures in Nigerian politics, that is, state building. For example, he starts with a brief history on the character of the political chiefs who inherited the colonial state from the British overseers. They mimicked the governance genus of the departing imperial power.[6] Kieh, Jr., then makes a laconic allusion to the nature of the First Republic (1960–1966), the first military intervention (1966–1979), the Second Republic (1979–1983), the second military intervention (1983–1993), the aborted "Third Republic" (1993), the third military intervention (1993–1999), and then delved into the "Fourth Republic" (1999–present)—the nitty-gritty of the chapter and volume.

The genesis of the Fourth Republic began in 1999 under General Obasanjo, who exchanged his military uniform for *agbada* and became the first president of the Fourth Republic. Given his politico-military experience in Nigeria, many national and international observers had high hopes that he would lead Nigeria to the political promised land—flowing with milk and honey. He was nationalistic, spoke and wrote splendidly in support of democracy and human rights.[7] No sooner was he elected to power, however, than his advocacy for democracy and defense of human rights became hollow. Indeed, many scholars and admirers who cheered him on to power were bewildered by his sudden change to authoritarianism and self-delusion that he was a political messiah. He tried to abrogate the constitution so that he could run for a third term and failed. An explication of this peculiar political metamorphosis in leaders—especially political leaders—is explained poignantly by Farooq A. Kperogi accordingly:

> Almost everyone I know wonders why people in power change radically; why they become so utterly disconnected from reality that they suddenly become completely unrecognizable to people who knew them before they got to power;

> why they get puffed-up, susceptible to flattery, and intolerant of even the mildest, best-intentioned censure; why they appear possessed by inexplicably malignant forces; and why they are notoriously insensitive and self-absorbed. Everyone who has ever had a friend in a position of power, especially political power, can attest to the accuracy of the age-old truism that a friend in power is a lost friend. Of course, there are exceptions, but it is precisely the fact of the existence of exceptions that makes this reality poignant. . . . Abraham Lincoln once said, "Nearly all men can stand adversity, but if you want to test a man's character, give him power." Look at all the power brokers in Nigeria—from the president to your ward councilor—and you'll discover that there is a vast disconnect between who they were before they got to power and who they are now.[8]

Even though the centrality of this volume is on confronting the contemporary political, economic, and social quagmires in the Fourth Republic with a view to providing solutions, this chapter suggests that there is need to understand the past political developments. In other words, it is essential to comprehend the causes of past political, economic, and social pitfalls to design theories that might avert these difficulties in the present republic. This chapter exposes some of the faux pas in Nigerian political history so that they are mitigated or not deliberately repeated by future political leaders in the Fourth Republic.

Indeed, it was the character of the state in colonial Nigeria that determined the disposition of Nigerians who inherited the state from the departing administrators following home rule. Accordingly, the political, economic, and social problems of Nigeria in the Fourth Republic have their genesis or roots in the past. By fully acknowledging how they started and combating them, Nigerians can use her vast human capital and material wealth that she is endowed with to play a major role in Africa, the world, and like India explore the universe.[9]

The clamor for the breakup of the country by some groups in Nigeria in the Fourth Republic has a lot to do with the governance technique and attitude of those political actors who assume that being elected to office gives them license to exploit the national coffers. But this assumption is further from the truth. Arguably, if only the Gowon administration had used the wealth from oil proceeds in the late 1970s to develop the society, infrastructure, and institutions efficiently, probably the country would not be in the present political, economic, and social predicaments in the Fourth Republic. Today, restructuring and a return to true federalism have become the rallying cries of minority and marginalized groupings who because they are denied justice, equity, and fair play in the polity demand a change from the contemporary functioning unitary system.[10] In this way, each state can exploit its raw materials and use the proceeds to develop the state and pay taxes to the federal government a la the brief First Republic.

This chapter "'False Starts' and Missed Opportunities in Nigerian Politics" is highly relevant to the current nature of Nigeria's political system. It is a comprehensive analysis that informs the reader of the political character of the state, political class, and citizens reminiscent of Rene Dumont's book, *L'Afrique Noire est Mal Partie* (*False Start in Africa*), on the continent's development project. In this volume, Dumont suggested, among other things, that colonialists, political actors, and Africa's intelligentsia were culpable for Africa's underdevelopment. More importantly, he had hoped that African intelligentsia would collaborate evocatively with each other on how to solve Africa's problems. But they did not, and the rest is history on Africa's development trajectory. In fact, Dumont noted emotionally:

> It has become increasingly clear that there has indeed been a false start in Africa. It is a false start, which is part of the legacy from Africa's colonial past. . . . There has been a false start, too, by the academicians in their efforts to speak meaningfully to each other and to Africa's law makers.[11]

In addition to highlighting the false starts and missed opportunities in Nigerian politics, Kieh, Jr., suggests areas for the Nigerian intelligentsia to cooperate and fight for the purpose of promoting the country's illusive national unity and development. It has been over five decades since Claude Ake pointed out a false start and proffered a major solution to the republic's politics that if it had been implemented would have, sans doute, resolved Nigeria's political, economic, and social conundrums. He argued robustly that the establishment of a political culture that could command national legitimacy was and is needed for successful governing in Nigeria. Indeed, he contended that the fundamental problem of unity in Nigeria has two elements or features: (1) How to elicit deference and devotion to the claims of the state (suggesting the conversion of ethnic nationalism to nation-state nationalism or I am a Nigerian first notion or dogma)[12] and (2) How to boost normative consensus governing political behavior among citizens. This implies that to promote national unity necessitates developing a political culture—say democracy—and urging citizens' pledge or obligation to it.[13]

In sum, this chapter "'False Starts' and Missed Opportunities in Nigerian Politics" provides readers with succinct instances in which false starts were made and opportunities missed. In this regard, Kieh, Jr., assessed the performances of Presidents Obasanjo, Yar' Adua, Jonathan, and Buhari's regimes on human rights, corruption, and human material wellbeing and, overall, found them wanting and culpable. He found many "false starts and missed opportunities" in these administrations that together have made the governance project and praxis in the Fourth Republic problematic. Accordingly, if these three indices—human rights, corruption, and human material wellbeing—are to be improved in the Fourth Republic, major collaborative steps must be undertaken by patriotic politicos, citizens, and transformational leaders. In short, the improvement in these areas where the country has experienced false starts and missed possibilities would enable the country to shine. This development would enable citizens to claim the nation's greatness that has been squandered on the altar of political, economic, social, and religious insularity by many leaders in the Fourth Republic.

He concludes, however, that the panacea for ending the perennial cycle of false starts and missed opportunities in Nigeria is the democratic reconstitution of the state by patriotic politicians, citizens, and transformational leaders. [This process] includes structural transformation of the political economy, power relations (both in the state and society), and the emergence of a new generation of transformational and servant leaders.

Chapter 3, "Public Policy and Economic Development in Nigeria," is written by Kelechi A. Kalu whose scholarship is exemplified by his extensive publications in the areas of public policy, economics, conflicts, and conflict resolutions.[14] The crux of this chapter is the hypothesis that in Nigeria politics drive policy and consequently adequate policies formulated to advance good governance and development are inefficacious for most citizens. Indeed, this supposition is illustrated by Tunji Olaopa who in the Nigerian case revealed:

> Policymaking is the very essence of the government. It is the means by which the intention of government is communicated on how it wants to facilitate infrastructural development, [for example], that will improve the welfare of the citizens. And that process is unabashedly competitive, with significant bargaining involved that demands prioritization and opportunity lost and gained. In other words, policy preferences of one group are maximized against others i.e., no one group, or constituent can be made better off without others being made worse [i.e., zero-sum-game]. Thus, some interests are inevitably more satisfied than others, and whoever is most satisfied depends on who has most political clout and lobbying capacity.[15]

In politics the struggle for power reigns supreme and is frequently based on zero-sum game as the preceding view suggests. Subsequently, good policies are set aside by politicians who fear that not allowing "politics to drive policies" could make them lose the next election. The chapter contends that a government that implements policies to promote economic development for the citizenry would make investment in the infrastructure a sine qua non because it supports entrepreneurial investments which could in turn generate wealth and a tax base for the regime. This is so because businesses are likely to generate employment for the unemployed and thereby ameliorate national angst issuing from the effect of unemployment. Such a government policy could promote the "theory of economic circulation" which could advance development. In this project, the government will be advancing a development strategy that would be beneficial to most citizens and the nation-state itself.

In this chapter also Kalu historicizes and contextualizes the problems the republic has had with its development projects and suggests why some of the well-crafted plans have failed despite their noble intentions. One of such projects was the Ten-year Plan for Development and Welfare for Nigeria (1946–1955). Other plans were enacted in 1962–1968, 1975–1980, and so on. Moreover, measures undertaken to improve economic development in Nigeria were Operation Feed the Nation (1975–1979), Green Revolution (1980–1984), Vision 2020 (2007–2009), among others. These good plans and measures aimed at boosting economic development were not efficacious in part because leaders selfishly placed politics before policy.

This chapter went a step further to provide examples of the leadership genres of Generals Gowon and Obasanjo to illustrate how leadership matters if Nigeria is to tackle the problem of her leaders placing the cart before the horse—that is, politics before policy in decision-making. The issue that arises from their governance technique was and is that the process of development in the society is hampered and some of the political developments in the Fourth Republic could be traced to Gowon and Obasanjo's leadership genus. The chapter argues that in Gowon's (1967–1975) efforts to transform Nigeria, he launched two major programs, namely, the Indigenization Program and the National Youth Service Corps (NYSC).

The Indigenization Program, overall, was intended to encourage Nigerians to take charge and ownership of running the businesses in the country with a view to making them compete with other industrial economies globally. In Gowon's indigenization scheme, he adopted in narrow terms the Soviet or Stalinist model of de-nationalizing the light industries such as candle making and hairdressing and nationalizing the heavy industries such as steel, oil, and fertilizer enterprises. His laudable NYSC in which a college graduate serves the nation for a year in a state other than his or her state of origin was intended to improve the ethnic, religious, and sectional chasms that exist between the future leaders of Nigeria.

Obasanjo's attempt to transform the country happened when he courageously assumed power following the assassination of General Murtala Muhammed and transferred power to a civilian rule in 1979. Following the failed civilian regimes-cum-military juntas, Obasanjo experienced a political resurrection after he became a "born-again" democrat to serve as a civilian leader. He expressed his interest for civil society organizations, human rights groups, and pro-democracy troupes. For this gesture, hopes were high that Nigeria had finally found her political savior. But very much like other leaders before him, hopes that he would exculpate Nigeria from her economic quagmire dissipated.

This chapter suggests that both Gowon and Obasanjo depicted two forms of leadership genres—transformational and transactional—in their attempts to implement national policies. Transformational leaders are those leaders who place the interest of the society above parochial or sectional interest a la Abraham Lincoln and transactional leaders are those who believe in a quid pro quo or reciprocal relationship. Whereas Gowon, in his leadership style, seemingly portrayed himself as a transformational leader, Obasanjo was very much a transactional leader. The chapter suggests that for Nigeria to be successful she needs transformational leaders who would place policy before politics to advance economic development in the republic.

At the heart of this chapter is the quest to tackle the causes of the contemporary economic quandaries in the society by offering solutions. Put in another way, the chapter highlights the cocktail for Nigeria's economic developments that call for transformational leaders with the political courage to implement efficient policies. This is the case because they are more likely, than transactional leader, to take the risk of letting good policies and not politics inform their decisions, and therefore implement policies for the betterment of the country and not a sectional or ethnic group. It is in this regard that Kalu alludes to four challenges Nigerian economy, as articulated by Dr. Ngozi Okonjo-Iweala, the finance minister in President Obasanjo's administration, face. These are poor economic management, promoting private enterprise as the primary engine of growth, empowering people by improving the delivery of basic service, and investing in agriculture. The chapter then notes some strategies to alleviate the preceding problem and to place Nigeria on the path to the much-needed development in the Fourth Republic. Some of these are wealth creation, poverty reduction, strengthening the management of public finances, among other things. As is the case with similar recommendations, the foregoing solutions were not implemented by the incoming regime because politics trumped policy. Kalu, in his recommendations on the contemporary difficulties confronting the country, discusses comprehensively some solutions.

To promote sustainable economic development in Nigeria can be possible under the condition of what President Kennedy termed "competitive cooperation" in US versus Soviet relations. The suggestion here is that the various nationalities should compete in the production of resources that could assist in the development of a region and its collectivity. This was the case when the North was famous for its groundnut pyramids, the West for its cocoa, and the East for her palm oil and coal. The nationalities should cooperate in trade and in the defense of the motherland from external threats and other areas of national interests.

His other recommendation is that of sharing the oil revenue in such a manner as to cause less angst among the oil-producing states. It is a given that the revenue sharing formula changed when oil became Nigeria's "black" gold. In this process, the areas that produced crude oil were marginalized to their chagrin and consternation. Attempts to address the needs of the oil-producing states to their satisfaction on this matter have been inadequate. However, it would be necessary to confront this economic dilemma to advance political stability and peaceful coexistence in the Fourth Republic.

Chapter 4, "Strategic Reforms to Resuscitate the Nigerian Healthcare System," is written by two distinguished scholars Joseph A. Balogun[16] and Philip C. Aka.[17] This chapter is an excerpt from a compressive report on the healthcare dilemma in Nigeria compiled by these authors. The moral dimension of this chapter for Nigeria is that "the generation of wealth and development in a society happen when the citizens are healthy." This supposition is analogous to the cliché "Health is Wealth." Accordingly, Nigeria needs an adequate universal healthcare system to prosper in the Fourth Republic. The political tragedy of the republic is that despite the fabulous wealth it once produced from oil proceeds, ironically, the country does not have suitable state hospitals that can provide healthcare needs to ordinary citizens, let alone the president, wealthy, and powerful Nigerians. Thus, some of her political leaders have sought medical treatment overseas. This reality highlights the problematic condition of Nigerian healthcare system. In this chapter, these authors, among other things, expose and highlight some of the weaknesses in the healthcare system and provide recommendations on how to ameliorate these shortcomings in the Fourth Republic.

Indeed, as long ago as 2000, the World Health Organization assessed Nigeria's healthcare system and rated it as "dysfunctional, ineffective, undercapitalized, costly, and inaccessible." It ranked the country's performance at 187 out of the 191 countries evaluated. Paradoxically, in an oil-rich country, more than half of the citizens lack access to health services. Statistically, it has one of the highest infants, child, and maternal mortality rates and the average life expectancy rate is fifty-five years. This chapter suggests that one of the major causes of the weak healthcare system in the country is political. And as noted in chapter 3, politics often influence policy outcomes so much so that adequate policies are ignored by politicians in pursuit of political and self-interests. When government officials are paid allowances for receiving healthcare overseas, the incentive to construct adequate medical facilities at home becomes less attractive. This abusive practice is referred to in Nigerian parlance as "medical tourism."

To combat the contemporary healthcare quandaries in the Fourth Republic, the authors suggest and elaborate on the following: Nigeria's leaders should recommit themselves to the Abuja Declaration on Optimal Budgetary Allocation, promote increased participation in the National Healthcare Insurance Scheme, expand access to essential medicines and vaccine, strengthen the health information system, tackle the shortage of healthcare workers, improve the conditions of service for healthcare workers, curtail corruption in the healthcare industry, update the healthcare education curriculum, address the public health consequences of political violence, and promote research and development within the healthcare system. These authors are swayed that the reform strategies, as superbly articulated in this chapter, are critical for the renaissance of the current flawed healthcare system that has led to the popularity of medical tourism among the politico-economic elites.

The politicization of religion in Nigeria problematized the relative harmony that existed between members of these two major religions in the republic. Religious conflict became combustible when it was stressed during the writing of the 1999 Constitution and after. If I may wallow in reminiscences in the 1960s and 1970s, it was not uncommon for Christians to celebrate Muslim holidays with Muslims and for Muslims to Celebrate Christian holidays with Christians with pleasure and excitement.

Regrettably, in chapter 5, "Christian-Muslim Conflict in Post-Civil War Nigeria: Prelude to the Fourth Republic," Olufemi Vaughan alludes to the resurgence of religious politics. In short, it sheds light on how the politicization of religion exacerbates social and political tensions in Nigerian society historically and in the Fourth Republic. This academic whose scholarship is in the areas of Nigerian and African tradition, politics, and religion[18] brought his expertise to bear on the chapter.

In this chapter, the author attempts to historicize and contextualize the reasons for the current religious clashes in the Fourth Republic. In fact, religious conflict in the society started before the commencement of the present republic. He explains the development under the rubric of "Nigeria's Christian-Muslim conundrum: The Political Context, in the chapter." In doing so, he informs his readers of the combustible relations between these two major religions that started when politics became part and parcel of religion. In other words, politicos infused politics into religion, as they have done with ethnicity to be successful in electoral contestations.

Indeed, because of religious influence in the republic, the Nigerian Supreme Council for Islamic Affairs proclaimed its interest in national affairs following the Civil War and during the Gowon administration. The strategy during General Gowon and Muhammed's administrations was to legalize and nationalize *Sharia*, the Islamic form of jurisprudence in Nigeria. Following resistance by Christians from the South, the Middle Belt, and minorities in the

North, this political and religious move to nationalize *Sharia* was sabotaged and abandoned. The powerful pro-*Sharia* forces, however, did not relent in their efforts for its revival in the society.

Following the birth of the Second Republic in 1979 and the writing of a new constitution, the issue of the *Sharia* returned to the center stage. The two main political parties that emerged out of the political competition were the Unity Party of Nigeria (UPN) dominated by Southern politicians and the National Party of Nigeria (NPN) dominated by Northern politicos. The victory of NPN dominated by ethno-religious Muslim group meant that it could use its newly acquired power to foist the *Sharia* system on the country.

The UPN made up of fundamentally Southern-cum-Middle Belt Christians resisted this attempt aimed at nationalizing Sharia. At this point, it was clear that the battle line was drawn between ethno-regional and ethno-religious fault lines that continue to characterize the political and religious conflicts then and now in the Fourth Republic. Although the chapter suggests that efforts have been made by Muslims and Christians to resolve a few heated religious differences, such as Nigerian membership in the Organization of Islamic Countries, the process has not been entirely successful. This attempt to Islamize the country begs the question as to whether Nigeria is a secular state or about to become an Islamic Caliphate. Above all, in contemporary assessments, the activities of Boko Haram in the North and Herdsmen in the South are not reassuring signposts that religious conflicts will abate in the Fourth Republic. Be that as it may, it is irrefutable that the mitigation and eventual resolution of Muslim-Christian conflicts is critical to advancing political stability and peaceful coexistence in the contemporary republic.

Although corruption is said to be *semper et ubique* (always and everywhere), in the Nigerian case it has become pathological many observers would argue.[19] Indeed, it would be perverse to postulate that corruption is a twenty-first-century phenomenon in Nigeria.[20] The vexing problem is the irony that many of those same leaders who lambast the negative impact of corruption on the economy and polity are themselves some of the major culprits. Thus, it is a foregone conclusion, many contend, that unless the negative effects of corruption are reduced in the Fourth Republic, economic growth and development would be stymied. In fact, to point to her abundant natural resources and impressive human capital, one is compelled to pose the query: Why is the country not progressing in proportion to her abundant resources in the Fourth Republic?

Bennett A. Odunsi in chapter 6, "The Nigerian Police Highway Corrupt Practices: Strategies to Curb the Transgression," tackles an obvious aspect of corruption and its quagmire in the society. This author's interest in the police and its shenanigans in the areas of corruption and human rights is informed by his study of Criminal Justice and Law enforcement.[21] Additionally, he has written extensively on the matter of, and need for, reforming the police.[22]

The author's opening salvo in his chapter starts with the actions of the notorious Special Anti-Robbery Squad formed in 1992 whose raison d'etre was that of rooting out atrocious and nefarious criminal gangs operating within the country's commercial capital Lagos and in southern Nigeria. In no time, however, the rampancy of criminality in much of the country spread across the thirty-six states of the federation. Because of the new development, the SARS was given a mandate to arrest and prosecute armed robbers, kidnappers, and other criminal elements and gangs deemed to break the law. Problematically, overzealous members of the SARS literally took the laws into their own hands and in several instances failed to act judiciously. SARS iniquitous enforcement of ex-judicial laws has not only incurred the wrath of citizens but also the condemnation of human right organizations such as Amnesty International. Nevertheless Arguably, to further political stability and peaceful coexistence in the republic require a major reformation of this police force to make it more friendly to citizens than it is currently perceived to be in the society.

A critical issue raised in this chapter as it relates to combating a major challenge in the Fourth Republic, likely to advance peaceful coexistence, is the ubiquitous police roadblocks erected mainly for extorting bribes from motorists. It will not be hyperbolic to state that most Nigerian motorists in southern Nigeria have encountered police roadblocks on Nigerian highways where police officers demand bribe on flimsy charges. In truth, such an act by a police officer is illegal. Yet, they keep happening again and again.

After referencing case after case of police roadside extortions from citizens and sometimes civilians who are too slow to act on their request, Odunsi discusses some of the reasons why there exist antagonisms between the police and citizens. He does so under the following rubrics: (1) Nature of Public-Police Disaffection, (2) Police Checkpoints Menace, (3) Effects of Checkpoint Extortion on Citizens/Nation, (4) Consequences of Checkpoint Extortion, and (5) the Way out. Indeed, the author's suggestions on the way out are refreshing. His counsels include, but are not limited to, such measures as incorporating or coopting private citizens into police boards to advance accountability, increase transparency, enhance democratic governance, and stimulate public involvement in decision-making. Participation of civilians on the police board could enhance the legitimacy of the police force in the eyes of the population and promote peaceful coexistence and national cohesion in the Fourth Republic.

In the discourses in chapter 7 "Subaltern Voices and Implications for Nigerian Politics in the Fourth Republic: A Theoretical and Conceptual Analysis," Samuel Zalanga brings to the fore the essentiality of subalterns in global and Nigerian history even though because of their economic and social status in society, they are generally treated with disdain. Central to his contention, and that of this volume, is that subalterns should not be as marginalized as much as they are in Nigerian politics. This is so because the country needs their support to further political stability and peaceful coexistence in the Fourth Republic.

Indeed, instead of the political class and entrepreneurial elites manipulating or using some members of the subalterns in their political and economic battles, as a few of them have done in the Fourth Republic, and thereby exacerbating the current politico-social instability, they should be invited to participate in finding solutions. Thus, the key to Zalanga's hypothesis and contention is that if Nigeria intends to move forward in the Fourth Republic, in terms of development or modernization, attempts must be made to promote the welfare of subalterns. This measure could be undertaken by first respecting their human rights and then providing them with the basic tools to do so—that is, education, and full participation in political, economic, and social advancement. Failing to do so is likely to exacerbate her current political, economic, and social predicament in a polity that has the natural resources and human capital to catapult the country developmentally. Such national development could rekindle her attractive reputation in the late 1970s and early 1980s. During this epoch, the oil wealth made Nigeria an attraction to the rest of Africa and enticed some of the best and brightest Africans from other countries on the continent to the republic.

The United Nations define human rights, among other things, as "rights inherent to all human beings, regardless of race, sex, nationality, ethnicity, language, religion, or any other status. Human rights include the right to life and liberty, freedom from slavery and torture, freedom of opinion and expression, the right to work and education, and many more. Everyone is entitled to these rights, without discrimination."[23] The allure of the concept of human rights has made it so popular that practically every nation-state is a signatory to the Universal Declaration of Human Rights. Yet, it is safe to say that most states do not fully respect the rights of their citizens. Thus, those whose rights are violated agitate for their rights to be respected. In the developed world, citizens' rights are commonly appreciated and protected. In much of the developing world, however, citizens' rights continue to be infringed upon by law enforcement agents often at the behest of autocratic leaders and their lackeys.[24] For many political actors, the constraints to follow the law and respect the rights of citizens flow from politics defined as the struggle for power and the application of the politics of the zero-sum game in its wake.[25] A paradox on the question of human rights violations in much of the developing nations, and Nigeria in particular, is that the national constitutions are embroidered with splendid human rights tenets that are seldom enforced.[26]

Indeed, it is not astonishing that an agency of the Federal Government of Nigeria crafted an inspiring instrument on human rights—a human rights document with which to combat the vexing, recurring, and incessant human rights breaches in the country. The title of this unique text is National Action Plan for the Promotion and Protection of Human Rights in Nigeria (NAPPPHRN).

Because of the comprehensiveness of NAPPPHRN, it serves as the framework with which E. Ike Udogu examined chapter 8, "Human Rights Conundrums in the Fourth Republic: A Search for Solutions." This chapter also draws its analytic sap and supporting materials on human rights from Nigerian Constitution. This is so because political stability, peaceful coexistence, and national cohesion in the polity can be advanced if the human rights of all Nigerians, regardless of ethnicity, religion, wealth, status, and so on, are cherished and respected.

To underscore the importance of human rights in the discourses on how to promote peaceful cohabitation by her multiple ethnic troupes in the Fourth Republic, the chapter highlights some of the key human rights elements that when respected could advance national harmony and political stability desperately needed for economic development. To this end, he discusses the following rights foundations: right to life; right to dignity of human person; right to private and family life; right to freedom of thought, conscience, and religion; right to freedom of expression and press; right to peaceful assembly and association; right to freedom from discrimination; right to education; and the rights of women.

NOTES

1. Attahiru M. Jega, "Restructuring the Nigerian Federation: Challenges and Prospects," A presentation delivered as the No. 4 in the Public Lecture Series of Nasarawa State University, Keffi, on Wednesday August 4, 2021, Assembly Hall, Main Campus, p. 6.

2. Pita O. Agbese and E. Ike Udogu, "Taming the Shrew: Civil-Military Politics in the Fourth Republic," in E. Ike Udogu (ed.), *Nigeria in the Twenty-First Century: Strategies for Political Stability and Peaceful Coexistence* (Trenton, NJ: Africa World Press, 2005), pp. 25–26.

3. Jega, "Restructuring the Nigerian Federation: Challenges and Prospects," p. 9. See E. Ike Udogu, "The Allurement of Ethnonationalism in Nigerian Politics: The Contemporary Debate," *Journal of Asian and African Studies*, Vol. XXIX, No. 3–4 (1994), pp. 160–171.

4. USA Africa Dialogue Series – NADECO Writes UN, US, EU, on Looming Civil War in Nigeria (June 21, 2021)

5. See George K. Kieh, Jr. *Beyond State Failure and Collapse: Making the State Relevant in Africa* (Lanham, MD: Lexington Books, 2007); Pita O. Agbese and

George K. Kieh, Jr. (eds.), *Reconstructing the Authoritarian State in Africa* (Melton Park, UK: Routledge Publishers, 2018); Pita O. Agbese and George K. Kieh, Jr. (eds.), *The State in Africa: Beyond False Starts* (Chicago, IL: Third World Publishers, 2014); George K. Kieh, Jr. "Liberal Democratization and Democracy," in E. Ike Udogu (ed.), *The Developing World: Critical Issues in Politics and Society* (Lanham, MD: Scarecrow Press, 2012), pp. 1–22.

6. E. Ike Udogu, "Democracy in Africa: Fiction or Fact in the 21st Century," Paper presented at the Global Awareness Society International 25th Conference, Budapest, Hungary, May 2016, pp. 1–2. http://orgs.bloomu.edu2016_proceedings_pdsPDF (Retrieved 9/16/21).

7. E. Ike Udogu, "The Allurement of Ethnonationalism in Nigerian Politics: The Contemporary Debate," *Journal of Asian and African Studies*, Vol. XXIX, No. 3–4 (1994), p. 167; see "Kaduna Caucus," *West Africa* (February 14–20, 1994), p. 252.

8. Farooq A. Kperogi, "How Political Power Damages the Brain—and How to Reverse It." USA/Africa Dialogue Series, Saturday July 27, 2019.

9. Chinua Achebe, *The Trouble with Nigeria* (London: UK: Heinemann Publishers, 1983), p. 2.

10. E. Ike Udogu, "The Allurement of Ethnonationalism in Nigerian Politics: The Contemporary Debate," pp. 163–167.

11. Rene Dumont, *False Start in Africa* (New York: Praeger, 1969), pp. 18–23.

12. Claude Ake, *The Theory of Political Integration* (Homewood, IL: The Dorsey Press, 1967), p. 1; Achebe, *The Trouble with Nigeria*, pp. 5–6.

13. Ake, *The Theory of Political Integration*, p.1.

14. Kelechi A. Kalu, *Peacebuilding in Africa: The Post-Conflict State and its Multidimensional Crisis* (Lanham, MD: Lexington Books, 2021); Kelechi A. Kalu, et al., *Territoriality, Citizenship and Peacebuilding: Perspective on Challenges to Peace in Africa* (London, UK: Adonis and Abbey Publishers, Ltd., 2013); Kelechi A. Kalu, *Agenda Setting and Public Policy in Africa* (Aldershot, UK: Ashgate Publishers, 2004); Kelechi A. Kalu, *Economic Development and Nigerian Foreign Policy* (Lewiston, NY: Edwin Mellen Press, 2000).

15. Tunji Olaopa, "Opinion: Ibrahim Badamasi Babangida (IBB) in the Eye of History." http://www.newstimes.com.ng/2021/08/13/10275-ibrahim-badamasi-babangida-ibb-in-the-eye-of-history/ (Retrieved 8/13/21)

16. Joseph A. Balogun, *Healthcare Education in Nigeria: Evaluation and Emerging Paradigms* (Milton Park, UK: Routledge Publishers, 2020); Joseph A. Balogun, *Health Professions in Nigeria: An Interdisciplinary Analysis* (London, UK: Palgrave Macmillan Publishers, 2021)

17. Philip C. Aka, *Genetic Counseling and Preventive Medicine in Post-War Bosnia* (London, UK: Palgrave Macmillan Publishers, 2020); Philip C. Aka, *Human Rights in Nigeria's External Relations: Building the Record of a Moral Superpower* (Lanham, MD: Lexington Books, 2016); Philip C. Aka, "The Need for an Effective Policy of Ethnic Reconciliation," in E. Ike Udogu (ed.), *Nigeria in the 21st Century: Strategies for Political Stability and Peaceful Coexistence* (Trenton, NJ: Africa World Press, 2005).

18. Olufemi Vaughan, *Chiefs, Power, and Social Change: Chiefships and Modern Politics in Botswana, 1880s–1990s* (Trenton, NJ: Africa World Press, 2003); Olufemi Vaughan, *Religion and the Making of Nigeria* (Durham, NC: Duke University Press, 2016); Olufemi Vaughan, "Religion and State Formation," in E. Ike Udogu (ed.), *Nigeria in the Twenty-First Century: Strategies for Political Stability and Peaceful Coexistence* (Trenton, NJ: Africa Word Press, 2005); Olufemi Vaughan, *Nigerian Chiefs: Traditional Power in Modern Politics* (Rochester, NY: University of Rochester Press, 2006).

19. G. Osariyekemwen Igiebor, "Political Corruption in Nigeria: Implications for Economic Development in the Fourth Republic," December 16, 2019. doi: 10.1177/0169796X19890745 (Retrieved 8/16/21)

20. S. O. Osoba, "Corruption in Nigeria: Historical Perspective," *Review of African Political Economy*, Vol. 23, No. 69 (1996), pp. 371–386. doi: 10.1080/03056249608704203; Robert L. Tignor, "Political Corruption in Nigeria Before Independence," *The Journal of Modern African Studies*, Vol. 31, No. 2 (June 1993), pp. 175–202.

21. Bennett A. Odunsi, *The Role of the Ombudsman in Nigeria: Redress of Grievance* (Lewiston, NY: Edwin Mellen Press, 2007); Bennett A. Odunsi, "Law Enforcement Issues and Strategies for Reformation," in E. Ike Udogu (ed.), *The Developing World: Critical Issues in Politics and Society* (Lanham, MD: Scarecrow Press, 2012).

22. Bennett A. Odunsi, "Police and Human Rights Infractions: The Need for Reform," in E. Ike Udogu (ed.), *Nigeria in the Twenty-First Century: Strategies for Political Stability and Peaceful Coexistence* (Trenton, NJ: Africa World Press, 2005).

23. United Nations. https://un.org/en/global-issues/human-rights (Retrieved 8/16/21).

24. E. Ike Udogu, "Human Rights and Minorities in Africa: A Theoretical and Conceptual Overview," *Journal of Third World Studies*, Vol. 18, No. 1 (2001), pp. 87–104; E. Ike Udogu, "An Examination of Minority Groups and Human Rights Issues in Europe and Africa," *Journal of Political Science*, Vol. 28 (2000), pp. 21–43; E. Ike Udogu, "Theoretical and Analytical Discourses on the Human Rights of Indigenous Peoples of Africa," in E. Ike Udogu (ed.), *Human Rights Dilemmas in the Developing World: The Case of Marginalized Populations at Risk* (Lanham, MD: Lexington Books, 2018).

25. E. Ike Udogu, "Human Rights Constraints: Analysis and Potential Solutions," in E. Ike Udogu (ed.), *The Developing World: Critical Issues in Politics and Society* (Lanham, MD: Scarecrow Press, 2012).

26. E. Ike Udogu, "National Constitutions and Human Rights Issues in Africa," *African and Asian Studies*, Vol. 2, No. 2 (2003), pp. 101–123.

Chapter 2

"False Starts" and Missed Opportunities in Nigerian Politics

George Klay Kieh, Jr.

INTRODUCTION

Since the colonial era that ended the processes of autonomous development in the various indigenous polities, Nigeria has had what E. Ike Udogu poignantly refers to as a "checkered political history."[1] For example, the "first generation" of leaders had the opportunity to deconstruct and democratically reconstitute the neo-colonial and peripheral state that was bequeathed to Nigerians on October 1, 1960, when the country gained independence from the United Kingdom. However, the opportunity was squandered when the "first generation" of leaders chose to maintain the post-colonial state, which was a replica of its colonial progenitor. This meant the post-colonial Nigerian state was plagued by the contradictions it inherited from the colonial state as well as the emergent ones. The contradictions included the primacy of ethnicity and regionalism at the expense of the forging of a national identity, the centrality of the acquisitive impulse through the process of primitive accumulation, and the neglect of basic human needs.[2] The control of the state thus became an epic "life and death battle," because the faction or fraction of the emergent local wing of the ruling class that controlled state power used it to pursue factional interests.[3]

Amid the resulting "false start" and missed opportunity, the "men in mufti"[4] staged a military coup on January 27, 1966, thereby ending the "First Republic."[5] The consequences of the coup plunged Nigeria into crisis and laid the foundation for the countercoup on July 15, 1966.[6] After about nine years of the rule of the Gowon-led military junta, another coup was staged on July 29, 1975, that brought General Murtala Mohammed to power. Later, General Mohammed was assassinated on February 13, 1976, and replaced by his deputy, General Olusegun Obasanjo. By this time, military coups and military rule became mainstays of the country's political landscape.

After more than thirteen years of military rule, the military made the determination to disengage from politics as rulers.[7] Subsequently, election was held on August 11, 1979, for a new civilian president. Thereafter, on October 1, 1979, Alhaji Shehu Shagari was inaugurated as the president of Nigeria's "Second Republic." After serving the constitutionally required four-year tenure, President Shagari was elected to a second term in the controversial 1983 presidential election.[8] The sordid performance of the Shagari regime during both its first term and the interrupted second term provided the pretext for "New Year's Eve military coup" on December 31, 1983, and the resulting collapse of the "Second Republic."[9] The coup commenced the second cycle of military intervention in Nigerian politics as rulers. However, the Buhari military regime, which took power in the "New Year's Eve military coup," was overthrown by fellow military officers on August 27, 1985. The "palace coup" brought General Ibrahim Babangida to power. Interestingly, the Babangida military regime designed and implemented an elaborate transitional plan that was purportedly intended to return the country to civilian rule.[10] The transitional plan culminated in the holding of presidential election on June 12, 1993. According to the results, the presidential election was won by Moshood Abiola. However, in a brazen undemocratic act, General Babangida annulled the results of the presidential election, claiming that his action was intended to prevent the staging of a military coup.[11]

Having failed to provide the requisite leadership to address the country's multidimensional crises of development, including "false start" and missed opportunities, the Babangida military regime cynically disengaged from the rulership of the country on August 26, 1993. Amid the crisis of governance it created, on August 27, 1993, the Babangida regime ushered in Nigeria's "Third Republic" under the leadership of Ernest Shonekan as the interim president.[12] While the Shonekan regime was grappling with the whirlwind of protests from various sectors of the Nigerian society as a result of General Babangida's cynical schemes and actions, General Sani Abacha, the minister of defense, staged a coup on November 17, 1993, that overthrew the Shonekan regime and ended the "Third Republic." The emergent Abacha regime was quite notorious for, among others, the vitriolic violation of political human rights and the further entrenchment of the culture of primitive accumulation.[13] Amid the political turbulence, General Abacha died on June 8, 1998, and was replaced by General Abdulsalami Abubakar. Subsequently, the Abdulsalami regime presided over the formulation and implementation of the modalities that culminated in the ushering in of Nigeria's "Fourth Republic" on May 30, 1999.

Undoubtedly, after more than six decades of independence that have been shaped by the seemingly unending cycle of "false starts" and missed opportunities, Nigerians, especially the subalterns, have become engulfed in a sea of anger, cynicism, hopelessness, and a deep sense of betrayal by the Nigerian state and its various custodians, both military and civilian. In short, "things have fallen apart" in Nigeria.[14] Victor Eke Kalu provides a chilling summation of the Nigerian predicament:

> To say that the Nigerian condition is deplorable is an understatement of the negative proportions of the Nigerian problem. A condition in which there is a yawning gap between those who have access to the best possible necessities of life and those who have nothing to swallow but their pride, as they sneak around begging for a handout, is the most suicidal condition for a people. It is suicidal both for those who strive to perpetuate it, by "donating" millions of naira every week, as well as for its victims, for whom the art of living is a nightmare.[15]

Against this background, the purpose of this chapter is twofold. First, it will examine the ways the Obasanjo, Yar'Ardua, Jonathan, and Buhari regimes have addressed Nigeria's perennial crises of "false starts" and missed opportunities. Specifically, the focus is on three major policy areas: human rights, corruption, and human material wellbeing. Second, the chapter offers some suggestions for addressing the "false starts" and missed opportunities syndrome that has bedeviled Nigeria since independence to advance the good political life (human rights, material wellbeing, etc.) in the Fourth Republic. In order to address the research problems, the chapter is divided into five major parts. First, the chapter frames "false starts" and missed opportunities, which serve as the chapter's analytical framework. Second, the travails of the Nigerian state are examined. The rationale is that it is the failure of the state that has generated the multidimensional crises of underdevelopment. Third, using the "false starts" and missed opportunities model, the chapter interrogates the ways the various regimes in Nigeria's "Fourth Republic" have addressed some of the major dimensions of the crises of underdevelopment generated by the peripheral Nigerian state, as trajectories for addressing the legacy of "false starts" and missed opportunities. Fourth, some suggestions are proffered for addressing the "false starts" and missed opportunities syndrome in Nigeria. Finally, the chapter draws some major conclusions.

PROBLEMATIZING "FALSE STARTS" AND MISSED OPPORTUNITIES

The pivot of "false starts" is the failure of a regime to take corrective measures to address a societal ill or ills in a sphere or spheres—cultural, economic, environmental, political, religious, security, and social—when there is an opportunity to effect change.[16] Instead, a regime chooses to either continue pursuing the policy trajectory that has failed to address the problem or embarks upon the pursuance of a "new" policy path that similarly fails to address the problem. Consequently, the policy lacuna remains unresolved and entrenched with deleterious ramifications for the citizenry in the Fourth Republic.

The "false start" phenomenon is caused by both internal and external factors. At the internal level, the peripheral state is the *causa moven*. The peripheral state is the by-product of Euro-American imperialism and domination of the peripheral regions of the world, including Africa. Its major function, as an appendage of the world capitalist system, is to preside over the production of primary products such as coffee, diamonds, and oil to feed the industrial-manufacturing complexes of the "Global North" and create propitious conditions for metropolitan-based multinational corporations to engage in the predatory accumulation of profits. In addition, the peripheral state enables the faction or fraction of the local ruling class that is managing the state at a particular historical juncture to use it as an instrument for the primitive accumulation of wealth.[17] Hence, the members of both the local and external wings of the ruling class are opposed to the effecting of fundamental changes, including structural ones that will transform the relations of production, among others, thereby setting into motion the process of addressing "false starts." At the external level, the world capitalist system and its suzerains, including the United States, have and continue to play pivotal roles in subordinating the human development needs of peripheral states to the economic and related imperatives of the "Global North." Hence, the underdevelopment of the "Global South," including "false starts," and the development of the "Global North" are integral parts of the same dialectical process: The underdevelopment of the "Global South" leads simultaneously to the development of the "Global North."[18] Thus, state managers in the "global periphery" constantly experience pressure from the United States and the other suzerains of the world capitalist system not to undertake fundamental changes in their respective domestic political economy that will alter both their internal and the global "division of power."[19] Sometimes, too, leaders in the Global North and greedy leaders in the Global South are in cohort or alliance in exploiting the Global South.

Another major element of the "false start"-missed opportunities nexus is the lack of transformational and service-oriented leadership in most of the states in the "global periphery." As Fong Yi Lai et al. observe, transformational leadership, inter alia, entails "[diverting public servants] from self-serving to holistic goals."[20] Similarly, as Janice P. Tanno and David Banner assert, servant leaders are "change agents."[21] Importantly, leaders cannot be transformational and service oriented unless they have the political will that is imperative for effecting fundamental change. In this vein, the seemingly unending cycle of "false starts" and missed opportunities in the "global periphery" is the consequence of the lack of transformational and service-oriented leaders at various levels of government, who have the political pluck to effect fundamental changes that will address societal problems, thereby ending the cycles of "false starts" and missed opportunities.

THE PERIPHERAL NIGERIAN STATE: THE FOUNDATION OF "FALSE STARTS" AND MISSED OPPORTUNITIES

Background

The sine qua non for understanding the perennial cyclical phenomenon of "false start" and missed opportunities in Nigerian politics is lodged in the peripheral Nigerian state. This is because like all social formations, the Nigerian state is the "arena of struggle."[22] That is, the state is the space in which various forces, including classes, engage in myriad contestations over sundry issues spanning the broad gamut, from cultural to social. Significantly, the state is not a neutral arbiter in these contestations. This is because the state embodies the vision of the dominant group. Hence, the dominant group's interests mediate the various contestations. As Makau Mutua asserts, "The state is an empty vessel in which a [dominant group deposits its vision of society]."[23]

Against this backdrop, the post-colonial peripheral Nigerian state, like others in the "global periphery," embodies the vision of the various groups that have and continue to dominate it since its creation. Thus, it is critical to decipher the development of the Nigerian state, especially the dominant forces that have and continue to shape and condition it. Such an approach will provide an understanding of the roots of the country's seemingly unending cycle of "false starts" and missed opportunities that are by-products of the crises of the state itself. Hence, this section of the chapter will briefly examine the historical evolution of the Nigerian state, culminating in its post-colonial phase.

Historical Evolution

The Nigerian state was conceived by British imperialism as a "commodity" for the production of surplus to help enrich the British government and the members of its ruling class. In other words, drawing from Benjamin Maiangwa et al. and P. J. Stern's formulations, the framing vision for Nigeria was that of a "corporatized entity"[24] or a "company state."[25] In this vein, as a "company state," Nigeria is a social formation that "binds a multitude of people together in a legal singularity, an artificial person that could maintain common rights, police, community standards and behavior, and administer over and on behalf of the collectivity."[26] Against this background, British imperial corporations such as the Royal Niger Company, United African Company, United Trading Company, and African Timber and Plywood Company played a pivotal role in the operationalization of the vision of Nigeria as a commodity to be exploited as an integral part of the process of predatory accumulation. Thus, these imperial corporations exploited Nigeria's resources for the benefit of their owners, who were members of the British ruling class and the British government.

When the United Kingdom established the Nigerian colonial state under the "Amalgamation scheme" of 1914, the vision of Nigeria as a "commodity" remained the dominant Weltanschauung. Accordingly, the colonial state exploited Nigeria's resources as part of the imperial United Kingdom's global strategy of capital accumulation. In order to resist the protestations of Nigerian nationalists, the colonial state developed architecture of oppression and repression. Organizationally, a colonial bureaucracy was established replete with a police force and other instruments of repression. In addition, as part of the classic colonial strategy of "divide and conquer," the colonial administration took steps to polarize Nigerians to divert their attention away from the venalities of British colonialism. One of the major measures was the establishment of the Native Authority (NA) comprising co-opted local elites. In turn, the NA was used as the colonial state's instrument for visiting repression and oppression on Nigerian nationalists throughout the colony. In addition, the colonial state engineered a rift between the northern region, on the one hand, and the other regions on the other. Similarly, the colonial state fomented division and rancor within the various regions between nationalists and pro-British elites. The British colonial state then took the side of and privileged those Toure Kazah-Toure refers to as "the most pro-British, conservative and feudalistic forces in the [colony]."[27] Ultimately, ethno-regional identities became ascendant, thereby undermining the creation of a pan-Nigerian national identity In addition, the colonial state extolled the importance of private capital accumulation through the instrumentality of the state and inculcated this orientation in the minds of the privileged local elites.

When Nigeria became independent on October 1, 1960, the "first generation" of leaders failed to deconstruct and democratically reconstitute the state, which was inherited from British colonialism. This was because they had internalized the British imperial framing of Nigeria as a "commodity" to be exploited by the wielders of political power. In addition or Moreover, the genre of British colonialism socialized the compradors to design and deploy the full battery of nefarious methods for retaining political power, including the instrumentalization of ethnicity, region and religion, the use of bribery, political violence, and election rigging. This set into motion the first cycle of "false starts" and missed opportunities. Similarly, the subsequent generations of Nigerian leaders also internalized the vision of Nigeria as a "corporatized state," whose overarching raison d'etre is to facilitate the process of the primitive accumulation of wealth by the faction or fraction of the local wing of the Nigerian ruling class that controls state power at a particular historical junction. As well, the subsequent generations of leaders adopted and expanded the ambit of the illicit and immoral instruments that are used to maintain state power. In essence, Nigeria "has remained imagined and governed not as a nation but as an industrial corporate entity."[28]

The Portrait of the Nigerian State

The development of the Nigerian state over the past six decades has resulted in the creation of its portrait with distinguishing features. One is the nature of the state: It is a weak, dependent, no-hegemonic, and non-autonomous peripheral formation that serves as an enclave for producing primary products, especially oil, to help facilitate the continued socio-economic development of the United Kingdom, the United States, and other imperial powers. In addition, it serves as the "executive committee for managing the affairs of the Nigerian ruling class."[29] As Julius Ihonvbere argues, "the fundamental [nature] of the Nigerian social formation as a dependent, foreign dominated, underdeveloped, crisis-ridden, and marginalized actor in the international division of labor remains constant."[30]

In terms of its character, the Nigerian state, like other peripheral formations, has a multidimensional character that can be described variously as "criminalized," "exclusionary," "negligent," "prebendal," and "predatory"[31] among others. At particular historical junctures, a particular dimension or dimensions of the state's character may become dominant, while the others are present but dormant. For example, the "criminalized" dimension becomes ascendant when the members of the faction or fraction of the local wing of the Nigerian ruling class that are managing the state engage in the primitive accumulation of wealth. Similarly, the "negligent" dimension comes to the fore when the Nigerian compradors ignore and neglect to address the basic human needs of Nigerians, especially the members of the subaltern classes,

The mission of the Nigerian state is twofold. One is to create propitious conditions for the predatory accumulation of capital by metropolitan-based multinational corporations like Shell Oil. This is done by, among others, suppressing the rights of workers as they advocate for better wages and living conditions, and the granting of tax breaks and an assortment of privileges that are designed to enable foreign businesses to reap huge profits. The other is to enable state managers and their relations to accumulate wealth through the processes of primitive accumulation; these include bribery, extortion, the awarding of contracts on the basis of quid pro quo between the state managers and the beneficiaries, and various fraudulent procurement schemes. As Pita Ogaba Agbese asserts, "those now in the [Nigerian] dominant class [use] control of state power to enhance capital accumulation."[32] In sum, the mission of the Nigerian state is analogous to a "buffer service" in which the members of both the external and local wings of the ruling class and their relations "eat all they can eat,"[33] while life for the subalterns is a "daily struggle for survival."[34]

As for the political economy, it has several major features. A key one is that it straddles both the world capitalist system and the domestic arena.[35] In the case of the former, as an appendage of the global capitalist system, the primary function of the Nigerian economy in the "international division of labor" is to supply the dominant states in the world system with primary products, especially crude oil. Similarly, in the domestic arena, as has been discussed, the managers of the Nigerian state at various historical junctures ensure that the social formation performs its service role to the owners of foreign capital and their dominant states. Another feature revolves around the myriad asymmetries in power relations in various spheres, including class inequalities and inequities and gender inequities and inequalities. In addition, neoliberalism serves as the dominant development trajectory. It is anchored on suzerainty of the "market and market forces."[36] This means the material wellbeing of Nigerians is subordinated to the accumulation of profits, especially by external and internal capitalists. Further, each Nigerian regime formulates and implements policies that are designed to serve the interests of the members of ruling class and their relations, while paying lip service to the human needs of the subalterns.

"FALSE STARTS" AND MISSED OPPORTUNITIES: CRITICAL JUNCTURES IN NIGERIA'S "FOURTH REPUBLIC"—THE OBASANJO REGIME (1999–2007)

Background

The end of Nigeria's third cycle of military rule (1993–1999) ended with the inauguration of Olusegun Obasanjo, a former military head of state, on May 29, 1999, as the first president of Nigeria's "Fourth Republic." An undemocratic nature of the constitution-making process culminated in the promulgation of the 1999 Constitution approved by the ruling military council without popular participation—a false start. Nevertheless, it goes without saying that despite the controversies over the results of the 1999 presidential election, Nigerians were already sick and tired of military regimes—not least the repressive Abacha regime. Thus, the Nigerian political class, citizenry, and nation were eager for a return to civilian rule for various reasons. Thus, President Obasanjo came to office with high expectations from Nigerians, who were hopeful that the regime's performance would produce the "dividends of democracy," given his prior impressive advocacy for democracy and democratization in the polity before he became a president.

Having served his first term, President Obasanjo was elected to a second term, after the 2003 presidential election, amid the controversy about electoral fraud that has historically characterized Nigeria's elections since the "First Republic."[37] However, after the characteristic court "battles" with the main opposition party, President Obasanjo was declared the winner and inaugurated for a second term on May 29, 2003. Many Nigerians entertained the hope that another term would provide President Obasanjo the opportunity to rectify policies that did not ensure the protection of human rights, the promotion of democratic governance, and the advancement of human material welfare, among others.

Leadership

President Obasanjo was a career military officer, who held various positions in both the army and military regimes that ruled Nigeria. For example, after the 1975 military coup that brought General Murtala Mohammed to power, General Obasanjo was appointed Chief of Staff, Supreme Military Council Headquarters, a member of the ruling "triumvirate" (comprising Military Head of State Murtala Mohammed and General Theophilus Danjuma), and the second in command on the ruling Supreme Military Council. After the assassination of General Mohammed in 1976, General Obasanjo became the military head of state of Nigeria and served in this capacity until the transition to civilian rule on October 1, 1979. Against this backdrop, the authoritarian military culture helped shape President Obasanjo's leadership style. In addition, President Obasanjo's personal characteristics framed his orientation toward leadership. As a civilian president, Obasanjo's leadership was characterized by two orientations: the real leadership style (the praxis) and the pretentious one (the theory—which was also equivocatory). The former is what Richard Joseph and Darren Kew call an "autocratic leadership style."[38] It was anchored on the pillars of infallibility and messianism.[39] That is, President Obasanjo insisted that his views on, inter alia, policy issues had to be unquestionably obeyed, because he has a monopoly over ideas and was the "messiah" of Nigeria, who alone knew what was the best for the country during his presidency. In this vein, President Obasanjo had absolutely no tolerance for alternative perspectives and viewpoints on policy matters. Hence, those who dared to disagree with his views were subjected to vitriol and alienation and were regarded as enemies. Clearly, President Obasanjo's leadership style was an anathema to democratization and democracy, because it asphyxiated rigorous debates, which are indispensable to the formulation and implementation of sound policies, and encouraged the thriving of a culture of sycophancy. For example, during his tenure, President Obasanjo was regularly locked in antagonistic conflicts with the National Assembly, the media, and various civil society organizations that were engaged in the exercise of vertical accountability.[40]

In terms of the pretentious leadership orientation, it falsely conveyed, especially to the United States and other Western countries, the image of President Obasanjo as a visionary and transformative leader, who was unswervingly committed to the promotion of democracy and development in Nigeria, and Africa at large. This has its roots in two major events in Nigeria's political history. One was the role President Obasanjo played as the military head of state (1976–1979) in presiding over the transition from military rule to a civilian one in 1979. The other was his imprisonment in 1996 by the military head of state General Sani Abacha on the charge of treason. The emergent widely held view was that the then former general Obasanjo was imprisoned because of his role as a champion of democracy, in contradistinction to the dictatorial regime of General Abacha. However, the venality of President Obasanjo's pretentious leadership style was exposed during his quest to amend the Nigerian Constitution, in order to seek a third term of office following the expiration of his second term in May 2007. This was because this anti-democratic and corrupt scheme, as Abubakar Siddique Mohammed aptly notes, "unmasked the masquerade."[41] In other words, President Obasanjo's third term scheme (which failed because it was rejected by the National Assembly) removed the veil of deception that had shielded his real leadership style as a quintessential autocrat.

Policy Spheres

Human Rights

Since President Obasanjo was a victim of human rights abuses during the Abacha military dictatorship, the expectation was that his regime would set into motion the process of addressing the root causes of the scourge as well as proffer solutions to them. President Obasanjo initially responded to the clamor for addressing past human rights abuses by appointing a Commission on Human Rights Violations Investigation headed by retired Supreme Court justice Chukudifu Oputa.[42] The "Oputa Panel," as it was popularly referred to, was mandated to investigate human rights abuses, including "mysterious deaths and assassinations" covering the period January 1966–June 1998.[43] The panel's work was inhibited by the failure of the Obasanjo regime to provide the requisite financial, material, logistical, technical, and human resources that were imperative for the panel to implement its mandate. For example, the panel could not conduct the required public education campaign that would have engaged the Nigerian citizenry in the work of the panel. In addition, the Obasanjo regime failed to implement the panel's recommendations. Thus, the appointment of the panel was more of a symbolic effort designed to placate Nigerians than a real plan that was intended to bring to justice the violators of human rights, and help end the scourge of human rights violation and the underlying culture of impunity.

Against this backdrop, human rights violations continued during the Obasanjo regime's two terms of office (covering eight years). For example, in November 1999, a contingent of Nigerian soldiers killed scores of unarmed civilians in the Odi Community in Bayelsa State as a response to the alleged killing of police officers by a group of youth in the community.[44] In June and July of the following year, extra-judicial killings were committed by the federal joint task force in the Niger Delta region against individuals, who allegedly engaged in oil bunkering and related acts.[45] Similarly, in 2001, military, security, and police units killed about 200 unarmed individuals in Zaki Biam in Benue State.[46] During the same period, police and security forces arrested and detained Movement for the Actualization of the Sovereign State of Biafra (MASSOB) without charge, including the group's leader Ralph Uwazuruike.[47]

During the final year of the Obasanjo regime's first term of office, the state-sponsored violation of human rights continued unabated. For instance, security and police units continued to commit extra-judicial killings. Moreover, under "Operation Fire for Fire," state security forces used deadly force in apprehending criminals. Several of them were killed without according them their due process rights.[48] In the area of the freedom of the press, also, three journalists from *Insider*, a weekly news magazine, were arrested and detained on November 24, 2003, for publishing an article about the involvement of high government officials in the Obasanjo regime in corrupt oil deals.[49]

In the same vein, in 2007, the final year of the Obasanjo regime's second term, state security forces continued to violate the rule of law with impunity, including committing violent acts against individuals, including extra-judicial killings.[50] Not to be outdone by its government, some chieftains of the ruling People's Democratic Party (PDP) organized armed gangs that committed sundry acts of violence during the 2007 elections.[51] The purpose was to, among others, create a culture of fear that would have ensured the party's victory, especially in the presidential election. During the same period, state authorities in the Federal Capital Territory—Abuja—demolished the new offices of the African Independent Television (AIT), a move that was widely seen as a reprisal for AIT's critical coverage of the 2007 elections and President Obasanjo's failed scheme to stage a "constitutional coup" and get a third term.[52]

Corruption

One of the major promises made by the Obasanjo regime was its commitment to provide the requisite leadership for tackling the menace of corruption and its resulting adverse effects. In this vein, the Obasanjo regime established two major anti-corruption agencies as the principal drivers of his administration's campaign against corruption: the Independent Corrupt Practices and Other Related Offenses Commission (ICPC) and the Economic and Financial Crimes Commission (EFCC) were established in 1999 and 2003, respectively. Characteristically, the Obasanjo regime did not provide adequate resources for the ICPC.[53] Hence, the anti-corruption agency's effectiveness was undermined. However, with its limited resources, the ICPC investigated 608 of the 1,270 corruption cases.[54] Based on the results of its investigations, several government officials were prosecuted.[55] However, the Obasanjo regime undermined the credibility of the anti-corruption body by proscribing the prosecution of government officials, who were politically connected to both President Obasanjo and the ruling party.[56] In the case of the EFCC, although it prosecuted several government officials, it was hamstrung by two major factors. One was its lack of independence: The anti-corruption body took its "marching orders" from the Obasanjo regime regarding the prosecution of those who were accused of corruption. In turn, this led to the politicization of the anti-corruption body and the undermining of its credibility as an impartial body. The second and related factor that tarnished the EFFC's image was the selective prosecution of those accused of committing corrupt acts: The major criterion for prosecution was political connection rather than the merit of the case.

With the Obasanjo regime paying lip service to combating the vexatious problem of pervasive and rampant corruption, government officials continued to use the state as what Frantz Fanon referred to as a "warehouse" from which to collect their share of the loot.[57] For example, in 1999, several corruption scandals rocked the National Assembly, the country's legislative body. One of the major cases revolved around the issue of "overinflated prices contracts awarded."[58] An investigation into the matter implicated both the president and deputy president of the Senate.[59]

Similarly, in 2003, three former officials of the Obasanjo regime and other senior officials of the ruling party were charged for bribery by the ICPC. According to the charge, the accused former and current officials accepted bribes for over $1 million from SAGEM, a French Company, for the bid for the national identity card project.[60] During the same period, Kelly, Brown and Root, a subsidiary of Halliburton, an American energy service corporation, bribed several officials of the Obasanjo regime to the tune of $3 million to "obtain a favorable tax assessment" for their investments in Nigeria.[61]

Significantly, President Obasanjo undermined his regime's purported anti-corruption campaign by committing various corrupt acts. A key one was that President Obasanjo waived the required due process for awarding government contracts to selected companies.[62] The other was that he sold government properties to himself below the "market price."[63] Also, he did the same for his cronies in the private sector.[64] In addition, in 2006, President Obasanjo bribed several members of the National Assembly to support his third term bid. Claire Soares describes President Obasanjo's corrupt scheme thus: "[President Obasanjo] gave some members of the Nigerian National Assembly plots of land and about $500,000 each to vote in favor of amending the constitution to allow [his] third term."[65]

Regrettably, in terms of assessment of the regime during his two terms, Transparency International consistently ranked Nigeria as one of the most corrupt countries in the world. This captured the core of the schism between the Obasanjo regime's anti-corruption rhetoric and praxis. In addition, it was a testimony to the regime's demonstrated lack of political will to address the scourge of corruption.

Human Material Wellbeing

During his tenure, President Obasanjo also pledged to formulate and implement the requisite policies designed to improve the material wellbeing of Nigerians, especially the subalterns. In this vein, the administration, for example, established the National Poverty Eradication Program that was overseen by a National Poverty Eradication Council. In addition, it undertook various economic reforms, including the privatization of state assets. On the global front, the regime pursued and secured debt relief. The professed purpose was to free up the money that was used for debt repayment for financing various human needs projects.

What were the results of the economic reforms? In the area of poverty eradication, the majority of Nigerians remained poor. For example, in 2003, about 56 percent of the population lived in poverty (based on $1.90 per day).[66] As for the distribution of income, Nigeria's Gini coefficients were quite high. For example, in 2007, it was 0.42,[67] which meant that the distribution of income remained skewed in favor of the members of the ruling class. In terms of unemployment, the official rate was about 12.7 percent in 2007.[68] Clearly, this was an underestimation of the depth of unemployment in the country, especially among the youth. Overall, the state of the material conditions of the members of Nigeria's subaltern classes remained quite poor, as evidenced by, for example, Nigeria's 2007 Human Development Index of 0.478.[69] This placed the country in the lowest rung of countries in terms of the material wellbeing of their citizens.

Outcomes

The Obasanjo regime's policies on human rights, corruption, and human material wellbeing were mediated by two major contradictory trends. On the one hand, the regime formulated and implemented policies on the protection of human rights, the promotion of accountability by combating the scourge of corruption, and the advancement of human material wellbeing. However, on the other hand, the regime took various steps to obstruct, stymie, and undermine the successful implementation of policies that were reformist in their appearance. Importantly, this demonstrated that the regime simply paid lip service to the pursuance of genuine socio-economic and political reforms that could have helped address Nigeria's socio-economic and political crises of development, among others.

Hence, overall, the Obasanjo regime failed to provide the requisite leadership in setting into motion the process of ending the seemingly endless cycle of "false starts" and missed opportunities that has engulfed Nigeria since the "First Republic." Instead, the Obasanjo regime's neoliberal policy favored a "minimalist state," and privatization that fortuitously exacerbated human misery, as evidenced by the persistence of mass abject poverty and unemployment amid the concentration of wealth and income in the hands of the few members of the local wing of the Nigerian ruling class.

THE YAR'ARDUA ADMINISTRATION (2007–2010)

Background

Umaru Musa Yar'Adua was elected the second president of Nigeria's "Fourth Republic" on April 27, 2007, in an election that was characteristically plagued by fraud. As the European Union Observer Mission to Nigeria asserted, "the 2007 election was not credible, and in view of the lack of transparency, and evidence of fraud, there can be no confidence in the results."[70] In addition, the main opposition political party protested the results. However, despite the fraudulent results of the presidential election, Yar'Adua was inaugurated as the president of Nigeria on May 29, 2007.

The Yar'Adua regime inherited the country's perennial crises of underdevelopment, including their exacerbation by the Obasanjo regime. Nonetheless, the Yar'Adua regime had the opportunity to address the country's labyrinth of problems, especially human rights, corruption, and human material wellbeing. In addition, the regime had the opportunity to end the country's perennial cycle of "false starts" by charting and implementing a transformative policy agenda. How did the regime perform? Like the previous section, this is the central question that framed this section of the chapter.

Leadership

Prior to his ascendancy to the Nigerian presidency, Yar'Ardua held various positions in the academy, government, and private sector. For instance, he served as a university lecturer, corporate executive of Sambo Farms Ltd., and governor of Katsina State for two terms (1999–2007). In addition, he was quite active in party politics during both the "Second" and "Third" Republics. During the former, he was a member of the People's Redemption Party. In the case of the latter, he was the secretary of the Social Democratic Party for Katsina State.

In terms of his leadership style, it can be characterized as democratic. This was because he, among others, was tolerant of alternative perspectives as an integral part of the policy-making process. In addition, he was highly regarded for his personal integrity, as evidenced by the fact that during his tenure as the governor of Katsina State, he declared his assets, among other actions.

Policy Spheres

Human Rights

State-sponsored human rights abuses continued during the Yar'Ardua regime. Indeed, in 2008, state agents violated the rule of law and the freedom of the press. In the case of the rule of law, the police and state security service continued to engage in the practice of torturing prisoners and committing extra-judicial killings with impunity.[71] In the area of the freedom of the press, in September 2008, Channels Television, a private media outfit, was shut down by state security personnel, and several of its personnel were arrested.[72] The offense was the television station's reporting on the prospects of President Yar'Adua completing his term of office, due to his poor health. A month later, two US-based Nigerian journalists, who worked for an online media organization, were arrested and detained, while in Nigeria, for publishing stories deemed as unfavorable to the Yar'Adua regime.[73]

Similarly, in 2009, military, police, and security personnel violated the rule of law in various ways, including arrest and detention without charge, torture, and the commission of extra-judicial killings.[74] These state-sponsored human rights violations were committed against private citizens, journalists, and the leaders of various organizations, including civil society ones.[75] As Human Rights Watch lamented, "President Yar'Adua . . . has done little to rein in an abusive police force . . . there have been setbacks . . . in addressing Nigeria's chronic human rights problems."[76]

Corruption

Given his demonstrated personal integrity, Nigerians expected that President Yar'Ardua would be well positioned to provide the moral and political leadership for addressing the legacy of corruption in the country. President Yar'Ardua made Nigerians even more hopeful when he made the addressing of corruption one of the major planks of his regimes' "Seven Point Program."[77] The evidence shows that the regime had a mixed record on corruption. On the one hand, there were prosecutions of some government and ruling party officials, who engaged in corruption. But, on the other, those government and party officials, who were politically well connected, never faced prosecution for their commission of corrupt acts. Two major cases are instructive. In October 2009, a high ranking official of the ruling party and several officials of the Central Bank of Nigeria were indicted for corruption.

For the second example, Nuhu Ribadu, the chair of the EFCC, was dismissed by President Yar'Adua because of his efforts to prosecute James Ibori, the former governor of Delta State, and a major financier of President Yar'Adua's 2007 presidential campaign.[78] This was a vivid demonstration of the continuing saga of selective prosecution of government and party officials, as well as others for corruption. Undoubtedly, this approach, especially the case of former Governor Ibori, undermined the Yar'Adua regime's anti-corruption crusade. In this vein, for example, in 2009, Transparency International ranked Nigeria as one of the most corrupt countries in the world.[79]

Human Material Wellbeing

The improvement of human material wellbeing was a centerpiece of the regime's "Seven Point Plan." However, the emergent evidence showed that there were no significant improvements in the material conditions of Nigerians. Problematically, in 2010, the poverty rate stood at about 69 percent.[80] During the same period, the distribution of income remained unequal as reflected in the Gini coefficient of 0.43.[81] As for unemployment, the official rate stood at about 21.1 percent.[82]

Overall, in 2010, the state of human development in Nigeria was ranked low in the United Nations Development Program's Human Development Report.[83] This meant that the material conditions of Nigerians did not experience significant improvement during the Yar'Adua regime. As Robert Oghenedorn Dode argues, "the [Yar'Adua] administration lack[ed] the political and administrative will to implement the seven point agenda with the zeal it deserve[d]."[84]

Outcomes

President Yar'Ardua was plagued by health problems, which required him to seek medical attention on a regular basis during his tenure. In turn, this affected his capacity to devote the required time to governing the country. Unfortunately, he died on May 5, 2010, during the third year of his term.

However, despite his plans to address human rights abuses, curb corruption, and improve the material conditions of Nigerians, the country did not make progress in terms of ending the cycle of "false starts" and missed opportunities. Several reasons accounted for this. One was the failure of the Yar'Ardua regime to set into motion the required process of the democratic reconstitution of the Nigerian state, including the structural transformation of the political economy. Another factor was that the regime focused on elite pathologies as the drivers of the crises of development in Nigeria, without locating them within the broader context of the peripheral Nigerian state. Further, President Yar'Ardua did not demonstrate the political will to make transformative changes that would have fundamentally altered the course of the respect for human rights, combating corruption, and the improvement of the material conditions of ordinary Nigerians. This was because he was unwilling to take on the major internal and external forces and factors that are responsible for the crises of underdevelopment in Nigeria, including the vitriolic violation of human rights, the primitive and predatory accumulation of wealth through corruption, and the sordid state of human material wellbeing.

THE JONATHAN REGIME (2010–2015)

Background

Goodluck Jonathan was elected as the vice president of Nigeria in the controversial 2007 presidential election, as the running mate of Umaru Musa Yar'Ardua. When President Yar'Ardua became gravely ill, Vice President Jonathan assumed the role as the acting president. This action by the Nigerian Senate under the "Doctrine of Necessity" generated controversy. However, the decision remained. Then, on May 5, 2010, Acting President Jonathan succeeded President Yar'Adua as president, following the latter's death at a hospital in Saudi Arabia (President Yar'Adua's term was set to expire in

2011). The Jonathan regime was faced with the unresolved problem of state-sponsored human rights abuses, run-away corruption, and the deteriorating state of the material conditions of ordinary Nigerians, including mass abject poverty, and real high unemployment, including among the youth.

Since President Jonathan served for one year in completing his predecessor's term, the Nigerian electorate made the determination that this was not sufficient time to evaluate his performance. Hence, President Jonathan was elected in his own right as president of Nigeria on April 19, 2011, and inaugurated on May 29, 2011.

Leadership

Like his predecessor, President Jonathan was a university lecturer, prior to entering politics. His first major political position was deputy governor of Bayelsa State, from 1999 to 2005. He became the governor on December 9, 2005, when his boss Governor Diepreye Alamieyeseigha was impeached and removed from office by the Bayelsa State Assembly for corruption, centered around a money laundering case in the United Kingdom. In 2006, he was selected as the vice presidential candidate for the ruling party for the 2007 presidential election. Subsequently, he became vice president, then acting president, and finally president.

President Jonathan was known for his laissez-faire leadership style that was characterized by allowing his officials to perform their duties with minimum oversight. In addition, he was known for his receptivity to divergent perspectives. However, such a leadership style was not viewed favorably by some of the powerful forces in the ruling party, who did not regard him as a "leader."[85]

Policy Spheres

Human Rights

Nigeria's dismal human rights record did not improve during the Jonathan regime. Several cases are noteworthy. During the one year he served as president completing Yar'Adua's term, the police and state security agents continued to violate the rule of law, as evidenced by arbitrary arrest and detentions without charges, torture, and extra-judicial killings.[86] In addition, journalists continued to be subjected to intimidation and harassment by state security personnel.[87] To make matters worse, the perpetrators were never brought to justice. This led Human Rights Watch to charge that the Jonathan regime "lacked the political will to reform the police force and hold officers accountable for . . . serious abuses."[88]

Similarly, on February 9, 2015, military and police personnel used live ammunition against the supporters of the Indigenous People of Biafra (IPOB) during the group's rally.[89] This violation of the constitutionally guaranteed freedom of assembly resulted in the death of about nine protesters.[90] However, the perpetrators were never held accountable for murdering citizens, who were exercising their democratic right to protest.

Corruption

The primitive accumulation of wealth through the use of various corrupt means by state managers continued under the Jonathan regime. For instance, in 2014, a payroll padding scheme was unearthed at the Federal Civil Service. The scheme involved the placement of the names of "ghost employees" on the payroll and the collection of their salaries by the perpetrators of the scheme.[91] In another major case, the minister of petroleum and the members of the Board of Directors of the Nigerian National Petroleum Corporation (NNPC) were indicted for embezzling the corporation's funds.[92] Interestingly, President Jonathan dismissed the indicted members of the Board of Directors, but left the minister of petroleum in office.[93] In addition, there was a fuel subsidy scandal worth $7 billion that involved several officials of the Jonathan regime.[94] However, no action was taken to bring the culprits to justice.

In 2015, amid widespread reports that President Jonathan was beneficiary of some of the major corruption schemes, such as the embezzling of the funds of the NNPC by his minister of petroleum, he was accused of being involved in the illegal awarding of a government contract worth about $15 million.[95] Unsurprisingly, President Jonathan denied the charge and downplayed the various corruption cases that rocked his regime.[96]

Human Material Wellbeing

The material conditions for most Nigerians got increasingly worse during President Jonathan's tenure in office. Data suggests that in the measurement of poverty in the polity, from 2010 to 2011, the rate stood at an alarming 71.5 percent.[97] About a year later, it was estimated that about "100 million people [were] living on less than $1 a day."[98]

The increase in the rate of poverty was powered by inequities in the distribution of income, and unemployment, among others. In the case of the distribution of income, in 2015, Nigeria's Gini coefficient was 0.47.[99] In terms of unemployment, the official rate stood at about 19 percent.[100] Again, the official rate of unemployment underreported both the breadth and depth of the problem, especially among the youth, including college graduates.

Outcomes

The Jonathan regime failed to provide the requisite leadership to address the country's multidimensional crises of development, particularly in the areas of human rights, anti-corruption, and the advancement of the material wellbeing of the people. By so doing, it could not end the cycle of "false starts." Instead, the regime's policy responses contributed to the continuation of the saga of "false starts" and missed opportunities.

The failure of the Jonathan regime can be attributed to two major factors. One was the lack of a transformative vision for democratically reconstituting the peripheral Nigerian state, including its associated structural pathologies. In other words, President Jonathan like his predecessors was committed to the maintenance of the peripheral Nigerian state, because it benefited him and his supporters. Paradoxically, the presidency gave President Jonathan control over the dispensing of Nigeria's oil revenues, especially for the purpose of the primitive accumulation of wealth. Moreover, this mindset was clear in the way President Jonathan addressed the massive corruption scandal at the NNPC. He shielded the minister for petroleum from prosecution, despite the overwhelming evidence that she had stolen money from the oil revenues. The other was the lack of political will: President Jonathan lacked the courage that is imperative for societal transformation.

THE BUHARI REGIME (2015–PRESENT)

Background

Retired Major General Muhammadu Buhari competed for the Nigerian presidency during the 2003, 2007, 2011, and 2015 elections. He lost the 2003, 2007, and 2011 presidential elections, but insisted that they were rigged in favor of Obasanjo, Yar'Ardua, and Jonathan. Undaunted, he was the main rival of the incumbent President Jonathan during the 2015 election, which he won, thereby ending the reign of the PDP. Thereafter, he was inaugurated as the fourth president of the "Fourth Republic" on May 29, 2015.

On February 23, 2019, President Buhari was elected to a second term in a hotly contested election in which former vice president Abubakar Atiku was the candidate of the former ruling party (PDP). Characteristically, Atiku and the PDP charged that the election was rigged and took the matter to court. However, the court ruled against them, clearing the way for President Buhari to be inaugurated for a second term on May 29, 2019.

Leadership

President Buhari, like former president Obasanjo, is a career military officer, who held several positions both in the military, and military regimes. For example, after the 1975 coup, he was appointed the military governor of the North-Eastern State (from August 1, 1975, to February 3, 1976). After the state was divided into three new ones, he became the military governor of Borno State and served in this capacity from February 3, 1975, to March 15, 1976. He was appointed the federal commissioner of Petroleum and Natural Resources in the Obasanjo military regime. Following the "New Year Coup" on December 31, 1983, that overthrew the Shagari regime and ended the "Second Republic," he became the military head of state. However, he was overthrown in a "palace coup" in August 1985, led by General Ibrahim Babangida.

In terms of President Buhari's leadership style, it was shaped by his long career in the military as well as his personal traits. In the military, he was socialized into the command structure that is based on the order-obedience dyad: An officer with a higher rank gives an order to one of a lower rank, and the latter is required to obey without question or debate. In terms of his personal traits, they shaped his sense of humility and avoidance of an ostentatious live style. However, the military tradition is more dominant in his autocratic leadership style that is euphemistically referred to as "Buharism." Like former president Obasanjo, President Buhari's autocratic leadership style is antithetical to the building of a democratic Nigerian society for several reasons, including the centrality of pluralism both ideationally and organizationally.

Policy Spheres

Human Rights

As has been discussed, given President Buhari's autocratic leadership style, the respect for human rights was neither a priority area during his first term nor during his current second term. Hence, the Buhari regime did not, and has not provided, the requisite leadership to end human rights abuses, including holding perpetrators accountable. Several cases were noteworthy during the first term. On December 12 and 14, 2015, a military contingent killed about 347 members of the Shite Islamic Movement of Nigeria in Zaria, Kaduna State.[101] The perpetrators were never brought to justice by the Buhari regime. In May 2016, state security officers were accused of killing about forty members of two pro-Biafra organizations—IPOB and MASSOB.[102] Again, the culprits were never brought to justice. In 2017, the regime took several steps to curb the freedom of the press, including the monitoring of social media for so-called hate speech, the shorthand for news stories that are critical of the regime. In addition, the Nigerian Broadcasting Commission was empowered to monitor radio and television stories for "hate speech."

During the current second term, there are also some noteworthy examples of human rights violations by the state. For example, in 2019, the broadcasting licenses of the AIT and Ray Power radio were suspended by the Nigerian Broadcasting Commission for broadcasting information critical of the Buhari regime.[103] On October 20, 2020, soldiers shot at peaceful protesters at an anti-SARS (the notorious Special Anti-Robbery Squad) rally in Lagos. The rally was an integral part of protests in various Nigerian cities against the human rights violations that were committed by SARS.[104]

Corruption

The Buhari regime pledged to tackle the continued scourge of rampant corruption. The pledge resonated well with the majority of Nigerians, whose lives are adversely affected by corruption. In addition, many Nigerians remembered President Buhari's effort to combat corruption during his tenure as the military head of state of Nigeria from December 31, 1983, to August 27, 1985. During its first term (2015–2019), several government officials were prosecuted for corruption. For instance, in 2016, several former officials of the Jonathan regime were prosecuted for corruption. This was against the backdrop of the Buhari regime's allegation that "between 2006-2013, 55 public officials stole US$9 billion, amounting to more than 25 percent of their annual national budget."[105] During the same period, several government officials were prosecuted for embezzling $2 billion intended to purchase weapons to help wage the counter-terrorism campaign against Boko Haram.[106] Similarly, in 2017, the secretary to the federal government was dismissed for corruption, and the head of the National Intelligence Agency was sacked for stacking away $43 million in his home.[107] Overall, between 2015 and 2018, more than 603 public officials have been convicted on corruption charges.[108] In addition, the Buhari regime has made efforts to recover money stolen by government officials and kept in banks overseas.

Undoubtedly, the Buhari regime has made some laudable strides in combating corruption. However, these efforts have been undermined by two major factors. One is the politicization of the anti-corruption campaign, and the resulting selectivity in choosing the accused public officials to prosecute. In this vein, the efforts have focused heavily on the prosecution of officials of past PDP-led governments (Obasanjo, Yar'Adua, and Jonathan). The related problem is that officials of the ruling All Progressives Congress and others, who are politically well connected, including the former national chairman of the ruling party, who was accused of corruption, have been shielded from prosecution.[109]

Human Material Wellbeing

Over the past six years, the emergent evidence is that the Buhari regime's policies have not helped improve the material conditions of Nigeria. In the area of poverty alleviation, in 2019, about 54 percent of Nigerians lived perilously below the poverty line.[110] In 2020, Nigeria was dubbed the "poverty capital of the world," surpassing India.[111] This was because about 86.9 million Nigerians lived in severe poverty.[112]

The strangulating effects of mass abject poverty were made worse by the skewed distribution of income. In 2016, Nigeria's Gini coefficient was 0.48, which meant that the members of the ruling class owned disproportionate share of the national income.[113] In short, without sustained efforts to ensure the equitable distribution of income, mass abject poverty continues to plague the country.

In terms of unemployment, in 2020, about 33.3 percent of Nigerians were unemployed.[114] The official unemployment statistic is quite high, because it translates into millions of Nigerians. In addition, when underemployment is factored in, the situation is even much bleaker.

Outcomes

In the area of the protection of human rights, the Buhari regime's record has not been better than those of its predecessors. This means that human rights abuses, especially by state agents, have continued in the country. Clearly, the Buhari regime has missed the opportunity to formulate and implement policies that are designed to help ensure the protection of human rights, including reining in state agents, who have been the leading abusers of human rights since the post-independence era in the country. Accordingly, the regime is helping to continue the cycle of "false starts" in the human rights sphere,

As for corruption, the regime has made progress in holding the culprits accountable. However, as has been discussed, the politicization and resulting partisan nature of the anti-corruption campaign has adversely affected the regime's ability to seize the opportunity and end the cycle of "false starts" in this critical area. Thus, unless the regime pursues a blanket policy of "zero tolerance" for corruption that is applicable to all Nigerians, irrespective of their political and other affiliations and connections, the gains that have been made in this area will be undermined.

As for the improvement in the human condition, this is another area in which the regime's record is quite dismal. This is evidenced by the spiraling rates of poverty and unemployment, and the widening of the income gap between the rich and the poor. In addition, the horrendous socio-economic conditions in the country have contributed to the spikes in crimes like armed robbery, and the emergence of new criminal strategies for extorting money, such as kidnapping and seeking ransom as the precondition for releasing the captives.

BEYOND "FALSE STARTS" AND MISSED OPPORTUNITIES IN NIGERIAN POLITICS: SOME SUGGESTIONS

How can Nigeria end the cycle of "false starts" and missed opportunities in the Fourth Republic? The pivot is the democratic reconstitution of the peripheral Nigerian state.[115] This is because as has been discussed, the peripheral Nigerian state is the generator of the multidimensional crises of underdevelopment that have enveloped the country since the post-colonial era. In other words, a peripheral, dependent, and non-hegemonic state that lacks autonomy cannot create propitious conditions for ending the cycle of "false starts." Specifically, the democratic reconstitution of the peripheral Nigerian state will entail the transformation of the state's portrait. Indeed, as has been suggested previously, the nature of the current state should be deconstructed and reconstituted into an independent and autonomous social formation that is, among other things, not the handmaid of any class or group. In this way, the state will be able to exercise its authority over all classes and groups for the betterment of all Nigerians, irrespective of the class and social identities. But, to do this, the state will require an informed and engaged citizenry that is committed to the promotion of human-centered democracy and development coterminous with visionary, patriotic, and transformative leadership. These are women and men at the federal, state, and local levels that have the political nerve and courage to shepherd the process of systemic transformation, including the political economy, its relations of production, and power relations at all levels and spheres.

Similarly, the character of the Nigerian state needs to be changed so that it could be more productive. And this can be done, inter alia, by establishing an enabling environment for job creation as well as other socio-economic opportunities for all Nigerians. Further, the Nigerian state should collaborate with the private sector to provide the basic social needs of all Nigerians. This will help address the problems of mass abject poverty, inequalities in income and wealth, and unemployment.

Another major structural transformation that is required is the imperative of changing the mission of the Nigerian state from creating propitious conditions for both predatory and the primitive accumulation of wealth to the generator of wealth to benefit all Nigerians. This would mean that state resources, especially the revenues from oil and other exports, should no longer be used to enrich metropolitan-based multinational corporations and the members of the local wing of the Nigerian ruling class and their backers. Instead, the state should devote substantial resources to the betterment of human material wellbeing such as education, healthcare, decent public housing, and public transportation.

Further, the political economy should be transformed. Nigeria should diversify its economy by transcending the preponderant reliance on oil as the major revenue earner. Instead, other sectors of the economy, including agriculture, manufacturing, and service, should be fully developed. These will provide other sources of revenues for undertaking human development and national development in general. Also, it will help insulate Nigeria from the fluctuations in the prices of oil and the resulting adverse impact on the national budget. As well, the relations of production should be transformed so that workers, among others, can be paid more decent wages for their labor. Similarly, power relations in the various spheres and levels should be democratized.

Importantly, the democratic reconstitution of the state will also impact the various spheres of Nigerian society, including the cultural, economic, environmental, religious, security, and social. In other words, the establishment of a new democratic social formation that embodies the cultural and historical experiences of all the groups that constitute the Nigerian mosaic is imperative. Such a reconstituted state should be based on an inclusive and transformative vision that seeks to serve the interests of all Nigerians first. This innovative state structure will ultimately lead to improvements in all areas and thereby advance political stability and peaceful coexistence in the Fourth Republic.

CONCLUSION

The post-colonial Nigerian state is the major source of the multidimensional crises of development, including human rights violations, corruption, and the human needs deficit, that have plagued the country for more than six decades. In addition, the various generations of leaders that have run the state since the "First Republic" have not provided the requisite leadership to formulate and pursue a transformative vision. Hence, the country has experienced an unending cycle of "false starts" and missed opportunities. This is because each succeeding leadership has either maintained the status quo or made it worse.

Similarly, the "Fourth Republic" provides a golden opportunity for Nigeria to change course for the better. However, the Obasanjo regime that was expected to lay the foundation for ending the process of "false starts" and missed opportunities betrayed the hopes and aspirations of the majority of Nigerians. Instead, based on his messianic complex, he embarked on an abortive attempt to impose himself on the country for a third term. As for the Yar'Ardua and Jonathan regimes, they, too, did not address the "false starts" and missed opportunities they inherited. Instead, particularly the Jonathan regime could not muster the political will to even modestly address human rights violations, corruption, and the sordid state of human material wellbeing. In the case of the Buhari regime, while it has made progress in addressing the issue of corruption, its policy of selective prosecution has undermined the credibility of the crusade. On the other hand, the Buhari regime has not performed well in the areas of the protection of human rights and improvement in human material wellbeing. Overall, the crux of the collective failure of all the regimes that have managed the Nigerian state during the "Fourth Republic" is the lack of leadership fortitude to democratically reconstitute the state to serve the political, economic, and social interests of all Nigerians.

Finally, Nigeria will overcome her unending cycle of "false starts" and missed opportunities if nationalists, patriotic politicos, and transformational leaders amply democratize the state. A major precondition is that ethnic, regional, and religious fault lines must be transcended so that Nigerians can work together in harmony for the wellbeing of all in the Fourth Republic.

NOTES

1. E. Ike Udogu, "Liberal Democracy and Federalism in Contemporary Politics in Nigeria," in Toyin Falola (ed.), *Nigeria in the Twentieth Century* (Durham, NC: Carolina Academic Press, 2002), p. 344.
2. See Larry Jackson, "Nigeria: The Politics of the First Republic," *Journal of Black Studies*, Vol. 2, No. 3 (1972), pp. 277–302.
3. Ibid.
4. See Eric Nordlinger, "Soldiers in Mufti: The Impact of Military Rule Upon Economic and Social Change in Non-Western Societies," *American Political Science Review*, Vol. 64, No. 4 (1970), pp. 1131–1148.
5. See Pita Ogaba Agbese, "With Fingers on the Trigger: The Military as a Custodian of Democracy in Nigeria," *Journal of Third World Studies*, Vol. 9, No. 2 (1992), pp. 220–253; George Klay Kieh, Jr. and Pita Ogaba Agbese, "From Politics Back to the Barracks: A Theoretical Exploration," *Journal of Peace Research*, Vol. 30, No. 4 (1993), pp. 409–426.
6. Agbese, Ibid; Kieh and Agbese, Ibid.

7. See Toyin Falola and Julius Ihonvbere, *The Rise and Fall of Nigeria's "Second Republic"* (London: Zed Press, 1985).

8. Ibid.

9. For a discussion of the collapse of Nigeria's Second Republic, see Ihonvbere and Falola, *The Rise and Fall of Nigeria's Second Republic*, op. cit.

10. For a discussion of the Babaginda military regime's transitional scheme, see Pita Ogaba Agbese, "The Impending Demise of Nigeria's Forthcoming Third Republic," *Africa Today*, Vol. 37, No. 3 (1990), pp. 23–44; Pita Agbese and E. Ike Udogu, "Taming the Shrew: Civil-Military Relations in the Fourth Republic," in E. Ike Udogu (ed.), *Nigeria in the Twenty-First Century: Strategies for Survival and Peaceful Co-existence* (Trenton, NJ: Africa World Press, 2005), pp. 15–40.

11. See E. Ngwuta Okone, "Annulment of June 1993 Presidential Election and the Elusive Question of democracy in Nigeria," *South East Journal of Political Review*, Vol. 5, No. 1 (2020), pp. 27–40.

12. The New York Times, "A Court in Nigeria Declares Interim Government is Illegal," November 11 (1993), Section A, page 11.

13. See Agbese and Udogu, op. cit.; Julius Ihonvbere, "Are Things Falling Apart? The Military and the Crises Democratization in Nigeria," *The Journal of Modern African Studies*, Vol. 34, No. 2 (1996), pp. 193–225.

14. The expression was borrowed from Chinua Achebe's book *Things Fall Apart* (London: William Heinemann, Ltd., 1958).

15. Victor Eke Kalu, *The Nigerian Condition* (Enugu, Nigeria: Fourth Dimension Press, 1987), 1.

16. For a discussion of the "false starts" model, see George Klay Kieh, Jr., "False Start and the Crises of Underdevelopment in Africa," in Pita Ogaba Agbese and George Klay Kieh, Jr. (eds.), *The State in Africa: Beyond False Starts* (Ota, Nigeria: Third World Publishers), pp. 23–52; and Rene Dumont, *False Start in Africa* (Oxford, UK: Earthscan Publisher, 1988).

17. See Pita Ogaba Agbese, "With Fingers on the Trigger: The Military as Custodians of Democracy in Nigeria," *Journal of Third World Studies*, Vol. 9, No. 2 (1992), pp. 220–253.

George Klay Kieh, Jr., "The States and Political Instability in Africa," *Journal of Developing Societies*, Vol. 25, No. 1 (2009), pp. 1–25; George Klay Kieh, Jr., "Private Accumulation in Liberia's Iron Ore and Rubber Sectors," in Emmanuel Oritsejafor and Allan Cooper (eds.), *Africa and the Global System of Accumulation* (London: Routledge, 2021), pp. 54–69.

18. See Andre Gunder Frank, *The Development of Underdevelopment* (Boston: New England Press, 1966).

19. For a discussion of the machinations of neo-colonialism in the "global periphery," including Africa, see Claude Ake, *Democracy and Development in Africa* (Washington, DC: The Brookings Institution Press, 1996).

20. Fong Yi La et al., "Transformational Leadership and Job Performance: The Mediating Role of Work Engagement," *Sage Open Journal*, January–March (2020), p. 1.

21. Janice P. Tanno and David Banner, "Leaders as Change Agents," *Journal of Social Change*, Vol. 10, No. 1 (2018), p. 1.

22. For a discussion of the travails of the African state, see Kieh, "The State and Political Instability in Africa," p. 10.

23. Makau Mutua, "Savages, Victims and Saviors: The Metaphor of Human Rights," *Harvard International Law Journal*, Vol. 42, No. 1 (2009), pp. 203 and 220.

24. Benjamin Maiangwa et al., "The Nation as Corporation: British Colonialism and the Pitfalls of Post-Colonial Nationhood in Nigeria," *Peace and Conflict Studies*, Vol. 25, No. 1 (2018), p. 3.

25. P. J. Stern, *The Corporate State: Corporate Modern Sovereignty and the Early Modern Foundations of the British Empire in India* (Oxford, UK: Oxford University Press, 2011), p. 7.

26. Ibid.

27. Toure Kazah-Toure, "Nigeria: Challenges of the Stateand Ways of breaking Through the Quagmire," in George Klay Kieh, Jr. (ed.), *Beyond State Failure and Collapse: Making the State Relevant in Africa* (Lanham, MD: Lexington Books, 2007), p. 153.

28. Maiangwa et al., op cit., p. 3.

29. For a discussion between the state and the ruling class, see Karl Mark and Frederick Engels, *The Communist Manifesto* (Moscow: Progress Publishers, 1848), p. 15.

30. Julius Ihonvbere, *Nigeria: The Politics of Adjustment and Democracy* (London: Routledge, 1994), p. 7.

31. For some of the major studies on the character of the African and Nigerian state, see Pita Ogaba Agbese, "The Political Economy of the African State," in George Klay Kieh, Jr. (ed.), *Beyond State Failure and Collapse: Making the State Relevant in Africa* (Lanham, MD: Lexington Books, 2007), pp. 33–50; George Klay Kieh, Jr., "The State and Political Instability in Africa," *Journal of Developing Societies*, Vol. 25, No. 1 (2009), pp. 1–25; and Richard Joseph, *Democracy and Prebendal Politics in Nigeria: The Rise and Fall of the Second Republic* (Cambridge, UK: Cambridge University Press, 2014).

32. Pita Ogaba Agbese, "The Impending Demise of Nigeria's Forthcoming Third Republic," *Africa* Today, Vol. 37, No. 3 (1990), p. 26.

33. See Kieh, "The State and Political Instability in Africa," ibid., p. 10 for an excellent discussion of the duality of peripheral states.

34. See Jeffress Ramsay, "Introduction," in Jeffress Ramsay, *Global Studies: Africa* (New York: McGraw-Hill, 2003), pp. 1–3.

35. See Magdalene David, "The Love of Liberty Brought Us Here: An Analysis of the Development of the Settler State in 19th Century Liberia," *Review of African Political Economy*, Vol. 11, No. 31 (1984), pp. 55–70.

36. For an excellent discussion of the travails of the neoliberal development policies in Nigeria, see Pita Ogaba Agbese, "Moral Economy and the Expansion of the Privatization Constituency in Nigeria," *The Journal of Commonwealth and Comparative Politics*, Vol. 30, No. 3 (1992), p. 335.

37. For a discussion of contested elections in Nigeria's history, see E Ike Udogu, "Building Sustainable Democracy and Political Stability in the New Millennium in Nigeria," in E. Ike Udogu (ed.), *Nigeria in the Twenty-First Century: Strategies for Political Survival and Peaceful Co-existence* (Trenton, NJ: Africa World Press, 2005), pp. 161–185.

38. See Richard Joseph and Darren Kew, "Nigeria Confronts Obasanjo's Legacy," *Current History*, Vol. 107, No. 708 (2008), p. 167.

39. See Vanguard, "Obasanjo and the Limit of messiah Complex," August 7, 2018, p. 1.

40. See *Human Rights Watch, World Report* (New York: Human Rights Watch, 2000).

41. Abubakar Siddique Mohammed, "The Masquerade Unmasked: Obasanjo and the Third Term Debacle," in Said Ademujobi (ed.), *Governance and Politics in Post-Military Nigeria* (New York: Palgrave, 2010), pp. 173–203.

42. See Phillip Aka, "Nigeria Since May 1999: Understanding the Paradox of Civil Rule and Human Rights Violations Under President Olusegun Obasanjo," *San Diego International Law Journal*, Vol. 4, No. 1 (2003), p. 232.

43. See *Human Rights Watch, Human Rights in Nigeria*, August 22, 2000, p. 1.

44. Ibid.

45. Ibid.

46. See *U.S. Department of State, Country Report on Human Rights Practices 2001—Nigeria* (Washington, DC: U.S. Department of State, 2002).

47. See *Human Rights Watch, World Report* (New York: Human Rights Watch, 2002).

48. See *U.S. Department of State, Country Report on Human Rights Practices 2003—Nigeria* (Washington, DC: U.S. Department of State, 2004), p. 1.

49. Ibid.

50. See *Human Rights Watch, World Report* (New York: Human Rights Watch, 2008).

51. Ibid.

52. Ibid., p. 142.

53. See *The New Humanitarianism*, "Why Obasanjo's War on Corruption is Faltering," July 30, 2004, p. 1.

54. Ibid.

55. Ibid.

56. Ibid.

57. Frantz Fanon, *The Wretched of the Earth* (New York: Grove Press, 1965).

58. *Human Rights Watch*, op. cit., August 22, 2000, p. 1.

59. Ibid.

60. *The New Humanitarian*, op. cit.

61. Ibid.

62. See Ogbewere Bankolo Ijewerene, "Anatomy of Corruption in the Nigerian Public Sector: Theoretical Perspectives and Some Empirical Explanations," *Sage Open Journal*, April–June (2015), p. 5.

63. Ibid.

64. Ibid.

65. Claire Soares, "Obasanjo's Bid for Third Term Rejected by the Senate," *Independent*, May 17 (2006), p. 1.

66. See the *National Bureau of Statistics, Poverty in Nigeria* (Abuja, Nigeria: National Bureau of Statistics, 2004).

67. See *World Bank, Gini Index—Nigeria* (Washington, DC: World Bank, 2021).

68. See *National Bureau of Statistics, Statistics on Unemployment* (Abuja, Nigeria: National Bureau of Statistics, 2008).

69. See *United Nations Development Program, Human Development Report* (New York: UNDP, 2008).

70. European Union Observer Mission to Nigeria, Press Release, April 23 (2007), p. 1.

71. See *Human Rights Watch, World Report* (New York: Human Rights Watch, 2009).

72. Ibid.

73. Ibid.

74. Ibid.

75. Ibid

76. Human Rights Watch, Nigeria: Abusers Reign at Mid-Term, June 7 (2009), p. 1.

77. See Ezeibe Christian Chukwuebaka, "Relevance and Limitations of President Yar'Ardua's 7-Point Agenda," *African Renaissance*, Vol. 6, Nos. 3 & 4 (2019), p. 35.

78. Human Rights Watch, Corruption is on Trial? The Record of Nigeria's Economic and Financial Crimes Commission, August 20, 2011; Ijewereme, op. cit.

79. *Transparency International, Corruption Perception Index* (Berlin, Germany: Transparency International, 2010).

80. See *National Bureau of Statistics, Poverty in Nigeria* (Abuja: National Bureau of Statistics, 2011).

81. See World Bank, op. cit.

82. See *National Bureau of Statistics, Unemployment in Nigeria* (Abuja: National Bureau of Statistics, 2011).

83. *United Nations Development Program, Human Development Report* (New York: UNDP, 2011).

84. Robert Oghenedorn Dode, "Yar'Ardua's 7-Point Agenda, the MDGS and Sustainable Development in Nigeria," *Global Journal of Human Social Science*, Vol. 10, No. 4 (2010), pp. 7–8.

85. See *BBC News*, "Nigeria's Goodluck Jonathan, Profile of a Defeated President," March 31, 2015, pp. 1–2.

86. *Human Rights Watch, World Report* (New York: Human Rights Watch, 2012).

87. Ibid.

88. Ibid, p. 150.

89. *U.S. State Department, Nigeria: 2016 Human Rights Report* (Washington, DC: U.S. State Department, 2016), p. 3.

90. Ibid.

91. Ijewereme, op. cit.

92. Ibid.

93. Ibid.

94. See Tim Cocks, "Nigeria's Jonathan Brushes Off Scandals to Lead 2015 Election Race," *Reuters*, October 27 (2014), pp. 1–2.

95. See John Sunday Ojo, Looting the Looters: The Paradox of Anti-Corruption Crusades in Nigeria's "Fourth Republic (1999–2014)."

96. See Cocks, op. cit.

97. See Inibehe Ukpong and Mohammed Kabiru Ibrahim, "Implication of Leadership Change on Poverty Trends in Nigeria," *International Affairs and Global Strategy*, Vol. 20 (2014), pp. 6–11.

98. Joe Brock, "Nigerian Poverty Rising Despite Economic Growth," *Reuters*, February 13 (2012), p. 1.

99. See World Bank, op. cit.

100. See *National Bureau of Statistics, Unemployment in Nigeria* (Abuja: National Bureau of Statistics, 2016).

101. See *Human Rights Watch, World Report* (New York: Human Rights Watch, 2017).

102. Ibid.

103. *Human Rights Watch, World Report* (New York: Human Rights Watch, 2020).

104. *Human Rights Watch, World Report* (New York: Human Rights Watch, 2021).

105. Ibid., p. 451.

106. Ibid.

107. Ibid.

108. See https://www.Allafrica.com/stories2018 (Accessed on August 1, 2021).

109. See Oludayo Tade, "Why Buhari's Government is Losing the Anti-Corruption War," *The Conversation*, March 7, 2021, p. 1.

110. See Omololu Ogunmade and Adebayo Akinwale, "Buhari: I Am Aware 54% of Nigerians Live Below the Poverty Line," *This Day*, September 25 (2019), p. 1.

111. *Bergen Magazine*, "The Poverty Capital of the World: Nigeria," August 28, 2020, p. 1.

112. Ibid.

113. See World Bank, op. cit.

114. *National Bureau of Statistics, Unemployment in Nigeria* (Abuja: National Bureau of Statistics, 2021).

115. For a comprehensive discussion of the democratic reconstitution of the state in Africa, see George Klay Kieh, Jr., "Reconstituting the Neo-Colonial State in Africa," *Journal of Third World Studies*, Vol. 26, No. 1 (2009), pp. 41–55.

Chapter 3

Public Policy and Economic Development in Nigeria

Kelechi A. Kalu

INTRODUCTION

Comprehensive knowledge of a country such as Nigeria, with its multiple ethnicities and deeply politicized religious institutions, is useful to understand how public policies are structured to achieve current economic development challenges and issues. When policymakers understand how politics is contextualized in a governance framework that promotes adequate policymaking, and how it can best be implemented by competent and skilled public officials whose values transcend ethnic and sectional interests, economic development policies work well and better.[1] For example, a government that works to advance economic development for all its citizens will make public investments in infrastructure that supports entrepreneurial activities by the private sector, knowing that their actions can create gainful employment for the masses and generate tax revenue for the government. And through social investments in education and healthcare, such a government ensures that political and economic development policies improve the lives of its citizens. An effective government provides its citizens access to good education, healthcare services, good and navigable roads that link different communities, an efficient and steady supply of energy in the form of electricity, and appropriate technologies for food preparation and preservation without destroying the environment. Furthermore, an effective government prioritizes its security function above other duties and ensures that everyone is treated equally before the law and that competent public servants eschew temptations for corruption in discharging their duties. A government led by individuals whose desires for the greatness of their nation trump their individual and group identities ensures that while *politics* is a good vehicle for mobilizing resources for development, it is *policies* that guide the design and implementation of national development goals.

Consequently, an effective government ensures equal access to resources for citizens to pursue their entrepreneurial ideas without undue bureaucratic constraints. Promoting a policy environment that grants citizens access to necessary economic inputs in their entrepreneurial activities also requires that the country's natural and human resources be exploited for the benefit of all citizens. Maintaining such a policy environment protects citizens' relative economic advantage against international competition and promotes employment and wealth creation as sources of pride for them. In exchange, an effective government is rewarded by citizens' patriotism and willingness to pay taxes and work collectively for enhancing local, regional, and international reputation of their country.

This chapter argues that contemporary public policy and economic development in Nigeria have largely been characterized more by politics—the struggle over power—and less about policy, which is the translation of ideas into real life practices that impact the lives of the people. Put differently, the politics of sectionalism has trumped the policies of contemporary national economic development in Nigeria. Thus, Nigeria's economic development is mainly held back by four structural factors, namely: (a) ethnic/regional sentiments that manifest as federal character policy in political, economic, and social policies, but in practice excludes minorities from governance and effective economic participation; (b) authoritarian rule that under civilian administrations is best seen as a "Selectocracy" cloaked as electoral politics; (c) inequity in the political and economic arrangement of powers, evident in federal revenue sharing formula; and (d) weak institutional capacity and the rule of law for effective governance and management of basic conflicts in the country. These structural factors have and continue to undercut sustainable economic development in Nigeria. Effective public policies[2] that resolve these structural factors are likely to unleash untapped opportunities for Nigeria to meet the "giant of Africa" expectations its citizens continue to nurture since political independence.

Historically, several economic plans or policies intended to tackle economic development in Nigeria have failed. For example, a Ten-Year Plan of Development and Welfare for Nigeria 1946–1955, 1962–1968, 1975–1980, 1981–1985 was not efficacious. Other failed policies envisioned to improve economic development in Nigeria were Operation Feed the Nation (1975–1979), Green Revolution (1980–1984), Structural Adjustment Program (1986–1991), National Economic Empowerment and Development Strategy (2005–2007), and Vision 2020 (2007–2009). These failures happened despite Nigeria's abundant natural resources, namely, arable land, bitumen, coal, iron ore, limestone, niobium, lead, petroleum, natural gas, tin, and crude oil. The issue, among other things, is that post-independence Nigerian leaders have largely focused on pronouncements of policies but are driven by politics in their decisions and implementations.

Some of the causes of the failures are poor leadership, dysfunctional institutions, and inadequate infrastructures. Accordingly, I shall examine the following to illustrate my point: (1) discuss and evaluate two consequential periods of Nigeria's efforts at effective and efficient economic development, namely, the administrations of Gowon after the civil war and Obasanjo's civilian administration to demonstrate how politics continues to trump policy and undermine Nigeria's economic development; (2) compare the transformational and transactional leadership styles of both administrations to enable better understanding of current challenges with public policy and economic development in Nigeria; (3) provide recommendations that would promote sustainable development in Nigeria's Fourth Republic.

Below, we will examine two regimes under General Gowon and President Obasanjo. These are two leaders that have had opportunities to transform Nigeria from regional and ethnic fixation to a patriotic and true federal government with potential for effective reorganization of the country's foundations for real economic development.

ADMINISTRATIONS OF GENERAL YAKUBU GOWON AND GENERAL OLUSEGUN OBASANJO

Nigeria gained political independence from Britain in 1960. Following that, political crises of governance in the West and country led to coups, counter-coups, and a civil war. Since then, the country has undergone several political transitions with military officers at the center of those transitions. As national leaders, Yakubu Gowon and Olusegun Obasanjo are two individuals who have played pivotal roles in Nigerian politics. Gowon served as head of state from 1966 until he was overthrown in a coup in 1975. Obasanjo succeeded as head of state in 1979, after his predecessor Murtala Muhammed was slain in a coup. Both served as military officers during the civil war, and subsequently as Military Heads of State of Nigeria. In addition, Obasanjo served two terms as a civilian president of Nigeria starting with the 1999 elections and his subsequent reelection in 2003. During their respective periods of leadership, both Gowon and Obasanjo proposed progressive policies and enjoyed public goodwill and international support for their administrations. This chapter asks the following questions: (a) How successful were both administrations in their economic development policies? and (b) What lessons are there to learn from these two administrations that sought to transform Nigeria into an economically successful country?

Gowon's Effort to Transform Nigeria

General Yakubu Gowon is a Christian from Plateau state. He led Nigeria through the difficult period of the civil war (1967–1970). As that war ended in 1970, Gowon's administration, in a Five-Year Development Plan, proposed a series of policies to reform and reintegrate Nigeria into a cohesive industrially developed economy. That Five-Year Development Plan's goals included the completion of a national census, adoption of a new constitution, establishment of more states, reconstruction of the Igbo territories ravaged by the civil war, demobilization and reorganization of the armed forces, eradication of corruption, and a political transition program. Of particular interest was Gowon's policy of promoting Nigerian Enterprises through his Indigenization Program and the National Youth Service Corps (NYSC)—both of which targeted structural economic and political reforms in the country.

The 1972 Nigerian Enterprises Promotion Decree was aimed at reforming the ownership structure of the Nigerian economy. Before 1972, all sectors of the Nigerian economy (imports and exports businesses in all productions) were practically run by non-Nigerians from primary to finished product stages. In the service and manufacturing industries, no Nigerian occupied senior-level positions. Similarly, in most of the companies, fewer than 20 percent of mid-level managers were Nigerians. Essentially, agro-business, chemical, oil and gas, and basic activities such as bakeries were mostly in foreign hands.

According to the Gowon administration, as a strategy for consolidating Nigeria's political independence, there was a need to restructure the ownership of the economy so that certain business activities like candle making, hairdressing, newspaper, radio, and television broadcasting were reserved entirely for Nigerians. As such, Nigerians were to have at least 40 percent paid-up capital (equity) in such business activities as tire manufacturing, interstate transportation, shipping and forwarding, and in most technologically related manufacturing concerns. Lastly, the government reserved other business activities like iron and steel, petroleum and petroleum services, fertilizer manufacturing/importations as potential state interests. These indigenization policies were aimed at creating conditions for Nigerians to assume ownership of their country and lay the foundation for a structurally sound framework for national economic productivity that would enable Nigerians to compete effectively with other industrial economies globally. Some of these policies were subsequently revised in 1977 after General Gowon was overthrown, but the spirit and intent of the original policy remained.

Similarly, Yakubu Gowon's broad perspectives on how to advance Nigeria were reflected in one of his legacies—the NYSC. Through education and public service, the NYSC aimed to bridge the ethnic, religious, language, and sectional divides in Nigeria that are often argued to have caused the civil war. The NYSC aimed to ensure that every Nigerian university graduate served one year in a part of the country other than his/her state of origin. The logic is simple—the more educated Nigerians interacted among themselves during university studies and after graduation, and the more interactions between them, the more individual, language, religious, and regional differences would decline. Consequently, the more likely young Nigerians from all backgrounds would see themselves first as Nigerians and comfortable with each other in finding common solutions to the nation's challenges. Thus, with young people more focused on national issues, the less attention they would pay to personalities and differences, thereby embedding the goodwill that would increase patriotism across the country.

While the NYSC as a national program remains a major legacy of Gowon's administration in Nigeria, its effects have been minimal as religious, ethnic, and regional agitations of marginalization continue to grow, especially in the western, north-eastern, eastern, and Niger Delta areas. Given that General Yakubu Gowon was overthrown in a bloodless military coup while attending an OAU meeting in Kampala, Uganda, in 1975, it is important to begin to understand why his colleagues in both the military and civil society did not share Gowon's vision for Nigeria. This development begs the question: Was his failure a function of leadership ineptness and weakness or the absence of broad-based consultations? Did the General have competent advisers with national patriotism as their paramount interest or did he surround himself with sycophants and regional, ethnic, and religious entrepreneurs? These questions will be addressed and their answers compared with the successes and failures of President Olusegun Obasanjo's administration.

Obasanjo's Effort to Transform Nigeria

Arguably, one of the most experienced and knowledgeable leaders on the intrigues of politics from military barracks to civilian office suites that Nigeria has ever had is Olusegun Obasanjo. He first ruled Nigeria as a military leader (1976–1979) after the assassination of Murtala Muhammed in 1976. Under Murtala Muhammed, Obasanjo served as the chief of Army Staff. He retired from public service amid general dissatisfaction, especially among the Yorubas, because of his alleged complicity with the Hausa-Fulani to deny another Yoruba man, Chief Obafemi Awolowo, the presidency in 1979.

For his singular act of transferring power from the military to civilians in 1979, Obasanjo earned the respect and accolades of the international community, especially from Washington and London. However, the last Nigerian dictator in military uniform, Sani Abacha (1993–1998), was not impressed with Obasanjo's claims to elder statesmanship and international respect. Abacha accused Obasanjo of complicity in an aborted military coup against his regime in 1995 and consequently threw him in jail. With Abacha's death in 1998, the transitional military leader Abdulsalam Abubakar released several political detainees, including Obasanjo, on June 15, 1998.

Even though on several occasions, Obasanjo denied any interest in political office, after a visit to him by Nigeria's former strongman, General Ibrahim Babangida, Obasanjo declared his party affiliation with the People's Democratic Party—a political club of the old northern and southern oligarchies. Consequently, Obasanjo was easily elected to a four-year term on February 27 and declared winner of the presidential election on March 1, 1999. He assumed office on May 29, 1999. He subsequently won reelection (amid charges of election frauds) in 2003. It should be noted that a few years before he was jailed and while in prison, General Obasanjo's interests had tilted toward civil society organizations, human rights groups, and pro-democracy organizations. As a result, those organizations worked to ensure that any political transition in Nigeria would help to embed democratic politics in the country. When he assumed the leadership of Nigeria for the second time, expectations were high for Obasanjo's administration to enshrine economic development. It had the capacity to provide leadership that would result in genuine political and economic reforms, deploy politics to mobilize the nation, and use public policy to guide national healing from unresolved traumas of the civil war and brutalities of military rule over the decades. These hopes were dashed by the administration's responses to two critical national issues that the masses had worked for: the institutionalization of a Sovereign National Conference (SNC) and embedding liberal democratic practices in Nigerian politics. Let us briefly consider these two issues.

Issues of SNC and Political Restructuring

As a self-proclaimed born-again Christian, a highly regarded former military officer, and an elder statesman, the expectation was that General Olusegun Obasanjo would utilize the second chance Nigerians afforded him as an elected president of the Federal Republic of Nigeria to address the fundamental issue that obstructed Nigerians of all ethnicities and regions from realizing their collective and individual goals within an independent African nation. For most Nigerians, convening a SNC was a strategy for negotiating and resolving challenges with the national leadership transition, revenue allocation, and unbalanced national development projects in the country. Although Nigeria's different major regions and ethnic groups had their reasons for agitating for the restructuring or non-restructuring of the country's political economy, ultimately it was all about a renegotiation of how politics—the distribution of scarce resources based on values—would be conducted in Nigeria for the foreseeable future.

President Obasanjo's ethnic group, the Yorubas, clamored for a SNC largely to ensure that the conditions that resulted in the annulment of the June 12, 1993, presidential election that was won by Mr. Moshood Abiola, a Yoruba man, would not be repeated in the future. Politically, the Yoruba groups were more interested in righting the wrongs committed against their man, Mr. Abiola. Thus, the SNC was mostly a tactic to be used to ensure a legally and institutionally sanctioned leadership transition that would give them the presidency, without which the Yorubas were willing to consider and, at least openly verbalize the possibility of an exit option from the Nigerian project, including the possibility of an independent Yoruba Nation.

The Igbos advocated for the SNC as a political strategy to achieve Gowon administration's promised reintegration and reconstruction of war-ravaged areas—mainly in the eastern region, whose inhabitants remain hopelessly unemployed and with death traps that serve as road networks, health, and education infrastructures that continue to deteriorate because of federal government neglect. For the Igbos, the SNC was expected to correct the neglect of their region and with a genuine opportunity for them to compete for the presidency of the country and, perhaps end the political marginalization at the national level and fully integrate them into federal executive, legislative, judicial, and security architecture of Nigeria and the national economy.

For the Hausa-Fulani, the situation was informed by the reality that (based on regional origins of Nigeria's heads of States) they had ruled Nigeria close to 80 percent of the period since independence in 1960 and were therefore quite concerned that any SNC conference might result in their loss of power and influence in federal appointments and the economy, especially if the Igbos, their perceived enemy from the civil war, were to be fully integrated into national politics, society, and economy without restriction.

It is important to note that while these agitations[3] were mainly at the level of civil society organizations across regions and articulated by such groups as the O'odua People's Congress [the Yorubas], the Arewa People's Congress [the Hausa-Fulani], and the Movement for the Actualization of the Sovereign State of Biafra (MASSOB) [the Igbos], most ordinary Nigerians got along well without the intense agitations orchestrated by the middle class and their elite political and economic sponsors. Also, given Nigeria's more than 250 ethnic groups, the three largest ethnic (Hausa-Fulani, Yoruba, and Igbos) mobilizations and organizations' mouthpieces simply did not account for the real effects of these politics of the three groups on smaller, yet important, ethnic groups across the country.

The 1995 tension galvanized by Abacha's execution of Ken Saro-Wiwa and eight other Ogoni activists from Nigeria's Niger Delta region where most of the country's crude petroleum comes from remained unresolved. The young, mostly unemployed, but effectively organized Ogoni activists demanded control of the resources from their regions without which they promised mayhem for oil companies and federal security forces. Some of the effects include the continuing incidents of the kidnapping of foreign oil workers for ransom in the region. What this suggests is that Obasanjo was offered a momentous opportunity to lead as an elder statesman who would initiate, if not a SNC, at least, a constitutional convention as a forum to guide dialogue on the political and economic restructuring of the country based on a broad-based consultative representation by regions, ethnic groups, distinctive social strata, religion, and other significant identities.

To further illustrate the administration's missed opportunities, it is important to note that shortly after the inauguration of President Obasanjo into office in May 1999, one of the unresolved issues—Nigerian citizenship versus religion, specifically, Islamic religion as the arbiter of national political identity—remained contentious. Since the 1999 constitution "served" as the basis for a National Sovereign Conference that could have publicly debated and resolved that issue of religion versus citizenship did not hold, Nigeria's politics trumped policy, yet again! For example, to test the resolve and wit of the Obasanjo administration's willingness to enforce the 1999 Constitution that would prioritize citizenship over other identities, including religion, Zamfara State in the northern region of Nigeria declared its intention in October 1999 to adopt Islamic Sharia law in the state with direct impact on all residents, including non-Muslims. Given no intelligible response to Zamfara from the Obasanjo-led federal government, in January 2000, Niger, another northern state, adopted Islamic Sharia law. By February 2000, many Nigerians (mostly Christians of Igbo descent) were killed in several riots in Kaduna because of that state's decision to adopt Islamic law. Consequently, some Igbos retaliated against Muslims in Aba, Abia State, over the killing of their kinsmen in the North.

By August 2000, rather than deal with the issue of what was a clear violation of the 1999 Nigerian Constitution, the Obasanjo administration took an easy way out of the unfolding constitutional crises. It granted the requests of National Youth Service Corpers who sought redeployment away from states that were establishing Islamic Sharia law, which led many prominent and ordinary Nigerians to conclude that the regime's constitutional inaction indicated acquiescence with the interests of the Muslim North. Given the foregoing, why did the Obasanjo-led government fail to accede to the popular demand for a SNC? Why did that administration fail to take legal action against the Northern state of Zamfara at the first instance of their action to operate against the national constitution using Islamic Sharia law? Why did Obasanjo's administration not use that opportunity to enable Nigeria's

Supreme Court to determine the legality of such practices? Was that administration's failure to ask the Supreme Court to weigh in on Zamfara's Sharia issue a function of leadership ineptness and weakness or a lack of adequate consultation, sheer tiredness, and lack of vision? These important questions go beyond the scope of this chapter. What remains clear is that Zamfara's action privileged politics over policy and provided Obasanjo time to complete his two terms in office. Thus, like Gowon, he left without accomplishing the policy goals of reforming Nigerian politics as a foundation for creating an effective and efficient environment for national economic development.

TRANSFORMATIONAL AND TRANSACTIONAL LEADERSHIP AND POLICY IMPLEMENTATION

As this chapter's opening vignette indicates, it is not whether or if a policy has moral content but the extent to which policymakers are aware that effective policy formation and implementation require strategic calculations, consultations, and compromises, particularly if such a policy is to survive the competitive governance processes. More significantly, effective consultation guided by efficient leadership within a framework of democratic governing processes ultimately make a difference in the success or failure of public policies. According to Peter G. Northouse, transformational leadership

> is concerned with emotions, values, ethics, standards, and long-term goals, and includes assessing followers' motives, satisfying their needs, and treating them as full human beings. Transformational leadership involves an exceptional form of influence that moves followers to accomplish more than what is usually expected of them. It is a process that often incorporates charismatic and visionary leadership.[4]

What is particularly important about transformational leadership is its emphasis on ideas and its capacity to change, not just individuals, but an entire nation. Based on enabling and ennobling ideas to enhance individual and group capacities for progressive and productive change, transformational leadership is devoid of rent-seeking, a cult of personality, and patrimonial tendencies. A transformational leader is open to honest dialogue with his advisers and ministers. Based on the overall goal of his or her administration, a transformational leader is not shy about taking risks by making bold decisions over the objections of perceived important advisers. Transformational leaders are excellent role models who articulate policies that have substantive and consistent moral overtones and a general expectation of excellence of themselves and others. Also, transformational leaders consciously use politics as a tool to motivate the citizens, their advisers, ministers, and the general citizens on the necessity of achieving identified national goals. Such leaders understand that all problems cannot be solved at the same time. They know that they cannot avoid all dangers but must confront each danger in the interest of securing the country and its citizens. In so doing, they can lay the foundation for an institutionalized and sustainable process of decision-making that values the citizens as people and the leaders as public servants.

In light of the foregoing, while General Yakubu Gowon had the vision and the charisma to establish the Nigerian Enterprises Promotion and the NYSC policies, his administration failed in one of the most important aspects of transformational leadership—clarity in understanding current challenges and issues to be resolved. The series of policies that General Gowon perceived as likely to transform Nigeria were mostly policies that would benefit the civilian politicians and perhaps some military officers. But those policies did not substantively address the root causes of why the civil war was fought. It was for the control of the Nigerian state and, therefore, its resources. Thus, with his Indigenization Program and NYSC policies as well as the demobilization and rehabilitation of the army after the civil war, among other policies, Gowon tried to address some of the core issues that would have helped to transform the country. He anticipated that a vibrant economy would offer demobilized civil war soldiers some post-war opportunities in the private sector, but those opportunities needed to have been first clearly identified and communicated to the military establishment and their support firmly secured. Such a strategy would have motivated the civil service to implement the indigenization policies more effectively. Gowon's political naiveté of using politics over policy reinforced existing tensions about the issue of who controls the Nigerian state. It consequently regenerated old fears that led to Gowon's overthrow by the Hausa-Fulani politico-military constituency who may have feared that Gowon was about to give away the barn in a semi-free market economy.

Additionally, although Gowon had the respect and support of the senior civil service officers, his administration's lack of attention to the poor salary structures and the conditions of service of most civil servants helped to orchestrate a strike that weakened the efficacy of his administration. That lack of attention to detail about the implementation of the post-civil war policies also provided some of the reasons that fueled the coup against him. In general, Gowon's failure was partly a result of poor decisions on personnel appointments, especially his cabinet officers who were generally perceived as both lacking adequate training and corrupt, especially in their implementation of national policies on import and export licenses. That lapse in judgment significantly undermined his efforts to provide a unifying vision that could have transformed the nation and its economy.

Finally, Gowon was perceived as more concerned about his image and power than the substance of his announced transition to civilian rule, and he was not prepared for the bitter politics that followed. To make things worse, rather than deploy a constitutional convention to attempt to initiate processes that would boost his administration's efforts to govern the Nigerian state effectively before transferring power to civilians, he unilaterally postponed the date for a return to civilian rule. Thus, Gowon underestimated his vulnerability within the army and the downfall of his administration resulted in the haphazard implementation of his NYSC policies and the collapse of the structures he tried to set up. Gowon's leadership style could be interpreted as transformational in intent but inefficient and ineffective in implementation. In general, it lacked consistent broad-based consultation strategies and was characterized by poor decisions on personnel appointments, frequent unilateral decisions, and a seemingly unprecedented mental fatigue from the civil war.

Rather than transformational leadership, President Olusegun Obasanjo's leadership style is best characterized as transactional.[5] In contrast to transformational leadership, transactional leadership reflects characteristics of personality cult and its processes do not invite participation based on merit or public service. Quite often, the outcome of transactional leadership is a close-knit leadership structure that tends to ignore input from outside the group. At the national level, it is a quintessential example of an authoritarian leadership structure exemplified by the president's personal involvement in matters from party politics to local government affairs. Such features suggest that President Obasanjo rarely consulted policy experts outside of his immediate circle of advisers and mostly sought information that was cognitively consistent with his preferred policy options and approaches. The cult of personality that surrounded him was such that he mostly believed that he was the best leader Nigeria ever had. Compared to others before him, that might very well be true, but there is scant verifiable evidence of sustainable and transformational accomplishments by his administration.

However, President Obasanjo is remembered for scuttling the idea of a SNC during his first term of office because his close-knit cabals were not interested in discussions that would result in the imagination of a transparent and accountable liberal constitutional governance system. Without transparent political restructuring, the interests and processes that guide policy design and implementation in Nigeria will continue to reflect a government, and therefore a state that is the main source of wealth accumulation in the country. Frequently, such a government is characterized by a transformational leadership style in policy making with implementation strategies that are transactional. What this suggests is that transformational and effectively implemented policies are likely in Nigeria when the private sector becomes the main employer of labor. Until then, transactional leaders, like Obasanjo and Buhari, will continue to use the national resources as tools for designing public policies that generate undue rent for a small group of individuals and regions without translating into Nigeria's economic development outcomes. Arguably, since he did not use a national or constitutional convention to remap and restructure leadership transition and, therefore, control of the Nigerian state, President Obasanjo left office without building a sustainable governance infrastructure for economic development in the country.

Similarly, President Obasanjo's political approach did not resolve the 1999 constitutional challenge that Zamfara State posed to the country and which was eventually followed by other northern states that reverted to Islamic Sharia law for civil and criminal offenses. The constitutional inaction by the Obasanjo administration was tantamount to subjugating the federally granted citizenship right of all Nigerians in the 1999 Constitution to the religious priorities of a sub-regional interest in Nigeria, at the expense of non-Muslim Nigerian citizens in those states. That privileging of politics over policy approach is consistent with the framework of the transactional leadership style and which maintained the value and importance of a rigid religion as a framework for governance in the affected states. His political approach of non-resolution of such a momentous constitutional issue assured Obasanjo reelection in 2003. In additional instances, this privileging of politics over policy was further demonstrated in the president's repeated use of the military in Odi, Jos, Ijaw, and other areas to resolve political issues that clearly demanded transparent policies to keep the peace and the government services needed by the citizens.

In the end, while President Obasanjo is popularly known as a strong leader against corruption, his administration's ineffective fight against corruption is largely because of the transactional nature of his leadership. In terms of personnel choice, President Obasanjo's second term in office is characterized by the selection of individuals who had excelled in their professions possibly to mute their criticisms of some of his inefficacious policies. There is no evidence that the president was either taking the wise counsel of those technocrats or allowing them free space to put their expert knowledge, talents, and experience to the best use in their service of the country.

Nigeria: The Impact of Population and the Economy

While socio-economic, political, and financial indicators do not tell us precisely how well particular individuals are coping with the challenges of economic and political environments, aggregate numbers permit a general evaluation of the trends of current and previous governments in their management of Nigeria's public policy to achieve economic development.

Politically, in 2021, Freedom in the World data[6] reveals that Nigeria is challenged with a political and civil rights score of 46 out of 100. This score indicates that Nigerians do not enjoy consistent rights to participate in politics or freely express their views and are not protected against other individuals and groups who may want to curtail their civil liberties. Data from the UNDP Human Development Index (HDI) 2020[7] reveals that more than 296,000 Nigerians flee the country annually for fear of different forms of insecurity, which include persecution by government security forces, physical harm by terrorists and bandits, and religious intolerance. That means that Nigerians are increasingly becoming refugees in other countries. The same sources of insecurity are largely responsible for more than 1.8 million[8] internally displaced persons in Nigeria. It is important to note that internal displacement is mainly attributed to the Boko Haram presence in the northeast region of Nigeria where the government remains unable to meet its basic responsibility to protect its citizens against physical and other forms of harm.

Economically, while Nigeria has the largest economy and population in the continent of Africa, over 53 percent of its working-age population live below the income line of $1.90 per day. Of those working, 62 percent of employed Nigerians are classified as working poor at Purchasing Power Parity value of $3.20 per day. And many of those lucky enough to have jobs lack access to healthcare privileges. This last indicator partly explains the maternal mortality ratio in Nigeria of 917 deaths per 100,000 women, which is the number of deaths due to pregnancy-related causes.[9] With regard to maternal mortality, only countries like South Sudan and Sierra Leone are worse off than Nigeria in sub-Saharan Africa!

Other economic indicators include trade and financial flows such as foreign direct investment (FDI) and remittances inflows into the economy. For example, in 2020 net FDI inflows as a percentage of GDP was 0.5, net official development assistance as a percentage of Gross National Income was 0.9, while private capital inflows were −3.3. However, remittances inflow by Nigerians working in foreign countries as a percentage of GDP was 5.31 in 2020, which is greater than FDI and net official development assistance combined. If Nigerians employed overseas are remitting at least 5 percent of the country's GDP annually,[10] it makes sense that with good leadership, trust in government capacity to carry out its basic security functions, Nigerians have the work ethic necessary for national economic development.

However, part of the challenge that Nigeria must deal with to achieve a positive transformation is the issue of inequality. A composite value of inequality in life expectancy, education, and inequality in income provides overall data on the extent of human inequality in Nigeria with an average coefficient of human inequality of 37.79 between 2010 and 2019.[11] With the adult literacy rate at 62 percent, it is troubling that more than 35 percent[12] of primary school children drop out of school annually, with a greater impact on young women, especially in the rural areas.

As Nigeria's population is projected to continue its upward trajectory, there is an urgent need to focus attention on taming the insecurity challenges across the country. For example, while Boko Haram and other bandits continue to raid schools to kidnap students for ransom and destroy communities in the northeast and northwest of the country, and Fulani herdsmen terrorize farming communities in the southwest and southeast regions of Nigeria, families and communities cannot settle down to safely enable their children to attend school or find sustainable employment that will be necessary to reduce human inequality in the country.

Generally, a population of more than 200 million people with a median age of 18.4 can serve as a competitive advantage for Nigeria to emphasize labor-intensive economic activities. One of the areas where this is possible is with improvement in the training and retention of healthcare workers in the country. The current 2.3 healthcare workers per 1,000 citizens is not sufficient to keep the population healthy. Nigeria needs to increase healthcare expenditure beyond the current 3.89 percent as a share of GDP and increase education expenditure beyond the current 7.04 percent as a share of the budget. These would enhance young people's education and health as a foundation for workforce training for economic development. Strategically, improving healthcare services and delivery as well as increasing opportunities for science and technical education training for Nigerian youths will unleash their entrepreneurial energies for innovation and job creation. It will also help to reduce the general unemployment rate of 33 percent and the 29 percent unemployment for those with bachelor's degrees.

Given the current projected population growth rate of 2.5 percent, Nigeria's total population will be approximately 400 million by 2050. With life expectancy at 60.87, it is imperative that Nigeria significantly increases its economic growth rate above 2.21 percent (2019 data), focuses on policies that enable competitive advantage for the youth, improves the healthcare services, and enhances education and workforce development of the citizens as a strategy to avert potential chaos in 2050.[13] Priority areas are to refocus on agriculture, small- and large-scale farming, and build efficient and effective petroleum refineries in the country with a petrochemical spinoff manufacturing that would create employment and serve as the basis for a fully industrialized Nigeria.

Consistent with the above, it is important to note that under President Obasanjo, Nigeria had a good opportunity to lay a solid foundation for economic policies and industrialization of the country. Led by the Finance Minister Dr. Ngozi Okonjo-Iweala, the economic policy team identified *four* challenges in the Nigerian economic policy environment:

1. Poor economic management, underscored by the volatile pattern of public expenditure, and the monocultural orientation of the economy . . . poor governance and weak public institutions undermined by ingrained and institutionalized corruption . . . inability of the state to deliver basic public services . . . and a hostile environment for private-sector growth, typified by bureaucratic hurdles and requirements.
2. Promoting private enterprise as the primary engine of growth by deregulating and liberalizing important sectors of the economy and incentivizing the private sector to invest and create jobs.
3. Empowering people by improving the delivery of basic services that matter for their lives—education, health, and essential infrastructure (clean water, sanitation, and so on).
4. Investing in agriculture to create jobs, and supporting micro, small, and medium enterprises . . . the livelihood for most Nigerians, especially women.[14]

To tackle the challenges, the team set goals and action items. These are wealth creation, employment generation, poverty reduction, and value reorientation. They further recommended the following: changing the way government works by strengthening the management of public finances, better prioritizing expenditures, restructuring the bloated civil service, introducing transparency in government business, and fighting corruption.[15]

The diagnoses of the roots of Nigeria's economic challenges, its goals, and actions that were done by the previous policy team, if effectively and efficiently implemented, can enhance economic development in the country. However, consistent with the nuances of Nigeria's political environment, most of the policy recommendations were abandoned with change in leadership and politics continue to trump policies in Nigeria. Thus, as indicated in the introduction to this chapter, there are four structural factors that work against economic development in Nigeria: ethnic and regional sentiments, authoritarian rule, inequity in the federal revenue sharing formula, and weak institutional capacity for the enforcement of the rule of law. The rest of this chapter provides further clarifications on these structural factors.

RECOMMENDATIONS—LEADERSHIP, INSTITUTION, AND INFRASTRUCTURE AS PRECURSORS FOR GOOD GOVERNANCE: A COMPREHENSIVE ANALYSIS

To establish the right kinds of public policy and at a level that would be significant for economic development in Nigeria's Fourth Republic requires improving the interrelated issues of Leadership, Institution, and Infrastructure.

That Nigeria has remained unable to rise to its capacity to produce sufficient food to feed its people, despite abundant agricultural resources and capacities, and reduce its food import bills is not surprising because it prioritizes federal character over merit in economic policies. Nigeria's economy continues to rely on revenues from the export of crude petroleum and its volatile international price structure that make it difficult for decision-makers to have reliable year-on-year budget plans for national development. Also, with a focus on the oil spigot for national revenue sharing and without a consistent governance structure and accountability for policy decisions and rent-seeking, the outcome is mostly transformational policy pronouncements and transactional implementation. It is important to propose "transformational policies" as both the Gowon and Obasanjo administrations did but it is even better when such policies have strategies for implementation on the basis of competence over "federal character." Such a strategy ensures that the "national cake is well-baked," expanded, and equitably distributed based on merit and need and to meet a social goal of reducing poverty and wealth inequality in the country.

Effectively implemented public policies, especially in a multiethnic state like Nigeria, require broad-based consultation with different constituencies, even if those constituencies are not necessarily in support of the current government. The brief description of previous national development plans and the examination of two policy periods—the Gowon and Obasanjo administrations—underscore how public policies need broad support and time to achieve the goals of economic development as measured by high GDP per capita, access to good healthcare services, equitable distribution of income, and stable domestic employment for Nigerians.

Thus, sustainable economic development in Nigeria can only be possible when different ethnic nationalities work together in an environment of competition, not fear, where basic services and access to a rules-based governance protect everyone equally. That means that policies, such as for recruitment for positions that require technical skills, are implemented without intentional bias but to generally grow "the national cake" with national appointments as a tactic. And, among other services, ensure that government-mandated standards guide road constructions, healthcare services, and food safety. Furthermore, policies should ensure that local, state, and national government institutions serve their regulatory functions, including to ensure consistent standards in Nigeria's educational institutions. Effective and efficient maintenance of national standards and adequate funding will enhance the capacity of higher education institutions to produce the stock of knowledge and human resources necessary for using abundant economic resources for local, regional, state, and national development. It starts with having people in the right positions who understand the national standards and can use the local contexts of politics to design and implement public policies to sustainably expand economic opportunities for everyone.

Consequently, at the national level, sustainable economic development starts with building effective and sustainable legislative, executive, and judicial institutions of governance that will enable Nigerians to collaborate with government and each other in efforts toward achieving economic and political development objectives. Such an effective governance structure is needed to enhance oversight and regulatory functions of government to make sure that policy designs are based on knowledge and capacity for successful implementation of projects that can verifiably meet national, and where necessary, international standards. The resulting governance and policy frameworks would be the basis for regulating important sectors such as construction across Nigeria to ensure, at a minimum, that the roads after construction can survive beyond the next rainy season and that buildings are not rendered unusable within months of their completion. In this respect, such a policy environment will ensure that university campuses that offer civil and mechanical engineering programs collaborate with contracting firms, both for opportunities for internships for their students and to ensure that completed buildings meet established standards that reflect institutional competence and the practical outworking of their mission as symbols of knowledge.

Clearly, effective and efficient leadership recruitment processes and a functioning governance infrastructure are needed to end impunity, ensure transparency, good governance, and patriotism, if Nigeria is to reach the fabled "giant of Africa" status rather than the "crippled giant"[16] that it has become. In addition, broad-based consultations/communication with the people and their representatives are critical to build the collaborative energy needed for effective implementation of government economic policies. One way this could play out is when security and efficient judicial institutions and staff resolve issues based on the rule of law to build confidence for Nigerians and foreigners to invest in diverse economic activities across the country. Without any of these, stemming from an effective, efficient, and transparent governance style, the nation's democracy will continue to exhibit a high level of autocracy as has become evident in the civilian administration of retired major general president Muhammadu Buhari. Indeed, the poor security and protection that continue to elude the nation under the Buhari administration have direct impacts on Nigeria's capacity to feed itself, to the extent that the government spent more than 1 billion dollars to import food items into the country in 2020 alone.[17] Also, Nigerians want their leaders to be successful and the most basic yardstick for judging political leaders' success is how well the state secures the safety and security of its citizens. Without such security, the citizens have no incentives for sustainable economic activities like farming, which impacts other aspects of their lives.

Thus, as part of its investments in economic development policies for the country, the Nigerian government needs to enforce policies that meet the needs for physical protection of its citizens against rogue government security agents, terrorists, secessionists, bandits, and ethnic vigilantes. Such policies must be based on the rule of law and be perceived to be fair across ethnic, religious, and regional lines. For example, if leaders circumvent the constitution and the judicial institutions, as Obasanjo did with the Sharia issue and Buhari with issues affecting the Southwest and Southeast regions by the Fulani herdsmen's violence against those communities, it becomes an invitation for other ethnic vigilantes to use violence as a tool for community protection, which then breeds an atmosphere of lawlessness, insecurity, and insensitivity that undermine efforts at national policy standards and development.

Ultimately, it takes visionary, committed, knowledgeable, competent, and goal-oriented leaders to appoint competent assistants and advisers whose integrity, transparency, and probity complement the leader's values and goals for the state. It requires even greater valor to respect the counsel of such advisers enough to heed them. This means that Nigeria needs to find a happy medium between federal character and merit, religious essentialism and citizenship, and politicized ethnic identities "son-of-the-soil" mentality that continues to undermine effective design and implementation of transformative public policies for economic development. For example, sensitivity to federal character in political appointments can coexist with merit in federal civil service selections and managerial appointments to parastatals that require technical knowledge and skills.

Similarly, ideas for effective economic development policies do not magically appear, especially from the international financial institutions. Such ideas must be contextually relevant to the Nigerian environment, contested and debated by those that desire to lead the country. In this context, Nigeria must reform how it selects leaders because the notion of good governance within the framework of free and fair elections remains a glorified "selectocracy" as elections do not make room for debating ideas about how best to manage Nigeria's economic development policies and conflicts in the country. What this means is that, when presidential candidates can openly debate each other on their ideas for leading Nigeria, the successful candidate's policies will have a better chance of success because ideas of state effectiveness and policy implementations would be based on the rule of law and transparently implemented by competent civil servants. Consequently, if Nigeria establishes (a) a sustainable framework for a constitutional democratic political system that respects and promotes human rights; (b) excellence in knowledge, leadership, and service as antidotes to ignorance, discrimination, poverty, and underdevelopment; and (c) promotes patriotism within the framework of the rule of law. Within the preceding context, Nigeria will have solid basis for meeting its economic development goals.

If the aforementioned factors are instituted at the local, state, and national levels of government, the consequences will be a cathartic release of energy that transforms the psychological perspectives of Nigerian citizens toward national, state, and local government officials and would likely result in progressive economic contributions and development by citizens across the board. A good governance environment makes transparent the knowledge of the rules that are expected for playing the game of politics. Such governance environment enables social interactions as bargaining processes, such that public policy becomes ipso facto, a contest for controlling the rules and therefore, the values, norms, and processes of maintaining and changing how Nigeria is structured and governed, without regard to the regional origins of public officials. Frameworks where the game, in public policy, is played mostly over the rules rather than the people have worked in advanced and new industrialized countries like the United States, Germany, Japan, and South Korea, among others. It can and will work in Nigeria when citizenship trumps other identities and merit grants access to employment, especially in technical fields requiring specialized knowledge. It will work for Nigeria when the rule of law guides the resolution of conflicts, ends impunity, and serves as the basis for the security of persons and properties. Lastly, it will work in Nigeria when rules of the game are observed by Nigerians such that competent civil servants, such as police officers, protect people without regard to states of origin. Additionally, when educational institutions live up to their mission to produce knowledge and develop competent Nigerians who would be able to find employment in private and public enterprises anywhere in the country.

The Politics of Sharing the Oil Revenue

In practical terms, with the end of the civil war in 1970 and the oil boom, the focus of every level of government has been on sharing the oil revenue from the federation account. Given the geopolitical decision that created the existing inequity in how oil revenue is shared, the consequence has been a marginal effort in the exploration and exploitation of natural resources across Nigeria, which continues to undermine sustainable economic development and expanding the "national cake" in the country. Centralization of the oil revenue in the federation account gives politicians and leaders from non-oil-producing areas undue control of a large portion of the revenue for their regions. This centralization with its resulting politics of "sharing the national cake" has essentially undermined thinking about alternatives and other potentially more viable sources of revenue for economic development in Nigeria. Also, a direct consequence of the inequity in the distribution of the oil revenue has been economic underdevelopment and persistent tensions in the Niger Delta region, kidnapping of foreign oil workers for ransom, merciless oil bunkering, and corruption at the highest levels of government, all of which continue to fuel political and economic grievances and insecurity in the region.

As Rotimi T. Suberu[18] notes, the demands and grievances articulated by Nigeria's oil-producing communities by their intermediaries are (1) the disposition of mineral land rents, (2) the application of the derivation principle to the allocation of federally collected mineral revenues, (3) the appropriate institutional and fiscal responses to the ecological problems of the oil-producing communities, (4) the responsibility of the oil-prospecting companies to the oil-producing communities, and (5) the appropriate arrangements for securing the integrity and autonomy of the oil-producing communities within the federal arrangement of powers.[19] Nigeria's 1999 Constitution obligates the states to protect the environment and maintain ecological health in their respective territories, but under the exclusive legislative list, section 39 grants the federal government all rights to "mines and minerals, including oil fields, oil mining, geological surveys and natural gas."[20] Indeed, I agree with Suberu's view that perhaps

> the most logically and legally compelling of the demands of the oil-bearing communities and states involves their claims to mineral land rents. Traditionally, for instance, land rights in Nigeria were vested in the respective local communities. Under the Land Use Decree of 1978, however, ownership of land in any state of the federation is vested in the State Governor in trust for the people of the state. Thus, both traditionally and legally, the Federal Government has no direct claims to land in the states.[21]

Hence, a federal guideline on land tenure reform is needed to spur sustainable economic development in each region. Such guideline will require each state to have in its constitution and laws, a clearly defined property rights and obligations of the various local and state governments. Such reform will also include provisions that each level of government must find sources of revenues for its administration and meeting the development needs of its constituency. And rather than the current constitutional structure that allocates funding from the federation account to states and local governments, the second and third tiers of government should be required to pay excise, import, and export taxes to the federal government on minerals exploration in their respective territories and on manufactured goods for export to other states and outside the country. This is an approach that is likely to compel state governors and local government chairpersons to explore other alternative sources of revenue within their jurisdiction, as Lagos State government has done with its taxation policies. Such reforms can free Nigeria from excessive reliance on revenues from production and price volatility of crude petroleum and the vicissitudes of international politics for funding its national economic development policies. Also, such reforms will likely end the contentious political, security, and development issues around crude petroleum revenues, subsidies, and endemic corruption, and therefore promote Nigeria's political and economic stability as a major plank for sustainable economic development.

Besides, Nigeria needs to move away from the lack of clarity on the issue of who owns the land, its resources, and financial responsibilities to local, state, and federal governments. To the extent that the federal government retains legal control to prescribe how much rent is paid and to collect such rents from the oil and other minerals prospecting companies for land use, the issue of ownership of mineral wealth versus ownership of land from which the riches come will remain unclear and contentious. These differences can be resolved with a constitutional amendment, and a restructured federal government that specifies responsibilities and obligations—for example, safety and security against external or interstate threats—as a federal government responsibility, and economic and general welfare issues as states and local governments' areas of responsibilities.

Collectively, these suggested reforms will change the role of the federal government over Nigeria's crude petroleum from primary owner of petroleum resources in the country to one of oversight and regulation of crude petroleum-related economic activities by private and quasi-government entities. This suggested change will bring to a relative end the attendant public corruption associated with federal government entities and parastatals, for example, NNPC, which continues to undermine government's credibility in the minority oil-producing regions at the national and international levels.

> [As the *National Concord* argued] . . . there have been disheartening contradictions and inconsistencies in Nigeria, a nation that recognized [*sic*] 100 per cent derivation as the basis for revenue allocation in 1950 but reduced it to 50 per cent at independence in 1960; to 45 percent in 1970; 20 per cent in 1975; 1.5 per cent in 1982 and 3 per cent in 1992 as crude oil, found in the Ijaw country, became the main source of national revenue.[22]

The principle of derivation has been a major strategy for revenue sharing in the country and seems initially to have been quite well balanced to meet the needs of the federal government and those of the states. What needs to be addressed is the increasing emasculation of the states and local governments by increased control of the one source of revenue in Nigeria—crude petroleum—and strategies for exploring, exploiting, and developing other revenue streams, especially in agriculture, across the country.

Political reforms that truly decentralize decision-making within a constitutionally granted authority in Nigeria can refocus national economic development strategies that start with a comprehensive cataloging of other abundant natural resources in Nigeria and agricultural activities. In the interim, effective and efficient running of the refining of crude petroleum in the regions where it is generated is needed to create employment for Nigerians. An efficient crude petroleum refining in Nigeria has the capacity to spinoff a petrochemical industry that takes advantage of economies of scale and simultaneously creates a massive infusion of technologies in Nigeria's educational and economic spaces, creates jobs for new graduates from universities and technical colleges, and provides employment opportunities for less-skilled Nigerians. Pointedly, the current 13 percent oil revenue allocated to the oil-producing communities is an improvement over the decades. It temporarily pacified the Niger Delta region but has not solved the resource-based ethnic conflicts and continues to threaten economic activities and security. This is not a sustainable economic development strategy.

An effective state capacity enables the designing and efficient implementation of economic development policies and has transparent institutional mechanisms for holding leaders accountable for how public resources are budgeted and spent. In such a state, rent-seeking and politics as vectors for revenue sharing are deemphasized while economic development policies are efficiently implemented. For example, based on federal revenue allocations to many states in Nigeria—Akwa Ibom, Delta, Rivers, Bayelsa, Lagos, Kano, Ondo, and Kaduna—the states should be, at least, as developed if not better than several African countries like Rwanda, Malawi, Togo, Liberia, Cape Verde, the Central African Republic, and the Gambia, whose overall GDP is comparable to the revenues of these states.[23] The question is, without a functioning and effective institutional and policy oversight, is the 13 percent oil revenue allocation from the federation account to oil-producing states sufficient to address economic, health, education, security, and other challenges in these states? And how likely are the custodians of state power and budgets to invest in sustainable projects that create employment, expand the generation of resources in their states, and unleash the entrepreneurial energies in their people?

Ultimately, Nigeria's public policies at the federal and state levels should be made based on strategic choices[24] that are rooted in the country's realistic efforts at internal resource mobilization. Nigeria's national economic development policies should aim to create opportunities for honest private sector employment, develop effective institutional structures for income tax mobilization at the local and state levels, fund infrastructural development, and gradually divest the government from economic activities. Nigerian government's active role in economic development policies and investments in specific industries in the country should be complemented by a robust regulatory and conflict management role in the economy. Such roles will help expand Nigeria's economic development efforts, promote collaboration between public and private sector economic activities, and preserve the legacies of *indigenous elites*, who will need to sacrifice their current urge for continuous accumulation without requisite productivity for a secure future of already accumulated wealth.

To reiterate, the foregoing suggestions are likely to yield intended development results if politics is used by leaders, especially presidents and governors, to mobilize resources for policies, and integrate regional, religious, and short-term interests into a national agenda. This will simultaneously ensure that policies trump politics in local, state, and national leaders' management of political conflicts as well as in decisions made to advance economic development. Such a framework requires significant enhancement of the capacities of state institutions in Nigeria to carry out their public policy functions that serve the economic, health, education, justice, safety, and security needs of the people. Also, a fair and transparent implementation of the rule of law requires an educated police service whose officers know the difference between civil and political rights and human rights and are not compromised by poor salaries to make them susceptible to bribery and corruption in discharging their duties. In addition, competent judicial staff and judges who can assess and rely on evidence to render decisions that are transparently fair to both the defendants and the prosecuting parties, without regard to wealth or positions in society, are needed for an effective existence of the rule of law.

Certainly, effective implementation of the rule of law can only exist in a constitutional environment where the military is subordinate to civilian authority in the discharge of their duties. The same rule of law and accountability applies at customs borders where Nigerians import and export goods and services, and at the immigration and customs desks at Nigeria's international airports as these have direct impacts on economic development activities in the country. According to Richard Carey,[25] the concept of state effectiveness is not new; it is a developmental state whose political legitimacy is based on the extent it can subordinate power to the rule of law and convincingly use public policy to advance "the welfare of the state and its people."[26]

A more nuanced argument for state effectiveness is presented by Ashraf Ghani and Clare Lockhart.[27] Ghani and Lockhart argue that state effectiveness requires the simultaneous performance of ten different but interlinked factors if the gains of sovereignty are to be realized by citizens globally, but especially in fragile and dysfunctional states like Nigeria. The presence of the following factors: (1) rule of law, (2) monopoly on legitimate means of violence, (3) administrative control, (4) sound management of public finances, (5) investment in human capital, (6) creation of citizenship rights through social policy, (7) provision of infrastructure services, (8) creation and expansion of the market, (9) management of public assets, and (10) public borrowing will enhance a state's capacity for economic development, and their absence will impede the implementation of development policies and achievement of possible outcomes.[28] Ghani and Lockhart's arguments are institutionally and substantively relevant to the argument advanced in this chapter that while politics can mobilize resources for policy advancement, policies have to trump politics to realize the goals of national economic development. It will take restructuring the inherited colonial Nigerian state and effective leadership, as well as competent and functional bureaucracies, to establish a sustainable framework for national economic development. Moving beyond the monocultural nature of Nigeria's economy, low level of development as previously noted, the politics of revenue sharing from the federation account, and persistent dependence of the annual budgets on the price of crude petroleum with Nigeria as a price-taker, will require restructuring at different levels and focused attention on increasing various levels of human capital in the country.

Investment in human capital is one of the major policies that effective states have used to build a middle class and secure the necessary manpower for sustainable development and management of their economies. According to Ghani and Lockhart, investment in human capital

> was the mechanism used to overcome the conflicts of the nineteenth century and provide a ground for stable democratic politics. As professions emerged, spurred on in part by the expansion of universities, they became critical to social mobility. Economic productivity and growth now depend on an educated and healthy population. As human capital becomes more critical to wealth creation than other forms of capital, public investment in universities also becomes more important. . . . The consequences of failing to invest in human capital are equally clear: an excessive degree of inequality, social immobility, and thus persistent poverty. Without access to health care and education, there can be no middle class. Growth becomes negative, stagnant, or slow and thus has no impact on development. Several of the poorest societies have had some of the highest rates of brain drain. Also, with the outbreak of the AIDS epidemic and failure to invest adequately in its mitigation, life expectancy in Africa has fallen to 1960s levels; and it threatens to wipe out the gains of the last five decades. Child mortality and childbirth death levels are still extremely high, populations continue to grow, and life expectancy in the poorest countries remains very low.[29]

Effective and functional education can be formal and informal. In Nigeria, it can take the form of apprenticeship to increase the stock of human capital in jobs that do not require formal university education. Also, most viable and effective states have efficient bureaucracies based on meritocratic recruitment processes which ensure that efficient and law-abiding citizens who take pride in their moral integrity as a foundation for their public service are consistently hired. Responsible and accountable stewards of public trust are more likely to have been well trained and therefore have a predisposition toward excellence that self-reproduces in their policies, whether those be for healthcare services, education, infrastructural development, or the efficient management of public finances. Thus, states that neglect human capital, for example, those that do not pay attention to higher education, are states that tend to have poor administrators and administration with inevitable low economic development outcomes.[30] Investments in education, for example, lead to innovation in public health, which leads to preventative health services and a healthier citizenry that becomes more productive. When states pay attention to the development of education and use of the competence of their citizens, as most of the South East Asian countries did during the Cold War, the outcome is remarkable economic growth. But states that do not pay attention to human capital investment in their countries will lack the capacity for effective development of contextually relevant policies and their implementations. The consequences are that such a state will be unable to use social policy as a tool for nation-building. Such is the case in Nigeria where inattention to human capital investment, especially since the 1980s, is evidenced in contemporary Nigeria with a growing population of over 200 million people and a 62 percent adult literacy level—mostly at the basic reading and writing level, and without a critical mass of technical and scientific cadres. Yet, its natural resources are vast—petroleum, bauxite, iron ore, natural gas, tin, coal, limestone, niobium, lead, tantalite, and zinc; and Nigeria has vast swaths of arable land for cocoa, cassava, yam, rice, palm oil, groundnut, and many other agricultural products that should make the country a net exporter rather than an importer of food items to the tune of over a $1 billion in 2020. With a life expectancy at birth of fifty-four years, GDP per capita of $2,028, 40 percent of the population living below the poverty line, and over 30 percent of the employed categorized as working poor, it becomes clear why Nigeria is one of the lowest-ranked countries in the HDI at an HDI value of 0.534 and ranked 158 out of 189 countries in 2018.

Unfortunately, while Nigeria earned 3.42 trillion Naira in 2020, it spent 3.3 trillion Naira on debt service[31] to external bilateral and multilateral entities. According to the federal government, "it made no revenue from stamp duties, domestic recoveries, assets, and fines,"[32] all of which are reversible with competent human capital, effective institutions, and policy framework that are needed to explore other alternative sources of revenue generation for Nigeria. Instead of defunding of education that led to brain drain with consequences for healthcare service deliveries, infrastructural development and maintenance, and further erosion of state capacity as was the case in the 1980s, Nigeria needs to refocus on getting human capital right as a sine qua non to getting economic development policies and implementations right. Today, the question is: quo vadis, Nigeria? Nigeria will go where her thought leaders take her. On the nation's economic policies given the continuing oppositional/confrontational strategies and politics at the national level in which each side is right, and no one is listening because "right" is generally the final word–Nigeria will most likely remain "dysfunctional and fragile!" Even so, it is our hope that Nigeria will produce transformational leaders after the current topsy-turvy politics under this Fourth Republic.

NOTES

1. See Kelechi A. Kalu and Jiyoung Kim, *Foreign Aid and Economic Development in South Korea and Africa: A Comparative Analysis of Economic Growth* (London: Routledge Publishers, 2022), Chapter 7.
2. See Ngozi Okonjon-Iweala, *Reforming the Unreformable: Lessons from Nigeria* (Cambridge, MA: MIT Press, 2012), p. 13.
3. See Sola Akinrinade, "Constitutionalism and the Resolution of Conflicts in Nigeria," *The Round Table*, Vol. 368, No. 41–52 (2003), pp. 42–43.
4. See Peter G. Northhouse, *Leadership: Theory and Practice, Third Edition* (Thousand Oaks, California and London, UK: Sage Publications, 2004), p. 170.
5. See Northouse, *Leadership: Theory and Practice, Third Edition*, p. 178.
6. Complete data and overview specific for Nigeria is available here: https://freedomhouse.org/country/nigeria/freedom-world/2021 (Retrieved July 9, 2021)
7. UNDP data on Nigeria is available here: http://hdr.undp.org/en/countries/profiles/NGA. (Retrieved July 9, 2021)
8. For the data on internally displaced persons in Nigeria, see the section on Transnational Issues in Moody's Analytics, https://www.economy.com/nigeria/indicators (Retrieved July 9, 2021).
9. UNDP op. cit. http://hdr.undp.org/en/countries/profiles/NGA (Retrieved July 9, 2021).
10. Ibid.
11. The average human inequality data, 2010–2019, is calculated by the author from the yearly data—40.7, 38.9, 41.2, 40.2, 37.5, 37.5, 36.6, 34.6, 35.5, and 35.2, as reported in http://hdr.undp.org/en/countries/profiles/NGA (Retrieved July 9, 2021).
12. Ibid.
13. Sources of data include Nigerian Bureau of Statistics at https://nigerianstat.gov.ng/ (last visited July 9, 2021); African Development Bank, *Nigerian Economic Outlook* at https://www.afdb.org/en/countries-west-africa-nigeria/nigeria-economic

-outlook (last visited July 9, 2021); and The CIA, *The World Factbook* at https://www.cia.gov/the-world-factbook/countries/nigeria/#economy (last visited July 9, 2021).

14. Okonjo-Iweala, *Reforming the Unreformable*, pp. 14–15.

15. Ibid.

16. The "crippled giant" term was coined by Eghosa E. Osaghae in *Crippled Giant: Nigerian Since Independence* (Bloomington, IN: Indiana University Press, 1998).

17. See Femi Asu, "$1.24bn spent on food imports despite Buhari's forex ban," at https://punchng.com/1-24bn-spent-on-food-imports-despite-buharis-forex-ban/ (Retrieved June 29, 2021).

18. Rotimi T. Suberu, *Ethnic Minority Conflicts and Governance in Nigeria* (Ibadan: Spectrum Books Limited, 1996), pp. 27–39.

19. See Kelechi A. Kalu, "Echoes of Instability: Implications for State, Society and Democratic Consolidation in Nigeria," *The Constitution: A Journal of Constitutional Development*, Vol. 5, No. 1 (March 2005), pp. 1–37.

20. Federal Republic of Nigeria, *1999 Constitution of the Federal Republic of Nigeria* (Lagos: Federal Government Press, 1999), p. 131.

21. Suberu, *Ethnic Minority Conflicts and Governance in Nigeria*, pp. 27–28.

22. Cited in Rotimi T. Suberu, *Ethnic Minority Conflicts and Governance in Nigeria*, pp. 29–30.

23. See Ngozi Okonjo-Iweala, *Fighting Corruption is Dangerous: The Story Behind the Headlines* (Cambridge and London: The MIT Press, 2018), p. 147.

24. Kelechi Kalu, "Nigeria: Learning from the Past to Meet the Challenges of the 21st Century," *Social Research*, Vol. 77, No. 4 (Winter 2010): 1367–1400.

25. Richard Carey, "Aid, Effective States and Development in the Busan Agenda and Beyond," p. 2.

26. Ibid. See Kalu and Kim, *Foreign Aid in South Korea and Africa: A Comparative Analysis of Economic Growth*, 2021.

27. Ashraf Ghani and Clare Lockhart, *Fixing Failed States: A Framework for Rebuilding a Fractured World* (New York: Oxford University Press, 2008), pp. 124–166.

28 Ibid.

29. Ghani and Lockhart, *Fixing Failed States: A Framework for Rebuilding a Fractured World*, pp. 139–142.

30. Ghani and Lockhart, *Fixing Failed States: A Framework for Rebuilding a Fractured World*, p. 142.

31. Temitayo Jaiyeola, "Nigeria made N3.42tn in 2020, debt servicing gulped N3.34tn – BudgIT." https://punchng.com/nigeria-made-n3-42tn-in-2020-debt-servicing-gulped-n3-34tn-budgit/ (Retrieved July 12, 2021)

32. Ibid.

Chapter 4

Strategic Reforms to Resuscitate the Nigerian Healthcare System

Joseph A. Balogun and Philip C. Aka

INTRODUCTION

The high mortality rates and enormous disease burden within the Nigerian healthcare system are overwhelming. First, measured in health outcomes, the health system ranks among the most suboptimal in the world; and, second, over time, coming to a head under the Fourth Republic since 1999, the health sector has endured further deterioration that places it on proverbial life support, mandating intervention of a type set aside for patients in the ICU. This chapter explores ten strategic reforms aimed at resurrecting Nigeria's dysfunctional healthcare system.

In 2000, the World Health Organization (WHO) assessed Nigeria's healthcare system and described it as "dysfunctional, ineffective, under-capitalized, costly, and inaccessible," in a global ranking that placed the country's performance at 187 out of the 191 countries surveyed.[1] A more recent study published in *Lancet* rated Nigeria at 140 of 195 countries on healthcare access and quality index, based on the number of deaths from thirty-two common preventable diseases, including tuberculosis (TB) and other respiratory infections, diphtheria, whooping cough, tetanus, measles, and maternal and neonatal disorders.[2]

More than half of the Nigerian population lacks access to health services. The deterioration goes back in time to decades. A few examples will suffice. In 2018, the top ten causes of death in Nigeria were lower respiratory infections, neonatal disorders, human immunodeficiency virus (HIV)/AIDS, malaria, diarrheal diseases, TB, meningitis, ischemic heart disease, stroke, and cirrhosis.[3] The health system endures a "double burden" from infectious diseases and non-communicable conditions that appears to be rising. For example, TB prevalence is 323 per 100,000, alcohol and tobacco use are exceptionally high at 9.1 percent in 2015 and 17.4 percent in 2016, and Nigeria has one of the highest road fatalities globally.[4] Road traffic accidents are the third leading cause of overall deaths, the leading cause of trauma-related deaths, and the most common cause of disability—an estimated 1,042 deaths a year for every 100,000 vehicles. Mortality due to household and ambient air pollution stands at 99 per 100,000 of the population.[5]

Malaria accounts for 27 percent of the global disease burden. It is a risk for 97 percent of Nigerians and accounts for more deaths than any other country in the world. Each year, the country reports about 100 million malaria cases, accounting for over 300,000 deaths. The mortality rate for malaria is 146 per 100,000 populations.[6] These gloomy statistics on malaria alone is compounded by morbidity figures from HIV/AIDS of about 215,000 deaths per year.[7] At 3.2 percent, Nigeria's HIV/AIDS prevalence rate is one of the highest in the world.

Nigeria has one of the highest infants, child, and maternal mortality rates; the second-largest number of children with delayed growth; and the third-lowest average life expectancy rate of fifty-five years in the world.[8] Nigeria ranked 153 out of 187 countries on the United Nations' human development index. At 814 per 100,000 live births, Nigeria also ranked 187 out of 191 countries on the maternal mortality indices. Paradoxically, Nigeria compares to low-performing countries like Chad (856), Central African Republic (882), and Sierra Leone (1,360). It performs below Somalia and the Democratic Republic of Congo. Overall, the maternal and infant mortality rate in Nigeria is worse than the average in sub-Saharan Africa. The statistics worsen for every 1,000 births in Nigeria: 108 infants (and children) die before five, the worst in Africa.[9] The dismal statistics in maternal and infant mortality are due to limited access to preventive programs in healthcare services (pre- and postnatal care, screening for specific diseases, and immunization) for pregnant women and children.

Due to underfunding, Nigeria lacks the infrastructure for treating non-communicable diseases. For instance, only seven of the thirty-six states in Nigeria have a specialist hospital or clinic for cancer treatment.[10] Globally, life-threatening contagious diseases have reduced substantially in the last decade, and performance on key health indices slightly improved. In Nigeria, however, poverty is at an all-time high, and malnutrition is still prevalent, with a 43.6 percent stunting rate. Health issues are further complicated by the fact that environmental change and air pollution are on the rise.

Currently, Nigeria's health system is weak, and the services are of low quality with inequitable distribution and insufficient infrastructures.[11] Moreover, the system is saddled with counterfeit medications and lack of state-of-the-art medical equipment. Due to widespread dissatisfaction with the healthcare system, 71 percent of Nigerians treat themselves before consulting a physician. When they seek treatment from doctors, they frequently did so with external financial assistance—sometimes from extended family members in the diaspora.[12]

Healthcare is profoundly political, and disadvantaged groups are often denied access to care. Nigeria ranks among the most richly endowed nations of the world in natural and human resources, but corruption and ineffective leadership have not made healthcare a number one priority. Since independence, some political parties have campaigned on providing free healthcare, but keeping the promise is where the rubber meets the road.

In the last decade, Nigeria's health system deteriorated further. Nigeria failed to meet the UN's eight health-related millennium development goals (MDGs) by the 2015 target date.[13] In September 2015, the UN adopted seventeen sustainable development goals (SDGs) to replace the expired MDGs. Due to a lack of political will, Nigeria has made little or no progress on the seventeen SDGs and is unlikely to meet the goals by 2030, without implementation of some drastic interventions. Regrettably, solutions to the high-disease burden and decrepit health system are not in sight, given that successive governments have consistently failed to implement a coherent national health plan. In 2016, President Muhammadu Buhari's government launched a plan to achieve 30 percent health insurance coverage by 2020. This goal has yet to materialize, and the health system appears currently to be on life support. This chapter explores the following ten strategic reforms aimed at resurrecting Nigeria's severely sick healthcare system.

NIGERIA'S LEADERS SHOULD RECOMMIT THEMSELVES TO THE ABUJA DECLARATION ON OPTIMAL BUDGETARY ALLOCATION

The first measure of strategic reform this chapter proposes is for Nigerian leaders at all levels, including non-governmental organizations (civil society), to recommit themselves to the Abuja Declaration on Optimal Budgetary Allocation in Africa. Globally, primary healthcare serves as the first point of contact for patients at communal levels, facilitating easy access to medical treatment and is the most efficient and cost-effective way to achieve universal healthcare (UHC). In Nigeria, the thirty-six states are responsible for providing secondary healthcare services in general hospitals, while the local governments are charged with coordinating primary healthcare delivery.[14] However, of the three arms of government, the local government is the least funded. The first casualty of a decline in oil revenue has always been the defunding of primary healthcare, followed by education. As a result, Nigeria has not been able to efficiently implement primary healthcare, the backbone of the health system.[15]

The tertiary hospitals have limited state-of-the-art diagnostic and therapeutic equipment to provide high-quality healthcare because 78 percent of the budget is allocated to personnel salary and welfare. In 2018, 93 percent of allocations to federal government-owned hospitals was spent on recurrent expenditure items, primarily personnel costs. In 2016, recurrent expenditure made up approximately 97 percent of total allocations to federal government-owned hospitals.[16] Consequently, tertiary hospitals have little money left to invest in capital projects, such as buildings, major diagnostic and therapeutic equipment, and power generating plants. Many tertiary hospitals lack well-trained healthcare specialists. For over two decades, healthcare spending in Nigeria has been lower than 10 percent of the national budget, even though the heads of African countries in 2001 committed to allocating 15 percent of their annual budget to the health sector.[17]

Nigeria's healthcare expenditure has been consistently lower than the average of 8.8 percent recommended by the Organization for Economic Cooperation and Development countries.[18] In 2011, only four African countries (Zambia, Malawi, Liberia, and Rwanda) met the 15 percent health budget benchmark. And as of 2017, only Sierra Leone (15.1 percent) and Liberia (15.5 percent) met the criterion. [19] Nineteen long years after the Abuja pledge, Nigeria is yet to redeem that pledge. Because of the poor state of health service delivery in the country, and the ubiquity of fake drugs, many affluent Nigerians seek medical treatment abroad.

The popularity of medical tourism among the politicians and aristocrats is problematic. Nigeria spends the equivalent of between US$1 and 1.5 billion annually on medical tourism to India, Egypt, Dubai, and the United Kingdom for cardiology, orthopedics, neurology, cosmetic and renal transplant surgeries, including cancer and renal dialysis care.[20] In 2019, the House of Representatives failed to approve a bill seeking to restrict public officials from taking foreign medical trips at public expense. Instead, the legislators argued that the proposed law discriminated against their human rights and punished them for the government's failure to develop the healthcare system.[21] Unfortunately, little has changed; instead, the elites, including President Muhammadu Buhari himself, ironically seek and receive medical treatment abroad.

Many health analysts expressed concern that Nigeria's 2021 budget allocated only 4.5 percent (about N592.166 billion of the proposed N13.082 trillion) to healthcare, compared, for example, to 12.5 percent by South Africa. More disconcerting, Nigeria made no direct allocations for epidemic prevention, despite the present and future threat of COVID-19.[22] Abdulaziz Abdullahi, permanent secretary in the Federal Ministry of Health (FMH), described the 15 percent health budget benchmark set under the Abuja

Declaration as an "aspirational" goal.[23] He attributed the paltry health budget to competing interests from different sectors, such as education, agriculture, insecurity in many parts of the country, and plummeting oil prices.[24] Against this backdrop, the following guides are proposed to ensure adequate funding for the health sector.

Recommendations

The Federal Government of Nigeria is a signatory to the Abuja Declaration and cannot describe the treaty as an "aspirational" goal. It should view the agreement as a valid benchmark that the government is under obligation to follow. To secure adequate capital funding to renovate buildings and purchase state-of-the-art diagnostic and therapeutic tools in tertiary hospitals across the country, Nigeria's national government should fund the healthcare sector at 15 percent. This recommendation is in sync with the Abuja Declaration.

Because of the decline in oil revenue, Nigeria's economic planning must include internally generated revenue, reining in on overhead costs, expanding tax brackets, and reprioritizing the areas in need of funding. The exorbitant cost associated with medical tourism is a significant waste of resources that the federal government could harness to develop the healthcare system. Accordingly, medical tourism should be strongly discouraged to upgrade the healthcare system.

The urban population in Nigeria has increased from 34.8 percent in 2000 to 46.9 percent in 2014, with an urbanization growth rate of 3.75 percent. At its current growth rate, the population will surpass that of the United States by 2050. Because the government has made little attempt to control population, Nigeria would be the world's third most populous country after China and India by the end of the century, with an estimated 400 million people.[25] For decades, funding for family planning has declined. This has contributed to the population explosion in the country.[26] As the population continues to grow unchecked, the health sector has not met the increased population growth. More funding is urgently needed for family planning and education (especially among teenagers).

About 33 percent of Nigerian children under five years evidence stunted growth. The incidence of severe acute malnutrition (particularly in the Northern sections of the country) contributes significantly to poor health outcomes.[27] A robust budget for the National Strategic Plan on Nutrition is needed to address the primary drivers of childhood illness and reverse malnutrition.

PROMOTE INCREASED PARTICIPATION IN THE NATIONAL HEALTHCARE INSURANCE SCHEME (NHIS)

The second strategic reform, necessary for improvement of Nigeria's healthcare system, is to promote healthcare through participation in the NHIS. The NHIS was introduced in 2005 by President Olusegun Obasanjo with the goals of providing access to quality healthcare and protecting Nigerians from financial risk by reducing the high burden of out-of-pocket (OOP) spending. Regrettably, fifteen years after its introduction, these goals remain unrealized. Indeed, less than 5 percent of Nigerians have the insurance needed to provide access to healthcare.[28] In addition, formal sector employers account for almost all the total enrolled persons under the NHIS.[29]

In Nigeria, OOP spending constitutes nearly 90 percent of total private health spending, placing a significant burden on households. About 60 percent of all health spending is financed directly by families without insurance. The low enrollment in the NHIS is partly due to the population's peculiar demographics. About 48 percent of Nigerians live in rural areas and 52 percent in urban areas.[30] Private vendors provide about 70 percent of healthcare, and the government offers only 30 percent, with over 70 percent of the drugs dispensed being adulterated or substandard.[31]

The revenue for financing healthcare is collected from pooled (i.e., budget allocation, direct and indirect taxation, and donor funding) and un-pooled sources, both contribute to over 70 percent of total expenditure. The un-pooled sources include OOP payments (informal or formal direct payments to healthcare workers (HCWs) following service provision) and payments for goods (medical products, such as bed nets, etc.). Despite these health financing options, spending is still unevenly distributed across the system, with regional inequity in healthcare expenditure.[32]

Odeyemi and Nixon compared Nigeria and Ghana's health and economic indicators after implementing the NHIS program for a decade.[33] In 2010, healthcare expenditure in both countries was about 5 percent of the Gross Domestic Product (GDP), but public spending was 38 percent of Nigeria's total expenditure, compared to 60 percent in Ghana. Over the ten years, the private OOP expense in Ghana fell from 80 to 66 percent of total expenditure but remained at over 90 percent in Nigeria. On the other hand, the population insurance coverage in Nigeria was a dismal 3.5 percent in Nigeria, compared to over 65 percent in Ghana. Additionally, Nigeria's health insurance package has variable benefits options depending on the membership category, while Ghana has the same benefits across all beneficiaries. In short, Nigeria can do better.

It is estimated that 93 percent of all employments in Nigeria is informal, with 95 percent of women working in the informal sector, compared to 90 percent of men.[34] The primary barrier in expanding health insurance coverage in Nigeria is the high percentage of employers in the informal economy and the low (3.5 percent) subscription to NHIS by the self-employed, private employers, and state governments.[35] The private voluntary health insurance has shown a low potential to expand coverage, decentralize health insurance to the states, and community-based health insurance, and has limited potential to extend access to the impoverished and vulnerable populations in the informal sector.[36]

Recommendations

Evidence from other nations worldwide suggests that it is challenging to attain UHC from contributory insurance schemes alone, particularly in countries like Nigeria with a large informal sector economy.[37] Thus, a tax-based, noncontributory, universal health financing system should be encouraged as the primary funding mechanism to accelerate progress toward achieving UHC in Nigeria. The main revenue should be supplemented by social health insurance and decentralized to states for the formal sector employees, and private voluntary health insurance should cover wealthy individuals. The low coverage of the NHIS is partly due to poor public awareness by the younger people, stereotypic ideas regarding the government's role in funding healthcare, cultural beliefs about health insurance attracting ill health, and lack of trust in the government.[38] Increased public awareness through conversation around health insurance using the media targeted to different social, economic, and occupational groups in the society will improve the low coverage in health insurance.

The Internet and other social media are used widely in Nigeria. About 113.3 million Nigerians comprising 59 percent of the population use mobile Internet, and many also use other social networks and messaging applications. Equally, about 41 percent use *Facebook* and *WhatsApp* platforms. Adults between eighteen and thirty-four years of age account for between 34 and 80 percent of the primary social media site users.[39] Thus, social media is a good source for health management organizations to disseminate information about health insurance. The oral word-of-mouth marketing strategy will be more effective in reaching Nigerians in the informal economic sector with only primary school education and those who lack access to social media technology. Leveraging the social networks of the different demographic and economic categories is expected to yield high gains in health insurance enrollment.[40]

To increase the revenue stream for the NHIS, the federal and state governments should expand job opportunities for the unemployed and provide a job training program for the youths. Failure to address extreme poverty in the country is among the reasons why previous healthcare reforms were unsuccessful. A citizen in search of the next meal will not be interested in purchasing health insurance coverage. Nigerian governments have an ethical obligation to provide health insurance coverage for the poor and improve the percentage of the insured population. The persistent and significant weakness of Nigeria's health financing system is due to low public spending, high levels of OOP expenditures (notoriously one of the highest in the world), and impoverishment due to healthcare costs. Consequently, different pragmatic efforts must be explored to increase public funding of healthcare alongside other options, such as public-private partnerships, and increased donor assistance, where practicable.

The Nigerian government can bolster NHIS revenue by leveraging private resources and promoting innovations and expertise. Only through improved funding of the health sector by the national government will expanded healthcare in Nigeria be a reality. To actualize this goal, the federal government must identify vital and alternative revenue streams to enhance the efficiency of the income collection mechanisms. Such incomes could be generated from the agricultural and mining sectors.

By 2015, six years after the federal government enacted the National Health Act (NHA), there was little traction on the ground related to implementation. Under the law, the NHA is expected to set aside 1 percent of the Consolidated Revenue Fund to provide primary healthcare, but this recommendation is yet to be implemented. President Buhari's administration has ignored recommendations by scholars, policy analysts, and civil society for the government to fund this component of the NHA.[41] To reduce the primary mortality indices in the country, implementing the NHA must be accorded the highest priority. Funneling local governments' allocations from the federal government through the state has failed because state governors often withhold such provisions for other state needs, thereby financially handicapping implementation of primary healthcare. The recently enacted arrangement that allows the local governments to receive their funds directly from the federal government is spot on and a viable way to go.

EXPAND ACCESS TO ESSENTIAL MEDICINES AND VACCINES

A third means of healthcare reform is expanding access to essential medicines and vaccines necessary to keep the masses in good health. Healthcare institutions in Nigeria lack essential resources, such as vaccine, medicine, and equipment. For over two decades, Nigeria has struggled unsuccessfully to address the production and distribution of counterfeit drugs. Successive administrations in the country lack the political will to enforce legislation related to counterfeiting. The growing numbers of deaths from adulterated medications prompted the public, led by the Pharmaceutical Society of Nigeria, to bring pressure to bear on the government to enact legislation (Decree No. 21 of 1998). The Decree prohibited the sale and distribution of counterfeit, adulterated, banned, fake drugs or poisons in open markets and without a license or registration.[42]

Founded in 1993, the National Agency for Food and Drug Administration and Control (NAFDAC) is responsible for controlling the importation, exportation, manufacture, advertisement, distribution, sale, and use of food, drugs, cosmetics, medical devices, bottled water, and chemicals by placing inspectors at various air and seaports to check these nefarious practices. In 2001, under Dora Akunyili as director-general, NAFDAC implemented thoroughgoing reforms. As a result, by 2006, drug failure rates fell to 16 percent from its high level in 2002, and the incidence of adulterated medications was reduced by 80 percent. However, despite NAFDAC's successes, counterfeit drugs remain prevalent. These are some of the reasons many Nigerians lose faith in their health system.[43]

Counterfeit drugs pose substantial threats to reducing infant mortality; improving maternal health; and combating HIV/AIDS, malaria, and other diseases. Proliferation of adulterated drugs causes treatment failures, organ dysfunction or damage, worsening chronic disease conditions, and many avoidable deaths.[44] Economically, and from a global standpoint, fake drug trade is worth US$200 billion, of which Africa accounts for about 42 percent of the nefarious market. In Nigeria, fake malaria medication accounts for 12,300 deaths annually and US$893 million in costs.[45] Fortunately, some private enterprises have come to the rescue in the fight against counterfeit drugs. These are *Medsafe*, *RxAll, Inc.*, *True-Spec Africa*, and *FD Detector*.[46]

Immunization rates in Nigeria are among the lowest in the world. In Northern Nigeria, barely 10 percent of children receive all their routine vaccines. Similarly, vaccination against tetanus is equally low among women.[47] Thousands of children still die annually from vaccine-preventable diseases because the primary healthcare system is highly ineffective and has deteriorated substantially in the last two decades.

In 2003, less than 1 percent of the infants in Jigawa, 1.5 percent in Yobe, 1.6 percent in Zamfara, and 8.3 percent in Katsina states were fully immunized.[48] The reasons accounting for the low rate of vaccination include rumors on the safety of the poliomyelitis vaccine. This misinformation disrupted the routine immunization services, created lack of public trust in the health services, and insufficient knowledge of the benefits of immunization by rural dwellers.

Despite the important improvements in response to disease outbreaks, Nigeria now faces a possible surge in "vaccine-derived" polio cases. Ironically, after three consecutive years without a natural poliovirus case, Nigeria was declared free of the disease by the WHO in 2020. This development was hailed as a milestone. Given that some northern states in 2003 banned vaccination, this is an achievement fraught with cautious optimism. In 2012, Nigeria accounted for more than 50 percent of all polio cases worldwide and nearly derailed the global drive to eradicate the disease in the country. Fortunately, WHO monitors the virulent strain of poliovirus.[49]

In 2020, the Nigerian government committed more resources to prevent vaccine-preventable diseases through immunization efforts. Of the nearly ₦91 billion capital budget, the FMH allocated ₦44.5 billion for the Basic Health Care Provision Fund and the remaining ₦46.5 billion for other activities. Specifically, ₦22.73 billion was budgeted for the Global Alliance for Vaccines and Immunizations, ₦4.8 billion for polio eradication initiatives, ₦815 million for procurement of non-polio supplementary immunization activities vaccine, and ₦4 billion for procurement of vaccines and devices.[50]

Recommendations

The primary drivers of fake drugs in circulation are the ineffective enforcement of existing laws, sales of medicine by unqualified vendors, high cost of genuine drugs, and sheer greed. Other factors are corruption, illegal drug importation, chaotic drug distribution network, demand exceeding supply, and lax control system in the economy.[51] Unfortunately, NAFDAC's forensic laboratory is inadequate to cope with the large volume of drug analysis requests, mainly imported medications. Counterfeiters exploit these inefficient quality control systems to manufacture, import, and distribute adulterated products.[52] Consequently, the federal government must fund NAFDAC to purchase high-tech equipment to test both imported and locally manufactured drugs to assure the market's quality and safety. More handheld spectrometers should be purchased and deployed for the authentication of products at the point of sale.

Although various laws regulate and control the manufacture, sale, and distribution of drugs, the weakest point in drug regulation is in the area of enforcement. Some drug laws conflict with each other, aiming more at deterrence and resulting in difficulty in bringing offenders to trial. Therefore, a review of the pharmaceutical laws is essential to help ensure stability in the regulations governing drugs. Pharmaceutical companies must focus more on developing better technologies to protect and identify genuine medications and produce complex labels and holograms difficult for counterfeiters to imitate. Furthermore, the penalties for drug traffickers must be commensurate with the severity of the crime. The maximum punishment for breaching the Decree on fake drugs is ₦500,000 (equivalent to about $2,500) or three months to five years in prison. Adopting stiffer penalties would make the practice less cost-free and lucrative for perpetrators.[53]

Untrained chemists and drug peddlers in the pharmaceutical business contribute to counterfeit because they lack the skill to identify fake medicines. The drug peddlers' sole aim is profit. They cannot educate patients on how to identify counterfeit drugs using visual security tools, including the print quality, the size and shape of tablets, and the examination of holograms. Therefore, healthcare professionals are in an excellent position to assist the government in fighting counterfeit drugs.[54]

The federal government should ban street hawking of drugs, unregistered chemist stores, and improve the registration and license of chemists and pharmacy outlets to ensure they follow good quality practices. In addition, government hospitals should not purchase drugs from open-chain enterprises. Instead, the federal government should support the local production of drugs and ensure their products go directly to hospitals and pharmacy outlets.

Despite the availability and effectiveness of many vaccines, the benefit is still highly dependent on a viable and sustainable health system, adequate funding, a motivated workforce, active community involvement, and strong partnerships. Currently, these conditions are lacking in Nigeria. If effectively deployed, available vaccines can, without doubt, accelerate the achievements of SDGs 3.8 (access to universal health coverage).[55]

The caveat must be entered that some vaccines are less effective in developing countries than in the industrialized world. Thus, clinical trials of vaccines in Nigeria are needed.[56] The federal government should, in the interim, increase funding for vaccine procurement and production of vaccines within the next three years. The activities of state governments toward reducing vaccine-preventable deaths should be made more transparent and better coordinated with the FMH.

STRENGTHEN THE HEALTH INFORMATION SYSTEM

The fourth strategic reform for rejigging Nigeria's faltering health system is strengthening the health information system. Although there is a high demand for mobile phones, Nigeria has the largest number of people without reliable Internet access in Africa: 53 percent of the population lacks reliable Wi-Fi connectivity.[57] An effective health information system is critical for providing care in hospitals and instituting measures that promote wellness and prevent disease.[58] However, the nation's health system is poorly developed and lacks functional medical intelligence and surveillance systems to provide timely information to combat possible public health menace.[59] Adequate medical intelligence and surveillance systems could have averted many of the shortcomings in the healthcare system. Unfortunately, the recommendations in this chapter related to addressing health security concerns did not positively affect the health system.[60]

Patients' medical records in many Nigerian hospitals are still processed manually instead of using computers. The FMH launched the National Health Management Information System (NHMIS) in the 1960s to coordinate the nation's medical statistics information for human resources, hospital activities, mortality, morbidity, birth, and death data in hospitals. National policy was introduced in 2006 and revised in 2014, but the health information system remains weak and ineffective due to underinvestment in health. The unplanned reporting demands resulted in the distortion of the nation's health information system, with many programs and institutions operating multiple or parallel systems.[61]

Today, the NHMIS focuses more on routine health data at the expense of other essential components and faces challenges, including lack of funding, staff shortage, limited resources, inadequate coordination of data flow, non-user friendliness, overlap of data collection instruments, lack of feedback to peripheral levels, and a massive backlog of unprocessed data.[62] In a nutshell, the data collection process is fragmented and inefficient. In addition, the health information system in the country is disease focused because of the requirements of foreign donor organizations and their specific reporting obligations toward diseases, such as HIV/AIDS, malaria, and TB. Nigeria's healthcare system has not effectively leveraged the growing penetration of information and communications technology in the country, nor has it explored opportunities for standardization and inter-system operation planning. Instead, perceptive assessments of the health information system unearth a range of major challenges, including weak governance, ineffective leadership, turf wars, duplication of roles and responsibilities, limited financial incentives for operators, poor technical skills, and an absence of interagency cooperation within the NHMIS.[63]

Recommendations

Electric power supply in Nigeria is generally unreliable, with better power, incredulously, available during the rainy season than dry season.[64] The irregular power supply produces unreliable health information systems, production losses due to damaged equipment, production downtime, severe injuries, and even death.[65] In addition, the safety of people living with disabilities (PLWDs) in high-rise buildings is compromised during power failure. The lack of reliable power and safe water supplies is common in many health institutions. More funding should be made to hospitals to purchase power generators to prevent frequent power outages that adversely affect healthcare delivery.[66] Additionally, to obviate reliance on generators for starters, the federal government must promote accessible power sources, such as wind, hydropower, and adopt co-generation of power using mini-grids and rooftop solar power generation.

Furthermore, the FMH should develop robust and functional medical intelligence and surveillance systems to prevent, detect, and treat diseases using remote sensor technology. The electronic health records created should be interfaced with mobile technologies to share data remotely. The platform will provide an array of new healthcare solutions to prevent and treat diseases. The Department of Public Health faculty in the universities must strengthen their curriculum to address the challenges of medical intelligence and surveillance systems. The FMH and tertiary hospitals should create an effective evidence-based research culture within their organizations. Additionally, the federal government should produce an integrated circuit (a smart) card for all citizens. The card will store medical records and foster efficient clinical documentation and processing of service claims by health providers.

TACKLING THE SHORTAGE OF HCWS

In addition to the preceding reform strategies, a fifth improvement would be to tackle the shortage of HCWs that Nigeria's healthcare system endures. Nigeria has 35,000 physicians to serve its estimated 211,400,708 million people—well below the 237,000 physicians that the WHO recommended in 2015.[67] Nigeria's physician-to-population ratio is at 0.3 per 1,000 persons, compared, for example, to Liberia at 0.1 physicians per 1,000 people, Sierra Leone at 0.2 per 1,000, Ethiopia at 0.2 per 1,000, and Uganda at 0.12 per 1,000. In contrast, countries like South Africa and Egypt stand at 4.3 and 2.8 per 1,000, respectively.[68] According to the United Nations, Nigeria's death rate in 2015 was 11.7 citizens per 1,000, the highest in West Africa and above 8.0 for all Africa.[69] The WHO rated Nigeria among the 44 percent of nations with less than 1 percent of physicians per 1,000 population.[70]

Besides physicians, there is also an acute shortage of other HCWs to deliver essential health services effectively. For instance, the ratio of psychologists and social workers is about two of these professionals to 100,000 clients or service recipients.[71] The WHO recommends one nurse per 700 population, but Nigeria has one nurse per 1,066 people. In 2014, Nigeria had 150,000 registered nurses for its estimated 160 million citizens.[72] The number surged to 240,000 nurses and midwives in 2017. However, based on WHO standard, Nigeria will need 471,353 nurses and midwives by 2030. Moreover, the demand and supply shortfall makes the healthcare system vulnerable if the production of HCWs is not substantially scaled up.[73]

There is an unequal distribution of HCWs, especially in the rural areas and in the northern region of Nigeria. Shortages of HCWs are more prevalent in the northeast, followed by the northwest. The northeast region, where 14 percent of the population resides, has only 4 percent of the physicians, vis-à-vis the southwest, home to 20 percent of the population, with 43.9 percent. Also, the northwest, a more populated region than the southwest and with a higher disease burden, has only one-fifth of the country's physicians.[74] To resuscitate Nigeria's dying healthcare system, the severe shortage of HCWs in these and other states should be tackled.

Given the HCWs shortage, it is disconcerting that many of them are emigrating abroad at an alarming rate for greener pastures unavailable at home. The "brain drain" has reached such new heights that some health analysts described the situation as a "ticking time bomb" for the country. The major destination countries that Nigerian physicians emigrate to, in ranking order, are the United Kingdom, the United States, Canada, Saudi Arabia, Australia, United Arab Emirates, Caribbean nations, Ireland, and South Africa.[75] About 90 percent of the physicians surveyed indicated they have plans to seek job opportunities abroad, while the nation's worsening health sector grapples with industrial strikes.[76]

Recommendations

Aside from the national shortage of HCWs, their distribution is of concern since they are concentrated in the southern part. The inequity in the distribution is due to the lack of coordination of the public and private sector activities and pressures in the private sector, leading to poor-quality work. In addition, the work environment has high attrition—mostly from rural areas and lack of planning, causing overproduction of some categories of HCWs and a shortage of others. These challenges are compounded further by the substantial increase in the migration of HCWs to other countries, the absence of an efficient and coordinated data collection system, and the explosion of medical tourism.[77] To address these issues, in 2011, the FMH partnered with the WHO, the United States Centers for Disease Control, and Carter Foundation to develop a functional human resources information system database to track HCWs' training, graduation, retirement, and exit from the country. At the time, Ruiz Gama Vaz, WHO's representative in the country, observed that the shortage and competence of HCWs posed the most significant challenges to the ability to deliver high-quality and affordable health services.[78] The FMH initiated a partnership project to develop a functional health information system, but ignored it to address the dire shortage of HCWs in the country.[79]

The FMH must provide technical support to professional regulatory bodies to put in place mechanisms that will allow for accurate tracking of exiting HCWs. The data management systems must be based at the state ministries of health and linked to healthcare education institutions. It should be integrated with the service delivery points, including the private sector, ports, and the professional regulatory bodies' computer system to ensure accurate tracking of the number of HCWs in the country. Such a monitoring system will facilitate health workforce planning.

The WHO's benchmark for optimal healthcare delivery stipulates one physician to every 600 people in the population. In 2019, there is one physician for every 5,000 Nigerians. This is one of Africa's notoriously highest rates. Despite this shortage, ironically, there are reported cases of unemployment of physicians/dentists and physiotherapists due to the reluctance of federal, state, and local governments to fund vacancies earmarked for hospital. The National Universities Commission (NUC) and medical professional regulatory boards should encourage the revision of healthcare education curriculum to include content in entrepreneurship. If implemented, this recommendation may provide graduates the skills to develop vibrant private medical practice.

Migration abroad is one of the primary causes of HCWs shortage in the country. For example, Nigerian universities have produced 4,748 bachelor's degree-prepared physiotherapists since the University of Ibadan first established a degree program in 1976.[80] Of this number, only about 1,000 are currently gainfully employed within the country.[81] Due to unsatisfactory service conditions at home and because the federal and state governments do not create positions annually, the remaining 3,748 physiotherapists have migrated to other countries. Thus, in a 750-bed hospital where seventy physiotherapists are needed, only six were employed.[82] Here again, Nigerian universities are training physiotherapists for export to other countries when they are highly in demand at home. The private and public education sectors must appropriately expand student enrollment in the existing healthcare academic programs to meet the need of HCWs in the country—and provisions should be made to find them jobs.

IMPROVE THE CONDITIONS OF SERVICE FOR HCWS

A sixth measure of reform, building on the five outlined above, is improving the conditions of service for HCWs. Multiple factors accounting for work stoppage (industrial action) in Nigeria's health system include bad leadership, timid labor administration, ineffectual policies, inadequate funding, turf battle among healthcare labor unions, uneven distribution of the HCW workforce, and poor working conditions and remunerations.[83] There are also massive discrepancies in the remuneration of HCWs on the same grade levels across the federal, state, and local governments.[84] Poor service conditions, including low salaries and benefits and long work hours, are the primary sources of conflict between management and the professional unions, often leading to industrial strikes.[85]

Over 1,000 Nigerian physicians emigrated to the UK between 2018 and 2019, seeking better pay for their skills. Mass immigration contributes to the low ratio of physicians to population.[86] Low wages, underinvestment in healthcare infrastructure, and the insecurity situation in some states in Northern Nigeria contribute to the inability to attract HCWs to their health facilities in those states. In 2020, during the COVID-19 pandemic, HCWs were promised an additional 50 percent of basic salary and an extra 20 percent for those working in the frontline. The package was not implemented, leading these HCWs to go on strike repeatedly during the crisis.[87]

Recommendations

HCWs in Nigeria earn substantially lower—three to five times—than their counterparts in South Africa. Comparatively, medical consultants in the United States make about ten times more than their counterparts in Nigeria and twice their peers in the UK (Balogun, 2020). The salary differentials between the United States and Nigeria are even higher for the other health professions. Astonishingly, the wages in Ghana and Nigeria are comparable. The finding suggests that some Nigerians leave their homeland for other reasons besides financial gains. Such factors probably include escaping the insecurity and chaos in everyday life, searching for high-quality education for their children, and avoiding the frequent school closures in Nigeria. Accordingly, the federal government must address the intractable security concerns and improve the educational system and conditions of service of HCWs to reduce the number of workers who take their services abroad.

With improved service conditions for HCWs in Nigeria, the brain drain phenomenon will be reduced substantially. Offering competitive compensation based on credentials will incentivize Nigerians in diaspora planning to stay permanently abroad to return to their homeland and contribute to national development. Employers must also provide annual continuing education opportunities for HCWs to acquire new knowledge and hone their clinical skills. Furthermore, tertiary hospitals in the country should ramp up their research infrastructure and offer grant incentives to support faculty engaged in transformative research that benefits the country.

CURTAIL CORRUPTION IN THE HEALTHCARE INDUSTRY

As a seventh strategy, along with the ones discussed above, every step needs to be taken to minimize corruption in the healthcare industry in Nigeria. Five corrupt practices in Nigeria that negatively affect the standard of care for patients are (1) procurement fraud, (2) under-the-counter payments, (3) health financing crime, (4) employment bribery, and (5) unreported absenteeism from work. Corruption in the health sector has a disproportionate pernicious effect on vulnerable populations—the poor, PLWDs, and the elderly.[88] They are shortchanged when resources are wasted or in short supply. The impact increases healthcare costs and reduces access to critical healthcare by people who need the services most. Corruption in the pharmaceutical and medical equipment industry manifests in the form of fraud and kickbacks, bribes to speed up the process for drug registration and certification of products, fake drugs allowed on the market, under-the-counter payments for medication, as well as theft and diversion of available drug supplies and equipment for personal use or resale. The corruption mentioned above drives up prices and leads to the delivery of substandard equipment or adulterated drugs.[89]

Health sector corruption is noticeable in various forms ranging from health financing crime to the use of public facilities and equipment to treat private patients. Corruption can also evince itself in diversion of budget allocations, lack of informed consent before starting a research study, unethical data collection including manipulation/falsification of data, employment-related bribery, jumping queues, failure to report absenteeism from work, malpractice, and referrals of patients to private clinics.[90]

Recommendations

There is no one best way to fight corruption. If it is simple to wipe it out, Nigeria would have found a solution because of its pervasiveness in the country. Even so, it can be detected through internal and external audits, reports by concerned citizens, investigative journalists, whistle-blowers, modern technology (blockchain, smartphone applications, and open data web platforms), and through asset and interest declarations.[91] The health organizations at the three levels of government can make progress in fighting corruption by implementing the following recommendations:

(a) Reform all major health institutions by focusing on improving financial management and strengthening auditors' power.
(b) Promote transparency and access to financial information at all health establishments. Public access to information will increase the responsiveness of administrators and board members.

(c) Support employees' demand for anti-corruption initiatives and empower them to hold health institution administrators accountable. This recommendation will break the cycle of impunity. Civil society organizations and journalists should assist in uncovering corrupt acts in the health sector.
(d) Close international loopholes in the global financial system to prevent money laundering and forestall hiding the proceeds of the stolen state assets to the developed countries.[92]
(e) Dismantle institutional red tapes to enable employees to initiate formal complaints about an ongoing act of corruption through the organization's Ombudsman (i.e., public complaints outfit).
(f) The organization must initiate appropriate sanctions following the detection of corruption. Sanction is a critical preventive component of any effective anti-corruption effort. The organization's Ombudsman must investigate and recommend appropriate disciplinary action. Progressive disciplinary action is an appropriate sanction for minor offenses, such as failure to report absenteeism or cut-in service line. However, egregious crimes such as bribes, kickbacks, theft, and diversion of hospital drugs, supplies, and equipment for personal use or resale should receive the more severe punishment, all the way to termination of appointment, and prosecution.
(g) Organizations' anti-corruption initiatives must be monitored using advanced technologies to apprehend, analyze, and publicly share information to prevent, detect, and deter corrupt behaviors.[93] Ongoing regular monitoring and evaluation are needed to determine the effectiveness of an organization's anti-corruption initiatives and any need for modification as the situations change.[94]

Additionally, the health institutions must demonstrate transparency and accountability to enhance taxpayers' confidence in their willingness to improve the health sector. Furthermore, taxpayers must have access to budgetary information and implementation documents and audit reports of health institutions. Finally, to attract much-needed funds from local and international foundations and donors, health institutions must present their case factually, communicating allegations of corruption with credible evidence, to prevent damaging the reputation of innocent workers.

UPDATE THE HEALTHCARE EDUCATION CURRICULUM

In addition to the preceding strategic measures of reforms outlined above, Nigeria should in its eight prudent scheme update the health education curricula in its universities. Besides the constant labor strikes, HCWs in Nigeria are divided and embroiled in a proverbial territorial or professional turf wars, as they repeatedly feud and interact with distrust of one another.[95] This negative competition takes away from the efficiency and effectiveness of the healthcare system and produces negative health outcomes. Repeated industrial action within the Nigerian health system is attributed to multiple factors that, besides the conventional poor working condition and remuneration, include ineffective leadership, effete governance style of union leaders, inadequate governmental funding, and uneven distribution of the healthcare workforce, among others.[96]

Conflict among HCWs is a recognized problem known to hinder quality healthcare service delivery.[97] In the hospital setting, authority does not usually come from single staff or personnel, nor is it exercised in a single chain of command, as in many large organizations. Physicians exercise substantial authority within the hospital structure and enjoy high autonomy. The independence within the medical and allied professions sometimes triggers conflicts within hospital settings.[98] The interprofessional conflicts cause dissatisfaction and suboptimal contributions of the feuding professional groups to patient care and encourage outbound medical tourism by affluent Nigerians who can afford it. It also contributes to patient dissatisfaction, increases job-associated stress and staff turnover, that ultimately results in the weakening of the health system.

As of June 2021, Nigeria has 174 universities accredited by the NUC. Of this number, the federal government owns forty-three, fifty-two were state funded, while seventy-nine were private.[99] The federal government funds seventeen (39 percent) of the healthcare education programs, nineteen (43 percent) are state funded, while the remaining eight (18 percent) are private universities.[100] Of the 174 universities, only forty-four (25 percent) offer healthcare education programs. Students receive their clinical experience primarily within the tertiary hospitals and community-based clinics located across the country.

The health system is the laboratory to test innovative curriculum and policy ideas; it is a crucial ecosystem to educate health professional students. Bearing in mind that an innovative educational system can bring about fundamental change within the larger society, the curriculum of all healthcare academic programs should be dynamic and subject to ongoing refinement informed by program assessments. Based on the evidence in the literature, the Curriculum reforms suggested here are needed urgently in Nigeria.[101]

Recommendations

The interdisciplinary team healthcare concept has been documented and shown to improve communication among HCWs, reduce medical errors and mortality rates, and improve patient outcomes and healthcare quality.[102] Based on the health model, the interprofessional teaching method creates a positive learning environment for students and fosters mutual respect between HCWs.[103] Adopting the interprofessional teaching method in all the existing forty-four Colleges of Medicine and Health Sciences in Nigeria will go a long way in sanitizing the health sector by decreasing the age-long stereotyping and improving the quality of communication among HCWs.[104] Studies of interdisciplinary teams in large health organizations revealed that improved communication modulates the disharmony and perennial conflicts among HCWs, thereby enhancing overall effectiveness. In addition, the existing literature revealed positive outcomes when health professional students and faculty work in tandem to provide primary care in local communities, particularly among the poor and rural dwellers.[105] The findings in the literature underscore the need to revise the curriculum of all health professions to include content on team dynamics, organization, and leadership theories, while faculty adopts the interprofessional teaching model.[106]

To provide healthcare graduates the knowledge and skills on how to develop private practice, while minimizing dependence on scarce government jobs, the NUC and professional regulatory boards should ensure that the curricula of healthcare education programs include entrepreneurship in its content. Furthermore, several scholars have advocated for the healthcare curricula in the Nigerian universities to include contents in the dynamics of administration, health economics, leadership, andragogy, and interdisciplinary team healthcare.[107]

To increase the number of tertiary hospitals which offers residency programs, within the last decade, the national government converted several general hospitals across the country to Federal Medical Centers. Regrettably, it did not adequately fund the hospitals to hire the personnel needed. As a result, the hospitals now have state-of-the-art edifices without the requisite workforce needed to run them.[108] To solve these myriad problems would require a well-articulated health policy backed by adequate funding and armed with adequate political willpower to implement them. Additionally, the government should set a target on the number of residents and house officers each tertiary hospital, Federal Medical Centers, and other accredited hospitals can employ. To achieve the target, this plan should be well funded. Many state-owned general hospitals can be accredited to offer residency programs in collaboration with the Federal Medical Centers and tertiary hospitals.

Additionally, carefully selected private hospitals should be accredited by the National Postgraduate Medical College and the West African Postgraduate Medical College to offer postgraduate programs. The utilization of private hospitals will expand postgraduate program opportunities for physicians, improve the quality of healthcare provided to patients, and stem the tide of brain drain that afflict Nigeria's healthcare sector. Implementing the above recommendations will go a long way to decongest the tertiary hospitals where residency programs are offered and alleviate unemployment among HCWs.

ADDRESS THE PUBLIC HEALTH CONSEQUENCES OF POLITICAL VIOLENCE

A ninth strategic reform, building on the preceding stratagem, would be to deal with the public health consequences of political violence in Nigeria. In the last decade, multiple security threats left civilians in Nigeria with psychological and physical maladies. These conditions resulted partly from the armed extremist group Boko Haram, recurring inter-communal violence in Nigeria's Middle Belt region, and disproportionate force utilized by security forces. Since 2009, activities of Boko Haram and the Islamic State in West Africa bandits have resulted in over 35,000 people killed and at least 2.4 million people internally displaced. Clashes between herders and farmers have left more than 8,000 people dead and displaced 300,000 across the country since 2011.

During the first half of 2020, more than 1,600 people were killed, and more than 300,000 civilians in Zamfara, Kaduna, Katsina, Sokoto, Niger, and Kebbi states were displaced.[109] In 2020, more than 1,531 people died, and thousands were displaced in inter-communal violence, mostly between herders and farming communities, and in attacks by gangsters in the north-central and north-western regions of the country. According to Amnesty International, thousands of people were internally displaced by inter-communal violence, and attacks by armed groups and security forces committed grave human rights violations, including torture and excessive force, resulting in injuries and unlawful killings. The military detained thousands of people suspected of links to Boko Haram in disease-infected jails. The HCWs were not adequately protected from COVID-19 infection. Accordingly, their health conditions were in peril due to shortages of personal protective equipment, dilapidated and over-stretched health establishments, low wages, and harassment by security forces.[110]

There is increasing tension between the law enforcement agents and the youths, particularly in the Middle Belt, Eastern, and Western states of the country. Living with violence or in fear of violence is a public health issue of utmost importance. The health consequences of violence include increased incidences of post-traumatic stress disorder, anxiety, depression, suicide, cardiovascular disease risk, and premature mortality.[111] Political violence in the country affects "citizens' health," those who witness the violence, family members, and society at large. Some of its casualties are left with permanent physical and mental disabilities.

Recommendations

The impact of violence on human health is of public health concern. Therefore, the federal government should create a Rehabilitation Task Force at the national level to coordinate social and rehabilitation services for the victims. In addition, the government should utilize the early warning system of the Economic Community of West African States to increase police and military deployments to vulnerable states and urgently reform the security sector, including incorporating international humanitarian and human rights law into all military and police training and ensuring sensitivity and accountability for human rights violations.

The psychological and physical problems sustained through violence in Nigeria have an immense negative socio-economic impact on the people. Some are forcibly displaced, and many lose their means of livelihoods. However, the government can improve their situation through emergency assistance, cash grants, healthcare services, and other social services. In addition, the FMH should set up information system databases for facilitating, identifying, monitoring, and evaluating the services provided for displaced people.

The state and local government authorities should work with community leaders to alleviate long-standing grievances between herding and settled communities. In addition, the federal government must address the root causes of inter-communal violence and the rise of armed extremism through political reforms and socio-economic initiatives. Such reform measures must tackle poverty, corruption, youth unemployment, and environmental degradation. In partnership with civil society (non-governmental organizations), these three levels of government should address the socio-economic conditions that breed political violence in Nigeria. They should also establish a national, priority health goal to eliminate violence and develop new methods of providing integrated health, social, and justice services to victims of violence. The FMH should accurately document the extent of violence in Nigerian society. The curriculum of all health professions should include statistics of violence and effective community-building strategies to curb them.

The national government should ensure that people with mental disabilities are institutionalized to receive psychiatric treatment and career training. Those with physical and other disabilities should be housed in community-based convalescent facilities to receive vocational education.[112] By establishing a Division of Medical Rehabilitation within the FMH, healthcare services for disabled persons can be better coordinated nationwide. The Division should also develop educational programs in medical sonography, medical social work, and rehabilitation counseling. These healthcare occupations are highly needed in the healthcare system and will complement the existing medical rehabilitation disciplines currently offered in the universities.

PROMOTE RESEARCH AND DEVELOPMENT (R&D) WITHIN THE HEALTHCARE SYSTEM

The tenth strategic reform this chapter analyzes would be promoting R&D in Nigeria's healthcare system. The change here is analogous to what one scholar perceptively called transformative research. Transformative research involves the application of innovative and creative ideas, discoveries, or tools that radically change the existing knowledge, challenge current understanding, and open pathways to new frontiers.[113] Such applications can change cultural values and society at large.[114] A transformative research approach is best suited to solve Nigeria's unresolved developmental health challenges aligned with the UN's SDGs. They include the ubiquitous issue of poverty, food insecurity, infectious diseases, maternal and child health, endemic non-communicable diseases, gender inequality, energy insufficiency, and climate change.[115] To confront these matters, two key issues need to be addressed. The first is how to ensure that scientists focus on finding solutions to local developmental challenges, what some analysts call "building on the indigenous." The second is to ensure that findings from scientific inquiry translate into policy and industry collaboration and action. Policymakers and scientists in Nigeria have yet to find an answer to these two problems. Instead, as Okonofua pointed out, most local research tends to focus on themes that describe the nature of a problem, rather than those that provide solutions to the developmental challenge.[116]

Development-driven scientific inquiries are expensive since they are often multidisciplinary, and high-tech equipment is needed to implement them. Unfortunately, the Nigerian government has invested limited resources for such research work. For example, the African Union recommends that African countries spend 1 percent of their GDP on R&D. To date, only South Africa, Malawi, and Uganda have reached this goal. Aside from funding, other constraints in applying innovative research in Nigeria include inadequate appreciation for intellectual work, execution of scientific inquiries for personal career advancement, and lack of political will to implement research findings that do not promote the interests of the politicos.

Production and timely dissemination of R&D are the tools for measuring the level of innovation within a healthcare system. Health research is a global endeavor, and investigators increasingly recognize that their research efforts are enhanced by collaborating with colleagues in other multiple centers and countries and engaging in joint training of HCWs. Unfortunately, the research outputs from Nigeria and other African countries have not matched those from other regions of the world. A study commissioned by the World Bank in 2014 revealed that, although Africa constitutes 16 percent of the world's population, the region produces only 1 percent of the global research outputs, with only 198 researchers for every 1 million people in Africa, compared to 455 in Chile and 4,500 in the United States and the UK. In addition, the study also found that all African countries produce about 27,000 research publications annually, equivalent to the total number of papers generated in a small country, such as the Netherlands. Three nations (Egypt, Nigeria, and South Africa) accounted for these publications in Africa. Most research publications in Africa now emanate from South Africa, Egypt, Nigeria, Algeria, Kenya, Morocco, and Tunisia, with South Africa as the most research productive country on the continent. The study estimated that, to catch up about halfway to the research momentum in Western countries, Black Africa (Africa below the Sahara) will require an additional 1 million PhD holders, especially those qualified to conduct cutting-edge research.[117]

Recommendations

Recommendations for a shift to transformative research, including ones beneficial to healthcare, have yet to bear fruits in Nigerian universities.[118] The sparse result is partly due to researchers' inability to identify the suitable approaches to achieve cooperation between industry and policymakers. Without further delay, the NUC should bring together researchers, technocrats, and industry partners in a new collaborative effort that provides interaction right from the research question's development phase until completing the inquiry. In addition, the universities should take a leadership role in training young investigators in transformational inquiry methods, including strategic communication methods on the social media platform to disseminate research findings to policymakers and industry audiences. For Nigeria to achieve sustainable support for high-quality research, the federal government must increase the R&D budget to 1 percent of the GDP in keeping with the African Union's recommendation.

CONCLUSION

Healthcare discourse is universally political, and conflict is frequently associated with how to tackle the issue within a broader economic and social system. Review of the scholarly literature unearthed multiple factors responsible for the suboptimal healthcare system in Nigeria. They include underfunding of the health sector, low wages, shortage of HCWs, corruption in the healthcare industry, and ineffective leadership. Other factors are antiquated infrastructures, outdated health information system, irregular power supply, brain drain, absence of a centralized planning system, insufficient vaccination against deadly diseases, and waste of scarce healthcare resources, among other reasons. Given these dismal scenarios, the 15 percent national budget recommended in the Abuja Declaration is imperative to boost the efficacy of Nigeria's healthcare system under the Fourth Republic.

NOTES

1. *The World Health Organization's Ranking of the World's Health Systems, By Rank* (Geneva, Switzerland: World Health Organization, 2000), https://photius.com/rankings/world_health_systems.html (last accessed October 10, 2020).

2. Nancy Fullman et al., "Measuring Performance on the Healthcare Access and Quality Index for 195 Countries and Territories and Selected Subnational Locations: A Systematic Analysis from the Global Burden of Disease Study 2016," *Lancet* 391 (2018): 2236–71. https://www.thelancet.com/journals/lancet/article/PIIS0140-6736(18)30994-2/fulltext (last visited October 10, 2020).

3. Centers for Disease Control and Prevention (CDC), *Global Health—Nigeria* (2018). https://www.cdc.gov/globalhealth/countries/nigeria/default.htm (last visited May 28, 2021).

4. N.O.C. Onyemaechi and Uchenna R. Ofoma, "The Public Health Threat of Road Traffic Accidents in Nigeria: A Call to Action," *Annals of Medical and Health Sciences Research*, 6, no. 4 (2016): 199–204. https://www.ncbi.nlm.nih.gov/pmc/articles/PMC5405630/ (last visited June 2, 2021).

5. *Global Health Observatory (GHO) Data: World Health Statistics 2016: Monitoring Health for the SDGs* (Geneva, Switzerland: World Health Organization, 2016). https://www.who.int/gho/publications/world_health_statistics/2016/en/ (last visited October 10, 2020).

6. Faisal Muhammad et al., "Major Public Health Problems in Nigeria: A Review," *South East Asia Journal of Public Health*, 7, no. 1 (2017): 6–11.

7. *The World Health Organization's Ranking of the World's Health Systems, By Rank* (Geneva, Switzerland: World Health Organization, 2000). https://www.photius.com/rankings/world_health_systems.html (last visited October 10, 2020).

8. See Ebuka Onyeji, "Analysis: Why Nigeria's Vision 20:2020 Was Bound to Fail," *Premium Times*, (January 19, 2020). https://www.premiumtimesng.com/news/top-news/373321-analysis-why-nigerias-vision-202020-was-bound-to-fail.html (last October 16, 2020); *Global Health Observatory (GHO) Data: World Health Statistics 2016: Monitoring Health for the SDGs* (Geneva, Switzerland: World Health Organization, 2016), https://www.who.int/gho/publications/world_health_statistics/2016/en/ (last visited October 10, 2020); *World Health Statistics, Part I: Global Health Indicators* (Geneva, Switzerland: World

Health Organization, 2015). https://www.who.int/gho/publications/world_health_statistics/EN_WHS2015_Part2.pdf, (last visited October 10, 2020); and *The World Health Report: Working Together for Health* (Geneva, Switzerland: World Health Organization, 2006), 1–15.

9. United States Embassy in Nigeria, "Nigeria Malaria Fact Sheet" (2011), https://photos.state.gov/libraries/nigeria/231771/Public/December-MalariaFactSheet2.pdf (last visited April 4, 2021).

10. Oluseun Onigbinde et al., "Nigeria: Health Budget Analysis," *Policy Brief in First Quarter* (2018), https://yourbudgit.com/wp-content/uploads/2018/04/Nigeria-Health-Budget-Analysis.pdf (last visited May 24, 2021).

11. *Half the World Lacks Access to Essential Health Services: 100 Million Still Pushed Into Extreme Poverty Because of Health Expenses* (Geneva, Switzerland: World Health Organization, and Washington, DC: World Bank, 2017); https://www.who.int/news-room/detail/13-12-2017-world-bank-and-who-half-the-world-lacks-access-to-essential-health-services-100-million-still-pushed-into-extreme-poverty-because-of-health-expenses (last visited October 10, 2020); *Current Health Expenditure Per Capita (Current US$)* (Geneva, Switzerland: World Health Organization, 2010), https://data.worldbank.org/indicator/SH.XPD.CHEX.PC.CD (last visited October 10, 2020); *Global Health Observatory (GHO) Data*, note 8; *World Health Statistics, Part I*, note 8; *The World Health Report*, note 8; and *The World Health Organization's Ranking of the World's Health Systems*, note 7.

12. "Nigeria: Laying the Groundwork for Safe, Quality Healthcare," *AXA Magazine* (May 24, 2019), ttps://www.axa.com/en/magazine/nigeria-laying-the-groundwork-for-safe-quality-healthcare (last visited October 16, 2020).

13. *Nigerian Health Sector Market Study Report* (Amsterdam, Netherland: PharmAccess Foundation, 2015). https://www.rvo.nl/sites/default/files/Market_Study_Health_Nigeria.pdf (last visited January 23, 2020).

14. Yusuff. A. Adebisi et al., "Assessment of Health Budgetary Allocation and Expenditure Toward Achieving Universal Health Coverage in Nigeria," *International Journal of Health Life Science* (2020), https://sites.kowsarpub.com/ijhls/articles/102552.html (last visited May 24, 2021).

15. *Country Policy and Information Note Nigeria: Medical and Healthcare Issues Version 2.0.* (London, UK: UK Home Office, 2018), https://www.justice.gov/eoir/page/file/1094261/download (last visited May 20, 2021).

16. Onigbinde et al., note 10.

17. "The Abuja Declaration: Ten Years On," *World Health Organization* (2011), https://www.who.int/healthsystems/publications/abuja_declaration/en/ (last visited February 10, 2020).

18. Anne B. Martin et al., "National Health Care Spending in 2017: Growth Slows to Post–Great Recession Rates: Share of GDP Stabilizes," *Health Affairs*, 38, no. 1 (2018), ttps://www.healthaffairs.org/doi/full/10.1377/hlthaff.2018.0508 (last visited January 4, 2021).

19. The World Factbook (Washington, DC: Central Intelligence Agency, 2021), https://www.cia.gov/the-world-factbook/countries/nigeria/ (last visited April 20, 2021).

20. See, for example, Adeteju Ajimotokan, "Korea Jostles for Slice of Nigeria's $1B Medical Tourism Spending," *This Day* (March 21, 2019), https://www.thisdaylive.com/index.php/2019/03/21/korea-jostles-for-slice-of-nigerias-1b-medical-tourism-spending/ (last visited October 10, 2020); "Nigeria Losing $1B Annually to Medical Tourism, Authorities Say," *VOA* (May 10, 2019), https://www.voanews.com/africa/nigeria-losing-1b-annually-medical-tourism-authorities-say (last visited October 10, 2020).

21. Abimbola Adelakun, "Nigerian Leaders Have Still Not Learned," *Punch Newspaper* (June 18, 2020). https://groups.google.com/forum/?utm_medium=email&utm_source=footer#!msg/usaafricadialogue/2YRl2gKUQGk/yM28m4VfAAAJ (last visited October 10, 2020).

22. Chukwuma Muanya, "Why 15% Budget Allocation to Health Is Tall Order, by FG," *The Guardian* (Lagos) (October 26, 2020), https://m.guardian.ng/features/why-15-budget-allocation-to-health-is-tall-order-by-fg/amp/ (last visited May 27, 2021).

23. Ibid.

24. Ibid.

25. United Nations Population Fund, *Sexual and Reproductive Health* (n.d.), https://www.unfpa.org/sexual-reproductive-health (last visited October 16, 2020).

26. Onigbinde et al., note 10, p. 10.

27. Ibid.

28. See, for example, Hubert Amu et al., "Understanding Variations in Health Insurance Coverage in Ghana, Kenya, Nigeria, and Tanzania: Evidence from Demographic and Health Surveys," *Plos One*, 13, no. 8 (2018): e0201833, https://journals.plos.org/plosone/article?id=10.1371/journal.pone.0201833 (last visited June 26, 2021); Bolaji S. Aregbeshola and Samina M. Khan, "Predictors of Enrolment in the National Health Insurance Scheme among Women of Reproductive Age in Nigeria," *International Journal of Health Policy Management* 7, no. 11 (2018): 1015–23, https://www.ncbi.nlm.nih.gov/pmc/articles/PMC6326643/ (last visited June 26, 2021).

29. Adeola A. Onasanya, "Increasing Health Insurance Enrolment in the Informal Economic Sector," *Journal of Global Health*, 10, no. 1 (June 2020), doi 10.7189/jogh.10.010329.

30. "Countries in the World by Population: Coronavirus Report," *Worldometer* (2020), https://www.worldometers.info/world-population/population-by-country/ https://www.worldometers.info/coronavirus/#countries (last visited October 10, 2021).

31. Menizibeya O. Welcome, "The Nigerian Health Care System: Need for Integrating Adequate Medical Intelligence and Surveillance Systems," *Journal of Pharmacy and Bioallied Sciences*, 3, no. 4 (2011): 470–78, doi 10.4103/0975-7406.90100.

32. B.S.C. Uzochukwu et al., "Healthcare Financing in Nigeria: Implications for Achieving Universal Health Coverage," *Nigeria Journal of Clinical Practice* 18, no. 4 (July–August 2015): 437–44, doi 10.4103/1119-3077.154196

33. Isaac A. O. Odeyemi and John Nixon, "Assessing Equity in Health Care through the National Health Insurance Schemes of Nigeria and Ghana: A

Review-Based Comparative Analysis," *International Journal of Equity Health*, 22 (2013): 1–8, doi 10.1186/1475-9276-12-9.

34. "A Rapid Diagnostics Assessing the Impact of COVID-19 on Enterprises and Workers in the Informal Economy in Nigeria," ILO Terms of Reference (n.d.), https://www.ilo.org/wcmsp5/groups/public/---africa/---ro-abidjan/---ilo-abuja/documents/genericdocument/wcms_749091.pdf (last visited June 29, 2021).

35. Odeyemi and Nixon, note 33.

36. Peter O. Okebukola and William R. Brieger, "Providing Universal Health Insurance Coverage in Nigeria," *International Quarterly of Community Health Education* (2016): 1–6, https://www.researchgate.net/publication/305039517_Providing_Universal_Health_Insurance_Coverage_in_Nigeria (last visited June 28, 2021).

37. Bolaji S. Aregbeshola, "A Tax-Based, Noncontributory, Health-Financing System Can Accelerate Progress Toward Universal Health Coverage in Nigeria," *MEDICC Review*, 20, no. 4 (2018): 40–45, en (scielosp.org) (last visited December 23, 2020).

38. Onasanya, note 29.

39. Ibid.

40. Ibid.

41. Onigbinde et al., note 10, p. 8.

42. Ibid.

43. Ibid.

44. Ibid.

45. Abi Millar, "The Rise of Fake Medicines in Africa," *Journalist Portfolio* (December 28, 2019), https://abimillar.com/2019/12/28/the-rise-of-fake-medicines-in-africa/ (last visited June 26, 2021).

46. Ibid.

47. Endurance Ophori et al., "Current Trends of Immunization in Nigeria: Prospect and Challenges," *Tropical Medicine & Health*, 42, no. 2 (June 2014): 67–75, doi 10.2149/tmh.2013-13.

48. Aishatu A. Abdulkarim et al., "Vaccines and Immunization: The Past, Present, and Future in Nigeria," *Nigerian Journal of Pediatrics*, 38, no. 4 (2011): 186–94, https://www.researchgate.net/publication/272342543_Vaccines_and_immunization_The_past_present_and_future_in_Nigeria (last visited June 28, 2021).

49. Debora Mackenzie, "Wild Polio Has Been Eradicated in Nigeria but Infections Will Continue," *New Scientist* (August 23, 2019), https://www.newscientist.com/article/2214302-wild-polio-has-been-eradicated-in-nigeria-but-infections-will-continue/ (last visited June 26, 2021).

50. Paul Adepoju, "A Breakdown of Nigeria's 2020 Budget for Health," *HealthNews.NG* (January 2, 2020), http://www.healthnews.ng/a-breakdown-of-nigerias-2020-budget-for-health/ (last visited June 26, 2016).

51. Angela Adebayo, "Fake Medicine in Nigeria—When the Drugs Don't Work," *Inventa International* (February 21, 2017), https://www.lexology.com/library/detail.aspx?g=6b2f05d6-1ecd-4e72-aba7-2c86ef70a8f9 (last visited June 26, 2021).

52. Ibid.

53. Ibid.

54. Ibid.

55. *Nigeria: Sustainable Development Goals* (New York: United Nations, 2020), https://sustainabledevelopment.un.org/memberstates/nigeria (last visited October 24, 2020).

56. Abdulkarim et al., note 48.

57. "Nigeria: Laying the Groundwork for Safe, Quality Healthcare," note 50; William Menchaca, "Crossroads: Top [Ten] Facts about Living Conditions in Nigeria," Borgen Project (Blog) (September 23, 2018), https://borgenproject.org/crossroads-top-10-facts-about-living-conditions-in-nigeria/ (last visited June 28, 2021).

58. Francis S. Collins, "Growing Importance of Health in the Economy," *We Forum* (2015), https://widgets.weforum.org/outlook15/10.html (last visited June 28, 2021).

59. S.A.J. Obansa and Akinnagbe Orimisan, "Healthcare Financing in Nigeria: Prospects and Challenges," *Mediterranean Journal of Social Sciences*, 4, no. 1 (January 2013): 221–36, doi 10.5901/mjss.2013.v4n1p221.

60. Welcome, note 31; Obansa and Orimisan, note 59.

61. F[ederal] M[inistry] [of] H[ealth], *Nigeria Health Information System Policy* (Abuja, Nigeria: 2014), https://ehealth4everyone.com/wp-content/uploads/2015/09/Nig-Health-Info.pdf (last visited October 10, 2020).

62. A.A. Abubakar, "Health Management Information System in Nigeria," *Study Lib* (n.d.), https://studylib.net/doc/10146504/health-management-information-system-in-nigeria (last visited June 26, 2021).

63. Emmanuel C. Meribole et al., "The Nigerian Health Information System Policy Review of 2014: The Need, Content, Expectations[,] and Progress," *Health Information and Libraries Journal*, 35, no. 4 (December 2018): 285–97, doi 10.1111/hir.12240.

64. Jide J. Popoola et al., "Reliability Worth Assessment of Electric Power Utility in Nigeria: Residential Customer Survey Results," *AU J.T.* 14, no. 3 (2011): 217–24, https://pdfs.semanticscholar.org/aebf/71eb57b215257620cf13fef48dae838c1ba3.pdf (last visited June 28, 2021).

65. Claudius Awosope, "Nigeria Electricity Industry: Issues, Challenges and Solutions," Covenant University 38th Public Lecture, Corpus ID 51901845 (2014), http://eprints.covenantuniversity.edu.ng/9474/1/Prof%20Awosope%20Public%20Lecture%20%2838th%29.pdf (last visited June 28, 2021).

66. Davies Adeloye et al., "Health Workforce and Governance: The Crisis in Nigeria," *Human Resources for Health*, 15, no. 32 (2017), doi 10.1186/s12960-017-0205-4.

67. "Countries in the World by Population," note 36; Gia Gambino, "Here's How Nigeria Can Improve its Sickly Healthcare System," *News Decoder* (October 6, 2020), https://news-decoder.com/heres-how-nigeria-can-improve-its-sickly-health-care-system/ (last visited June 26, 2021).

68. Kingsley Ighobor, "Diagnosing Africa's Medical Brain Brain: Higher Wages and Modern Facilities are Magnets for Africa's Health Workers," *African Renewal*

(December 2016–March 2017), 017/diagnosing-africa%E2%80%99s-medical-brain-drain (last visited June 26, 2021).

69. Gambino, note 67.

70. Onigbinde et al., note 10.

71. Akindare Okunola, "[Five] Facts Every Nigerian Should Know about Our Healthcare," *Global Citizen* (September 9, 2020), https://www.globalcitizen.org/en/content/health-care-facts-nigeria-covid-19/?utm_source=paidsearch&utm_medium=usgrant&utm_campaign=verizon&gclid=Cj0KCQiAtqL-BRC0ARIsAF4K3WGZxHt-Yz41A7plT75mK9ftJcCI-GjctLUo_rcIqLU_7fEgaOJGkZgaAry7EALw_wcB (last visited June 26, 2021).

72. Sola Ogundipe et al., "Shortage of Medical Personnel: Tougher Times Ahead for Nigerians (1)," *Vanguard* (Lagos) (January 27, 2015), https://www.vanguardngr.com/2015/01/shortage-medical-personnel-tougher-times-ahead-nigerians-1/ (last visited June 28, 2021).

73. "Nigeria Ranked [Seventh] among Countries Facing Shortage of Health Workers," *HealthFacts.NG* (May 11, 2017), https://www.physicianleaders.org/news/how-many-patients-can-primary-care-physician-treat (last visited February 10, 2021).

74. UK Home Office, *Country Policy and Information Note Nigeria: Medical and Healthcare Issues*, Version 2.0. (2018), https://www.justice.gov/eoir/page/file/1094261/download (last visited May 20, 2021).

75. See Mercy Abang, "Nigeria's Medical Brain Drain: Healthcare Woes As Doctors Flee," *Al Jazeera News* (April 8, 2019), https://www.aljazeera.com/features/2019/4/8/nigerias-medical-brain-drain-healthcare-woes-as-doctors-flee (accessed June 26, 2021); Molly Fosco, "Doctor Drain: An Exodus from Nigeria Threatens Its Healthcare System." *Ozy* (2018), https://www.ozy.com/around-the-world/doctor-drain-an-exodus-from-nigeria-threatens-its-health-care-system/87072/ (accessed December 23, 2020); "New Survey Reveals [Eight] in [Ten] Nigerian Doctors Are Seeking Work Opportunities Abroad," *NOI Polls* (December 11, 2018), https://noi-polls.com/new-survey-reveals-8-in-10-nigerian-doctors-are-seeking-work-opportunities-abroad/; and Bell Ihua, "Emigration of Nigerian Medical Doctors Survey Report," *NOI Polls* (January 2017), https://www.researchgate.net/publication/319546512_Emigration_of_Nigerian_Medical_Doctors_Survey_Report/link/59b2a7950f7e9b37434e8d2e/download (last visited June 26, 2021).

76. Ihua, note 75.

77. WHO Global Health Workforce Alliance (n.d.), https://www.who.int/workforcealliance/countries/nga/en// (last visited October 10, 2020)

78. Ruiz Gama Vaz, cited in Ogundipe et al., note 72.

79. Ogundipe et al., note 72.

80. See, for example, Joseph A. Balogun, *Nigerian Healthcare System: Roadmap to Universal and High-Quality Healthcare* (New York: Springer Nature, 2021).

81. Joseph Okoghenun, "Nigeria Has Only 1,000 Physiotherapists, Say Experts," *Guardian* (Lagos) (August 10, 2015), https://guardian.ng/news/nigeria-has-only-1000-physiotherapists-say-experts/ (last visited June 26, 2021).

82. Ibid.

83. Adeloye et al., note 66.

84. Chikwe Ihekweazu, "Three Reasons Strike Will Continue in Nigeria's Health Sector," *Nigeria Healthwatch* (September 1, 2015), https://nigeriahealthwatch.com/three-reasons-strikes-will-continue-in-nigerias-health-sector/#.XxeOd8LCGuU (last visited September 23, 2020); Ihua, note 88.

85. See Adeloye et al., note 66.

86. Okunola, note 71.

87. Ibid.

88. Udomoh Eshemokha, "Prof. Elusoji, UBTH Surgeon, Banned from Practicing Medicine for Life," *Nimed Health* (April 8, 2021), https://nimedhealth.com.ng/2021/04/08/prof-elusoji-ubth-surgeon-banned-from-practicing-medicine-for-life/ (last visited June 28, 2021).

89. *Combating Corruption* (Washington, DC: World Bank, 2020), https://www.worldbank.org/en/topic/governance/brief/anti-corruption (last visited December 26, 2020).

90. Eshemokha, note 88.

91. "Module 6: Detecting and Investigating Corruption," UNODC (2020), https://www.unodc.org/e4j/en/anti-corruption/module-6/key-issues/detection-mechanisms---auditing-and-reporting.html (last visited December 26, 2020).

92. Transparency International, *How to Stop Corruption: [Five] Key Ingredients* (2016), https://www.transparency.org/en/news/how-to-stop-corruption-5-key-ingredients# (last visited December 22, 2020).

93. *Combating Corruption*, note 89.

94. Robert Hunja, "Here are [Ten] Ways to Fight Corruption," World Bank (Blog) (2015), https://blogs.worldbank.org/governance/here-are-10-ways-fight-corruption (last visited December 22, 2020).

95. Obinna O. Oleribe et al., "Industrial Action by HCWs in Nigeria in 2013–2015: An Inquiry into Causes, Consequences and Control—A Cross-Sectional Descriptive Study," *Human Resource Health*, 14, no. 1 (2016): 46, https://www.ncbi.nlm.nih.gov/pmc/articles/PMC4962455/ (last visited September 23, 2020); see also Obinna O. Oleribe et al., "Interprofessional Rivalry in Nigeria's Health Sector: A Comparison of Doctors and Other Health Workers' Views at a Secondary Care Center," *International Quarterly of Community Health Education* (2017), https://doi.org/10.1177/0272684X17748892

96. Adeloye et al., note 66.

97. See Ademola Olajide et al., "Doctor-Nurse Conflict in Nigerian Hospitals: Causes and Modes of Expression," *British Journal of Medicine & Medical Research*, 9, no. 10 (2015): 1–12, doi 10.9734/BJMMR/2015/15839.

98. Taiwo A. Obembe et al., "Managerial Dynamics Influencing Doctor-Nurse Conflicts in Two Nigerian Hospitals," *Journal of Family Medicine and Primary Care*, 7, no. 4 (2018): 684–92, ttps://www.ncbi.nlm.nih.gov/pmc/articles/PMC6131988/ (last visited June 26, 2021).

99. F. Bolaji, List of All Universities in Nigeria Approved by NUC–2020 Latest List (2021), https://campusbiz.com.ng/list-of-universities-in-nigeria/ (accessed June 4, 2021).

100. Joseph A. Balogun, *Healthcare Education in Nigeria: Evolutions and Emerging Paradigms* (Milton Park, UK: Routledge, 2020).

101. See ibid.; Joseph A. Balogun, "The Case for a Paradigm Shift in the Education of Health Professionals in Nigeria," Second Distinguished University Guest Lecture, University of Medical Sciences, Ondo, Nigeria. (May 15, 2017), https://www.researchgate.net/publication/317387397_The_case_for_a_paradigm_shift_in_the_education_of_healthcare_professionals_in_Nigeria (last visited September 23, 2020); Ogoh Alubo and Vitalis Hunduh, "Medical Dominance and Resistance in Nigeria's Healthcare System," *International Journal of Health Services*, 47, no. 4 (2017): 778–94, doi 10.1177/0020731416675981; and Temitope O. Ojo and Adebowale F. Akinwumi, "Doctors as Managers of Healthcare Resources in Nigeria: Evolving Roles and Current Challenges," *Nigeria Medical Journal*, 56, no. 6 (2015): 375–80.

102. Elizabeth Manias, "Effects of Interdisciplinary Collaboration in Hospitals on Medication Errors: An Integrative Review," *Expert Opinion Drug Safety*, 17, no. 3 (2018): 259–75, doi 10.1080/14740338.2018.1424830;

Brooke Whitaker and Courtney Shrader, "Interdisciplinary Teams Reduce Errors and Improve Outcomes," *Lab Testing Matters* (March 5, 2019), https://www.labtestingmatters.org/home-page/interdisciplinary-teams-reduce-errors-and-improve-outcomes/ (last visited June 26, 2021); Heather Derrick, "Interdisciplinary Healthcare Teams," *SPNHA Review*, 14, no. 1 (2018), https://scholarworks.gvsu.edu/spnhareview/vol14/iss1/ (last visited June 26, 2021).

103. J.K. Singleton and C. Green-Hernandez, "Interdisciplinary Education and Practice: Has its Time Come?" *Journal of Nurse-Midwifery*, 43, no. 1 (January–February 1998): 3–7, doi 10.1016/s0091-2182(97)00116-x.

104. J.S. Katz et al., "Physical and Occupational Therapy Undergraduates' Stereotypes of One Another," *Perceptual and Motor Skills*, 92, 3 Pt 1 (2001): 843–51, doi: 10.2466/pms.2001.92.3.843.

105. I. M. Abdel Rahim et al., "Introducing Training in Primary Health Care Program Management into the Curriculum," *Medical Education*, 21, no. 4 (1987): 288–92, doi: 10.1111/j.1365-2923.1987.tb00365.x.

106. Simone V. Gill et al., "The Importance of Interdisciplinary Research Training and Community Dissemination," *Clinical Translational Science*, 8, no. 5 (2015): 611–14, https://www.ncbi.nlm.nih.gov/pmc/articles/PMC4625396/ (accessed September 23, 2020); Balogun, "The Case for a Paradigm Shift in the Education of Health Professionals in Nigeria," note 101; *Balogun, Healthcare Education in Nigeria*, note 100; and Balogun, *Nigerian Healthcare System*, note 80.

107. See, for example, Ojo and Akinwumi, note 123; Alubo and Hunduh, note 123; Balogun, "The Case for a Paradigm Shift in the Education of Health Professionals in Nigeria," note 101; Balogun, *Healthcare Education in Nigeria*, note 100; Balogun, *Nigerian Healthcare System*, note 80; Joseph A. Balogun, *Healthcare Professions in Nigeria: An Interdisciplinary Analysis* (Singapore: Palgrave Macmillan, 2021).

108. Shehi A. Abubakar, "Unemployment among Medical Doctors," *Gamji* (n.d.), http://www.gamji.com/article4000/NEWS4395.htm (last visited June 26, 2021).

109. *Nigeria: Population at Risk* (New York: Global Center for the Responsibility to Protect, 2021), https://www.globalr2p.org/countries/nigeria/ (last visited June 29, 2021).

110. Amnesty International, "Nigeria 2020" (2021) https://www.amnesty.org/en/countries/africa/nigeria/report-nigeria/ (last visited June 26, 2021).

111. Frederick Rivara, "The Effects of Violence on Health," *Health Affairs* (Millwood), 38, no. 10 (October 2019): 1622–29, doi 10.1377/hlthaff.2019.00480.

112. See *World Report on Disability* (Geneva, Switzerland, World Health Organization, 2011), https://www.who.int/teams/noncommunicable-diseases/sensory-functions-disability-and-rehabilitation/world-report-on-disability; https://www.who.int/countries/nga/ (last visited May 31, 2021).

113. J. T. Trevors et al., "Transformative Research: Definitions, Approaches and Consequences," *Theory Biosciences*, 131, no. 2 (2012): 117–23, doi 10.1007/s12064-012-0154-3.

114. Ibid.

115. Anonymous, "Drought Conditions and Management Strategies in Nigeria" (n.d.), https://www.ais.unwater.org/ais/pluginfile.php/629/mod_page/content/6/Nigeria_EN.pdf (last visited December 28, 2020).

116. Friday Okonofua, "IFA: A Quintessential Nigerian Patriot and Academic Icon," A Keynote Address Delivered at the Commissioning of the Isaac Folorunso Adewole Library of Tomorrow (IFA-LoT) at the University of Ibadan on Saturday, November 16, 2019.

117. *A Decade of Development in sub-Saharan African Science, Technology, Engineering, and Mathematics Research: A Report by the World Bank and Elsevier* (Washington, DC: World Bank 2014), http://documents.worldbank.org/curated/en/237371468204551128/pdf/910160WP0P126900disclose09026020140.pdf (last visited October 10, 2020).

118. Tertiary Education Trust Fund (TETFund, 2020), https://tetfund.gov.ng/ (last visited October 10, 2020).

Chapter 5

Christian-Muslim Conflict in Post-Civil War Nigeria

Prelude to the Fourth Republic

Olufemi Vaughan

INTRODUCTION

The years immediately following the imposition of Nigeria's fourth constitutional democracy in 1999—that marked the commencement of the Fourth Republic—saw a moment of intense religious conflict in southern and central Nigeria with problematic socio-political consequences for the republic. Much of these protracted and violent religious clashes revolved around the sharia crisis in Northern Muslim states, especially from 1999 to 2004. This chapter is not a discussion of the sharia crisis, a subject that I have analyzed extensively in two other publications.[1] Indeed, this chapter explores the prolonged Christian-Muslim conflict that set the stage for the horrific religious violence that consumed much of the attention of the first term of President Olusegun Obasanjo's civil democratic government from 1999 to 2003. Notionally, it contends that much of the religious violence in the earlier years of the Fourth Republic incubated in the three decades between the end of the Nigerian Civil War in 1970 and the birth of the Fourth Republic in 1999. Significantly, although communal hostilities, within localized sub-ethnic communities, were relatively common during the colonial era, especially during the decolonization epoch in the 1950s, Christian-Muslim confrontations were rare in Nigerian society from the colonial era until after the Nigerian Civil War in 1970s. Additionally, it is essential to note at the onset that violent conflicts between Christians and Muslims were virtually unknown in Nigeria's Southwest region (the Yoruba region) despite its large Christian and Muslim populations.[2] Accordingly, this chapter will underscore the regional context in which these protracted conflicts between Christians and Muslims have been sustained in postcolonial Nigeria. Moreover, this chapter will contextualize the persistent confrontations between Christians and Muslims in northern and central Nigeria within the wider framework of the historical processes of the formation of the Nigerian postcolonial nation-state. In this context, the chapter will underscore the appropriate structural framework for the manifestation of religious conflict in Nigeria, revealing the intersecting social, political, and economic contexts in which Christianity and Islam shaped social relations in these vast and diverse regions of contemporary Nigeria during the critical decades from the end of Nigerian Civil War and the imposition of the Fourth Republic.

Correspondingly, this chapter will analyze important Christian-Muslim reconciliation attempts to advance peaceful coexistence during this moment of intense religious confrontation in the republic. Regrettably, since most of these peace initiatives failed, the chapter will underscore their limitations, despite the spirited efforts of their advocates. Finally, this chapter will provide the foundation on which scholars of ethnic and religious conflicts in Nigeria will critically reflect on the structural framework for the devastating Sharia crisis that took center stage in northern and central Nigeria during the Fourth Republic, partially, providing a context for the rise of Boko Haram in Northern Muslim state of Borno in the early 2000s.[3] With firm roots in the Sokoto Caliphate and the impact of Christian missions in the Northern Nigerian provinces during the colonial period, the chapter will reveal how the structures of Christian-Muslim conflict in northern and central Nigeria are further complicated by the neo-patrimonialism of successive military and civil government, especially in the 1980s and 1990s. It is hoped that the outcome of these analyses would help scholars and politicos craft an efficacious framework on how to confront the issue of religious clashes in Nigeria during the Fourth Republic.

NIGERIA'S CHRISTIAN-MUSLIM CONUNDRUM: THE POLITICAL CONTEXT

The years immediately after the Nigerian Civil War were generally defined by scholars of Nigeria political studies as a time of post-war reconstruction and reconciliation, but these years also wounded up being a period when contending political and religious groups reasserted themselves within the framework of Nigeria's prevailing ethno-religious structure. As the military regime of General Yakubu Gowon embarked on post-civil war policies of reconstruction, Muslim activists, through various national organizations, especially the newly formed Nigerian Supreme Council for Islamic Affairs (NSCIA), proclaimed Muslim interests in national affairs.[4] These postulations and declarations opened up a space for the discussion of sharia, the Islamic code of conduct in the Nigerian legal system since its intense discussion in the defunct northern region during the decolonization process in the 1950s.[5] This process gained even greater momentum when the Gowon administration was overthrown in 1975. Gowon's successor, General Murtala Mohammed, a devout Muslim from Kano, openly embraced a public role for Islam in state affairs during his short period as head of state from July 1975 to February 1976. Following the outcry of Southern and Middle Belt Christians—as well as Christian minorities in predominantly Muslim Northern states—against Mohammed's attempt to establish a Federal Sharia Court of Appeal (FSCA), the Federal Military Government backtracked to create a unified customary court of appeal in 1975.[6]

As this agitation for post-civil war political and legal reforms intensified in the mid-1970s, the Federal Military Government created a committee to draft a constitution for a civil-democratic government in 1975. The deliberation of this constitution drafting committee ultimately led to the 1979 Nigerian Constitution. This act led to the country's attempt at constitutional democracy and the Second Republic, starting in October 1979. The drafting committee work opened the door for the assertion and infusion of religion into the public sphere; it encouraged an animated debate on the role of sharia in Nigeria's political and legal affairs.[7] This debate which brought Northern Muslim leaders into direct conflict with the political class of other regions of the country, notably the south east, south west, and Middle Belt regions, exposed Nigeria's deep political and religious fault lines. Consequently, sharia emerged as a critical medium for the articulation of Northern Muslim interests during the transition to a civil-democratic government in the mid-1970s.

Conflict between pro-sharia Northern Muslims, on the one hand, and south east, south west, the Middle Belt—as well as Northern-minority Christians—factions, on the other hand, intensified during the constitutional debates. During this period, a powerful Northern Muslim coalition emerged to petition for a FSCA that would have jurisdiction over both civil and criminal cases in Nigerian jurisprudence. Pro-FSCA Constitute Assembly members insisted that since religious injunctions require that the conduct of Muslims must be regulated by Islamic law, the proposed Nigerian Constitution must grant sharia courts authority to adjudicate on all legal matters that affect Nigerian Muslims.[8] But when it became apparent that the Northern Muslim pro-sharia delegates would not achieve their objective in the Constituent Assembly, they elected to boycott assembly deliberations. Eventually, the military administration of General Obasanjo pushed for a compromise by encouraging the judiciary subcommittee of the Constitution Drafting Committee to establish Sharia and Customary Courts of Appeal with limited authority in civil and criminal cases in Northern states.[9] Ardent anti-sharia activists from the south east, south west, and the Middle Belt—as well as Northern Christian minorities—contended that the subcommittee's compromise would infringe on the constitutional rights of religious minorities. This was especially so in Northern Muslim states and would undermine the secular principle of the Nigerian nation-state. Despite this limited constitutional victory by Northern Muslim elites, the Northern pro-sharia alliance was largely a marriage of convenience. It brought together various Northern Muslim elites—Hausa-Fulani, Kanuri, and other predominantly Northern Muslim ethnic groups—into a relatively coherent Northern Muslim ideological and political bloc. This national religious controversy at a critical moment in postcolonial Nigerian political history revealed a major ethno-religious fault line in the configuration of power in the Nigerian nation-state; it is one to be tackled in the Fourth Republic to further peaceful coexistence.

STATE CRISIS AND RELIGIOUS VIOLENCE UNDER CIVILIAN AND MILITARY RULE

Political parties in Nigeria's Second Republic (1979–1983) had their roots in the political alignment patterns during the decolonization process in the 1950s and the first decade of independence in the 1960s. Aware of the deep divisions among the major regions, and hoping to undermine alternative centers of power that led to the collapse of Nigeria's civil democratic government (the First Republic) in 1966, successive military regimes (Ironsi, Gowon, Mohammed-Obasanjo military governments) had all curtailed partisan political activities during the period of military rule, from 1966 to 1979. In the Northern states, the major site of Christian-Muslim conflicts, preexisting political associations provided the organizational node for the construction of political parties in 1978 when the Mohammed-Obasanjo regime lifted the ban on party politics. One of the most prominent political groups that shaped party political alignment during this period was the National Movement, precursor to the National Party of Nigeria (NPN). Although the NPN later embraced a diverse coalition of junior patterns, notably Yoruba, Igbo, and Edo politicians, as well as ethnic minorities from the Niger Delta, Rivers, and Cross Rivers States,[10] the party had its foundation in the Northern People's Congress (NPC)—the former Hausa-Fulani Muslim party of the preceding civilian government under the leadership of Ahmadu Bello, the Sardauna of Sokoto, during the First Republic.[11] Despite this national alliance, the NPN was firmly anchored to the *masu sarauta*, the Hausa-Fulani Muslim power structure.

The election that followed the new constitution saw voting primarily along ethno-regional lines, revealing prevailing geo-political alignments in which regional political parties such as the Unity Party of Nigeria dominated the southwestern states and the Nigerian National Party asserted significant influence in the south eastern states. Dominated by the Northern Muslim states, political NPN coalition asserted its hegemony, wining presidential and national legislative elections in 1979 and 1983. With the ascendancy of the NPN in national and Northern regional politics, Hausa-Fulani Muslim power and policies were anchored on the Islamization and northernization regimes of the erstwhile NPC's regional government during decolonization in the 1950s and the First Republic in the 1960s. This dominance in regional and national politics soon incited strong resistance from Christian activists, especially in Middle Belt and Southern states, as well as Christian minorities in Northern Muslim states. As Christians accused the NPN of advancing Northern Muslim interests, ethno-religious and regional divisions grew wider. Southern, the Middle Belt, and Northern Christian minorities trumpeted their opposition against what they considered the monopoly of state power by a Northern Muslim oligarchy. The NPN and other Hausa-Fulani Muslim elite, however, pushed back insisting on the establishment of a Sharia Court of Appeal that would have full legal authority in civil and criminal cases in Northern Muslim society. This stance and clash of interests between these groups further amplified Christian anxiety.

Under the domination of the NPN, growing ethno-religious and regional tensions brought religious violence, especially in Northern and Middle Belt states to the fore. Starting in the early 1980s under the political authority of the NPN, especially in Northern and Middle Belt states, a wave of religious violence by fringe Islamic movements ravaged several Northern communities. Although the origins of these violent conflicts are not always easy to discern, this religious violence tended to reflect several important social, demographic, and political factors.

First, it reflected the deepening religious and ethnic divisions in the Northern and Middle Belt states; second, it showed the growing alienation of the masses of Northern Muslims with the neopatrimonialism of the custodians of the Nigerian state; and finally it revealed the widening gulf among factions of Northern Muslim groups over claims of leadership in Northern states. These factors exacerbated prevailing fissures between Northern Muslim rulers and Northern Christian minority "indigenes," Northern Muslim "indigenes" and Christian "settlers" from Southern states, Northern Muslim elites and Southern Christian intelligentsia, and Northern Muslim elites of divergent ideological and political orientations.

Nevertheless, this growing politicization of religion, especially along prevailing ethno-regional and ethno-religious fault lines in Northern and Middle Belt states, was intimately connected to the structural challenges confronting the Nigerian state after the Nigerian Civil War in 1970.[12] With all of these religious crises going on in the 1970s and 1980s, the moral authority of the holder of state power was seriously compromised, severely undermining Nigeria's democratic and political process during the Second Republic. Compounded by deepening economic crisis from declining price of petroleum, the Shagari administration's entrenched neopatrimonialism aggravated ethno-regional and ethno-religious tension among Nigeria's diverse groups.[13] In addition, these religious conflicts reflect deeper structural crisis endemic to the Nigerian state and society. The tenuousness of Shagari's NPN government, and its administrative inefficacy, was revealed when a military coup brought the Second Republic to an end on New Year's Eve of 1983.

During this period of heightened politico-economic crisis, the first major religious conflict with national implications started in the early 1980s with a radical Muslim sect known as *Yan tatsine* (Hausa for, roughly, "those who damned"). Yan tatsine (*Maitasine*) deplored Islamic doctrine and Hausa traditions of protest to gain popular support among marginalized Hausa *talakawa* commoners in Hausa cities. While many analysts emphasized the fanaticism of Yan tatsine, Paul Lubeck perceptively traces the *gardawa*—the Quranic students who were the foot soldiers of the sect—to the era of the Sokoto Caliphate in the nineteenth century. As Nigerian society experienced rapid social transformation in the early decades following the attainment of independence in 1960, Lubeck contends, "semi-industrial capitalism" further undermined the *gardawa* in major Hausa cities such as Kano, especially in the dry season. Before the petroleum boom of the 1970s, the *gardawa* had been steadily integrated into labor market in Northern cities. The massive growth in oil wealth (from $1 billion in 1970s to almost $23 billion in 1980) only intensified the contradiction and social inequalities between an emergent commercial-bureaucratic class and the masses of Hausa *talakawa*, as semi-industrial production stagnated. With this economic transformation, the masses of dislocated "laboring poor" people were further marginalized from the mainstream economy, especially in the Northern Nigeria's principal city, Kano.[14]

It was in the context of these tensions in 1980, several months into the Second Republic, that Yan tatsine's opposition to state authorities exploded into twelve days of violent riots in Kano city that reverberated in various parts of Northern Nigeria.[15] With inadequate response from state authorities, the riot claimed many lives and destroyed property worth millions of naira. In 1981, another religious protest initiated by Yan tatsine discontent in Kano ended in a major confrontation between two Muslim sects that reportedly resulted in the death of several thousands. In Maiduguri in Borno State, 400 people were reportedly killed in 1982, as Yan tatsine rebellion spilled into the Kanuri region of Northern Nigeria. When Pope John Paul II visited Nigeria in 1982, growing tensions between Christians and Muslims rose to a boiling point, leading to widespread unrest, including the burning of eight churches in Kano by mobs of Muslim youths.[16] Two years later, in Jimeta in Yola State, in the northeast, over 750 people were reportedly killed. And in Gombe State, more than 100 people were reportedly killed in 1985.[17]

With Muslim and Christian identities further shaping boundaries of political mobilization by the late 1980s and 1990s, religious conflicts became outright confrontational. It was further complicated by a mix of political, social, and demographic conditions, especially in an environment where the legitimacy of the holders of state power was very much in doubt. The trigger for these violent confrontations tended to be the perceived encroachment of a religious minority—so-called non-indigenes—on the "ancestral" space of a dominant ethno-religious group. In this context, Christianity, and Islam, notably, in Northern and Middle Belt states, emerged as combustible and important framework for the articulation of local interests connected to the distributive resources of the state. This trend intensified the wave of religious conflicts in Northern Muslim states and in the predominantly Christian Middle Belt states.[18] Since these rigid Christian-Muslim religious boundaries are deeply embedded into the structures of society and rationalized access to state power, this trend has effectively posed a serious threat to peaceful coexistence between Christians and Muslims in Northern and Middle Belt states, especially since the turbulent 1980s.

During this period, another major bout of religious violence exploded on the national scene in Kafanchan, Kaduna State, with its significant Christian minority population, in March 1987, later spinning off to other parts of the state and several Northern communities. Kafanchan, headquarters of the Jema Local Government, is about 300 kilometers south of the city of Kaduna, the capital of the state. With a population of about eighty thousand at the time, Kafanchan consists of largely Christian indigenous ethnic groups and Hausa-Fulani Muslim "settlers." In a case which reflected the pattern in several sections of the state, Christian-Muslim confrontations would mark the peak of the religious violence in Northern and Middle Belt states in the turbulent 1980s. In this specific case, underlying Christian-Muslim tension turned into open attacks on churches when a recent Christian convert from Islam, Abubakar Bako, allegedly blasphemed against Islam at the city's College of Education.[19]

After a week of destruction, the Kaduna State military government convened a panel chaired by State Commissioner for Justice Hansen Donli to investigate the riots and to make recommendations to the state authorities. The Donli Panel, among other factors, noted: "From many submissions made, it is quite obvious that certain highly placed individuals and organizations, had in the past been in the habit of either making unguarded utterances or publishing provocative and sensitive materials in the media, capable of causing tension in the country."[20] However, the panel was unable to secure the confidence of both Christians and Muslim. Representing the interest of Christians in the state, the Christian Council of Nigeria claimed that the panel did little to address the plight of aggrieved Christians and kowtowed to powerful Muslim interests. On the other hand, representing the interest of Muslims, the Council of Ulama called for Muslim solidarity and argued that the governor should have done more to protect Muslims and requested the release of Muslims detained in police custody. A Committee of Concerned Citizens claimed that economic and social deprivation of Hausa-Fulani Muslims was the root cause of the violence, but Christian groups, the Kaduna State Government, and the Federal Government dismissed the Committee's claim. Eventually the Federal Military Government convened a judicial tribunal chaired by a renowned judge, Karibi-Whyte, to try those detained in the riots. In the end, little was done to provide either justice or reconciliation. Reflecting on this tragic riot, many years later, Rev. Dr. Matthew Hassan Kukah, one of the country's foremost theologian and later Catholic Bishop of Sokoto, concluded that the crisis further consolidated the power base of the Northern Muslim elite.[21]

Since this period of severe religious violence, Kaduna State, with its large Christian indigenous population, would continue as one of the major frontlines of Christian-Muslim confrontation in Northern and Middle Belt states. Indeed, Kaduna State would emerge as the frontline for the sharia crisis a decade later during Obasanjo's first term as civilian president in the Fourth Republic from 1999 to 2003.

Sporadic religious violence continued in some Northern communities in the late 1980s as the Northern Muslim political class asserted its power based during the transition to democratic government instituted by another Northern Muslim military head of state in the late 1980s and the 1990s. To this end, Northern Muslim rulers—especially Hausa-Fulani elites—created the Northern Elders' Committee, consisting of emirs, politicians, businessmen, and senior administrators, to exert politico-religious influence on the Federal Military Government. In the context of these efforts, internecine battles continued between Muslim and Christians, especially in Kaduna State, with its large indigenous Christian population. More widespread communal conflicts with religious overtones were reported during the 1987 local government elections. Christian leaders in Kaduna State and other Northern states with substantial Christian populations alleged that Muslims retained a stranglehold on state affairs. This allegation is exemplified by the Organization of Islamic Conference (OIC) crisis, Nigeria's involvement in the Islamic Development Bank, and the unrelenting push for expanded sharia in Northern states (as reported by Catholic Bishops of Nigeria). Northern Christian called for comprehensive reforms to ensure secularity and national unity, and for a prohibition against Nigerian membership in international religious organizations.[22]

During this period of intense religious conflict, intra-Muslim relations in Northern states also suffered as Muslim reformists, led by the charismatic Muslim cleric, Abubakar Gumi, rose to prominence by the late 1970s. Gumi who had been educated in elite Islamic schools in the 1940s and 1950s had formed alliances with prominent Northern Muslim rulers such as the Sardauna of Sokoto, Ahmadu Bello, former Northern Region Premier, Abubakar Tafawa Balewa, prime minister during Nigeria's First Republic. Gumi was also a protégé of Aminu Kano, leader of the Northern Element Progressive Union, the opposition party in Northern Nigeria during the First Republic, and Shehu Shagari, Nigeria's president during the Second Republic.[23] His political biography is intricately connected to the Northern Muslim power structure since Nigeria's decolonization process in the 1950s. After attending the renowned Kano Law School, Gumi briefly worked with the Sardauna of Sokoto and as a scribe for the chief alkali, thereafter, taking up a teaching position at his old school in the early 1950s.

In 1955, Gumi was made imam of the Sardauna's hajj group, and later in 1957, he oversaw the pilgrimage of Nigerians to the hajj. These notable accomplishments won him the appointment as deputy grand qadi of the Northern Region just before Nigeria's independence in 1960, and in 1962 he was promoted grand qadi. Gumi and the Sardauna of Sokoto (Ahmadu Bello, the premier of the Northern Region) founded the *Jama'atu Nasril Islam*, at the time the preeminent Muslim organization in Northern Nigeria; he established many Islamic schools in the Northern Region. After the assassination of the Sardauna in 1966 in a military coup, Gumi embraced a new Islamic reformism that questioned the authority of the *masu sarauta*, the Hausa-Fulani Muslim aristocratic class. In the early 1970s, he criticized the administration of General Gowon; this won him support from populist elements in Northern Muslim states. In 1975, Gowon's successor, General Murtala Muhammed appointed him grand mufti. During this time, he began to criticize the established *Sufi tariq* that dominate Northern Nigeria's Islam, reserving the strongest criticism for the *tijaniyya tariq* (most popular in Kano). He did so because of the association of the *qadiriyya tariq* with the nineteenth-century Sokoto Jihadists, such as Usman dan Fodio, the founder of the Sokoto Caliphate. Despite Sufism's long history arising from twelfth- and thirteenth-century mysticism, with *qadiriyya* coming first and *tijaniyya* emerging in the eighteenth century, Gumi claimed that their doctrines were inconsistent with the philosophy of Islam. Gumi averred that Sufi orders teach withdrawal from this world, practice mystical rites, canonize powerful local rulers, recognize saints, and organize the ummah (the Muslim community) into hierarchical, competing structures, all of which are unauthorized innovations to the Qur'an and the prophetic tradition.[24] In 1978, Gumi was instrumental in the establishment a new Muslim reformist movement that would become influential among Northern Nigerian Muslims, *Jama't Izalat al Bid'a Wasn't Iqamat as Sunna*, or *Izala*. Seeking to both revive and reform Nigerian Islam, Izala leaders preached a return to Muslim orthodoxy and defied Sufi thought and pedagogy (Northern Nigeria's dominant Muslim tradition of *qadiriyya* and *tijaniyya* Sufism) as deviating from holy texts.[25]

Nevertheless, Izala gained prominence among relatively well-educated professional in the public and private sectors, especially in cosmopolitan Northern cities of Kaduna, Jos, and Kano. With a focus on religious orthodoxy, Izala emphasized strict interpretations of religious texts, especially the Qur'an and Hadith, along with the widespread availability of classical texts in Hausa language.[26] Gumi, in his autobiography, frames the emergence of Izala as a regrettable necessity, given the corruption of many Northern Muslim rulers who had broken with piety of the founders of the Sokoto Caliphate: "They had brought back to life all the corrupt practices against which Sheikh dan Fodio went to war with the former Hausa rulers. They had become kings with big palaces full of servants and courtiers who required other people to bow down before them. They keep concubines and did not really fear God's anger."[27] Later, Gumi defends his Izala movement on grounds similar to those propagated by Usman dan Fodio and his followers during the Sokoto Jihad: "Certainly, one can draw a lot of parallels between the rise of some contemporary mass elements, like Izala Movement, and the forces that overthrew the Hausa kings during the jihad of 1804."[28] Indeed, it was from the tradition of the Sokoto Jihad, despite its qadiriyya doctrine, that Izala established its moral authority to inscribe sharia into the Nigerian politico-religious project and discourses in the Fourth Republic.[29]

Because of its transnational connections to the wider Muslim world and its modernist Muslim outlook, especially its emphasis on education for women and the masses of ordinary people, Northern Muslim youths flocked to the movement during a time of rapid social, political, and economic transformation. The movement's scathing critique of the Northern—Hausa-Fulani and Kanuri—Muslim establishment sparked a full-fledged resistance among a younger generation of Northern Muslims in the 1980s. Intra-Muslim conflict in the country was exacerbated when Saudi Arabia gave the prestigious King Faisal Award to Gumi in 1987 for service to Islam. Nigerian Christians were against the award because it underscored the influence of Saudi Arabia in Nigerian politics; in addition, some emirs frowned at it because the award elevated Gumi's brand of Islamic orthodoxy among Nigerian Muslims. Nevertheless, "infra-Sufi and Sufi-Yan Izala" differences mounted by the late 1980s,[30] resulting in the formation of *Jundullahi* (Soldiers of God) and the *Fityan al-Islam* (Muslim Youth or Heroes/Youth of Islam) by *qadiriyya* and *tijaniyya* clerics, respectively. Despite these countervailing forces, members of Izala were widely seen as forward-thinking Muslims because they denounced entrenched traditional Hausa and Fulani practices as un-Islamic, such as customary bride prices. Despite Gumi's death in 1992, and eroding Izala membership, the movement remained influential among Northern Muslims up until the beginning of the Fourth Republic in 1999.[31]

In other Northern cities, religious riots were triggered by several unfortunate incidents in the 1980s and the 1990s, notably, a case of an alleged inflammatory speech by a Christian preacher who had recently converted from Islam in Kaduna State; a Muslim protest in Kano in 1982 over the construction of a church near a mosque, which reportedly led to the death of forty-four Christians; and the visit by a German evangelist Reinhard Boonke in 1991, dubbed a "crusade," which resulted in two days of mayhem that led to the death of more than 200 people, most of them Christians. In addition, there were reports of a meeting at the Central Mosque at Ahmadu Bello University campus that called for the "destruction of Christianity in Zaria." This call led to riots in the university that spilled into local communities, resulting in the destruction of churches, mosques, and the homes of many Christians. In Kano city, in May 1995, a confrontation between two alleged Hausa thieves and Igbo shop owners led to religious attacks by irate Muslim youths in the Sabon Gari (settlers) quarters, resulting in the death of many Christians.[32] Significantly, these waves of religious crisis were widespread during the military regimes of three Hausa-speaking Muslims after the demise of Nigeria's Second Republic, namely, the military administrations of Generals Buhari, Babangida, and Abacha.

MUSLIM-CHRISTIAN RELATIONS: CONFLICT AND COMPROMISE UNDER MILITARY RULE

During General Babangida military regime from 1985 to 1993, Nigeria's Christian-Muslim conflicts took center stage over the country's controversial membership in the Organization of Islamic Conference (OIC, later Organization of Islamic Cooperation) in 1986.[33] While this crisis had all the qualities of political instability associated with Christian-Muslim relations during this period in Nigeria, it also featured the unusual attempt at the religious reconciliation and coexistence between prominent leaders of the two religions. When the Nigerian Federal Military Government joined the OIC, Christian leaders claimed that the regime made the decision to join the Muslim organization without consulting the Nigerian public. Nigeria's powerful Catholic bishops, expressing concern over the country's unity and the right of Christian minorities in predominantly Northern Muslim states, noted that the OIC charter undermined the essential tenet of Nigeria's plural and secular state.[34] Responding to the strong opposition of Christians throughout the country, General Babangida convened a Consultative Committee of leading Christian and Muslim leaders in 1986 to explore how Nigeria's national interest might "be affected by the recent change from observer status to full membership within the OIC" (Inaugural Meeting of the Committee on OIC). In the end, the report of the Consultative Committee was vague and inconclusive, revealing the frustration of Christian leaders over the growing influence of Northern Muslims over state affairs (Statement of the Consultative Committee on Nigeria's Full Membership in the OIC).

The following year, when Muslim mobs attacked churches in several Northern cities, Catholic bishops called on federal and state authorities to carry out a thorough investigation to bring those responsible to justice. And at the annual conference of Catholic bishops in Awka, the bishops again queried Nigeria's OIC membership. However, as Christian-Muslim tensions intensified, some Catholic leaders also encouraged peaceful dialogue with their Muslim counterparts, drawing on doctrines from the Second Vatican under Pope Paul IV from 1962 to 1965. Significantly, in a high profile meeting later in 1987, Catholic bishops, in collaboration with the Association of Episcopal Churches, in a communiqué titled "Christianity and Islam in Dialogue," identified common grounds between the two world religions; they called on Muslim leaders to reject discriminatory practices against Christians, including classifying non-Muslims as infidels and imposing heavy penalties on Muslims who converted to Christianity, and on Muslim women who marry Christians.

During this period of intense religious conflicts, some prominent Christian and Muslim leaders led peace initiatives throughout the country. No Christian leader exemplified this spirit of peaceful dialogue with Nigeria's Muslim leadership during this period than Cardinal Francis Arinze, a former archbishop of Onitsha and president of the Pontifical Council for Inter-religious Dialogue. As one of Africa's foremost Catholic priests, Cardinal Arinze, an ethnic Igbo, had gained fame for his humanitarian work in the defunct Republic of Biafra during the civil war. Having arrived at the Vatican only a year before the OIC crisis, Cardinal Arinze had extensive experience with Christian-Muslim conflicts in Nigeria. As Nigeria's religious crisis intensified in the 1980s, Cardinal Arinze called for reconciliation and understanding between Christians and Muslims.[35] In keeping with Cardinal Arinze's passionate plea for inter-religious dialogue, some other Catholic priests encourage constructive dialogue between Catholics and Muslims. In this regard, the work of a renowned Igbo Catholic theologian, Rev. Dr. Anih, is worthy of note. In a popular pamphlet *The Cathedral and the Mosque. Can they Co-exist in Nigeria*, Rev. Anih contends: "We believe that by healthy dialogue between Christian and Moslems a new religious sensitivity, called ecumenism . . . can give Nigeria peace and unity because dialogue is an eternal action."[36] Reflecting on the fallout of Nigeria's religious crisis in the 1980s, Anih called on people of all faiths, especially Christians to "listen" and "dialogue" carefully and work with Muslims to achieve a common good.[37]

Some mainstream Muslim organizations attempted to encourage constructive dialogue between Muslim and Christian groups. For example, the Council of Ulama tried to corral diverse Islamic interests into a peace movement, but its connection to the "radical" Muslim Student Society hindered the organization's claim as a reliable broker for peaceful dialogue between Muslim and Christian groups. Other peace efforts initiated by federal and state authorities took the form of seminars, workshops, and conferences to foster religious dialogues between Muslims and Christians in the late 1980s.[38] For example, in 1987, the Babangida administration convened the National Council of Religious Affairs (NCRA) as a statutory body to promote peaceful coexistence between Nigerian Christians and Muslims. This body, however, enjoyed little success. In practice the committee consisted of the NSCIA and Christian Association of Nigeria (CAN)—Nigeria's preeminent Christian association. When CAN alleged bias from federal authorities, toward Northern Muslim leaders on the committee and stopped participating in the body, the committee became obsolescent.[39]

Despite the peace initiatives, the divide between Christians and Muslims grew wider as the OIC controversy raged on with great intensity. Muslim leaders, most of them from emirate society, defended Babangida's decision to join the OIC, arguing that Nigeria is a majority Muslim country and thus should deepen its relationship with Muslim countries.[40] Muslim rebuttals to OIC critics further contended that the organization merely sought parity with Christian organizations; for example, Muslim activists argued that belonging to the OIC was no different from having diplomatic relations with the Vatican, as many countries did, including Nigeria.[41] However, the OIC's stated objectives revealed a major contradiction for a country with Nigeria's religious history. Indeed, the OIC's communiqué on this matter stated the organization's main objectives. They are, among other things, to spread Islam and familiarize the rest of the world with the religion, its concerns, and yearnings; and it emphasizes that Islam is the genuine path that can lead individuals to strength, self-esteem, affluence, and a better life. It is a promise and covenant of the authenticity of the ummah, safeguarding it from the cruel way of greediness. Christian leaders, for their part, argued that OIC held the force of international treaty. They contend that Nigeria, as an OIC member—like other OIC member states—would be duty-bound to provide financial resources to defend Islamic holy sites, support Palestinian liberation groups, and promote global Islamic solidarity.[42]

Embedded in the OIC conflict and contemporaneous national debate on the relations between Christians and Muslims were questions of how and by whom "Islam" and "secularity" is defined in a country where the vestiges of Western governance are steeped in Christian influences. The OIC saga thus exposed the fundamental contradiction in the discourse of the Nigerian state and society over the meaning of religion in Nigeria's purported secular state. To this end, the OIC affair and resultant controversy only hardened religious identities, especially as they affect Northern Muslim power structures, Northern Christian minority resistance, and Southern Christian intelligentsia insistence on Nigerian state secularity.[43] The OIC saga thus exposed a fundamental contradiction in Nigeria's equivocal secular state.

CONCLUDING REMARKS

The sharia crisis that consumed Nigeria's Northern and Middle Belt states in the early years of the Fourth Republic has its foundation in the protracted Christian-Muslim conflicts that dominated Nigerian society since the end of the Nigerian Civil War in 1970. This religious crisis is embedded in the structural fault line of the post-colonial Nigerian state-society system, reflecting the geo-politics of Muslim Northern Nigeria in relations to other geo-political blocs in the country, especially the Middle Belt states and Northern Christian minority communities. In this context, Christian-Muslim confrontations in Nigeria thus reflect how the structures of society embedded in the past reproduce Nigeria's deeply divided society that in part weakens the political structure of the Fourth Republic. The contemporary conflict and clamor by religious zealots and ethnic jingoists for restructuring the "Nigerian project" into ethnic states bears this postulation out.

However, this prevailing ethno-religious fault line created by Christian-Muslim conflicts in Northern and Middle Belt states—along with implications for the geo-politics of the Southern states—should not be taken for granted in the Fourth Republic. The role of religious doctrines, especially in Muslim Northern Nigeria where Islamic praxis or practices are deeply embedded into the "political" structures of society, boosts the probability of tensions. This transformative impact of Muslim doctrine was vividly reflected in the reformist doctrines of Izala under military junta and civilian rule in the 1980s and 1990s. As the crisis of the Nigerian nation-state deepened, Izala's reformist doctrines insisted on the imposition of sharia laws for the adjudication of civil and criminal cases in Muslim Northern states. This Christian-Muslim conflict finally came to a head with the civil democratic opening at the turn of the twenty-first century; and these major religions, given their invented irreconcilable differences, are on a collision course in the Fourth Republic.

The extensive analyses on Christian-Muslim conflicts in postcolonial Nigeria have, however, paid little attention to the spirited attempts at religious reconciliation and peaceful coexistence by Christian and Muslim leaders during these turbulent years of religious disputes in Nigerian society. Despite these peace initiatives, especially from Catholic bishops from South-eastern Nigeria, these laudable efforts experienced limited success because of the hardened and problematic structural divisions in postcolonial Nigerian society. As in the case of the ethno-regional structures that shaped the conflict between Christians and Muslims in Northern and Middle Belt states, the limit of these peace initiatives was apparent because the confrontations are intimately connected to the power configurations of post-colonial Nigerian state-society system. Shaped by the underlying structures of society among the contending communities in Northern Muslim and Middle Belt states, these entrenched religious structures are endemic features of the geo-politics in the Fourth Republic.

This chapter, in the context of this volume, suggests that the Christian-Muslim conflict in the Northern and Middle Belt states should be viewed holistically. It is a clash that has had the propensity for destabilizing the nation-state in the Fourth Republic. This is so because of religious (Christian-Muslim) penetration throughout the Nigerian society. Irrefutably, therefore, an amelioration and then resolution of Muslim-Christian clashes—that continue to simmer in the Fourth Republic—are critical to advancing peaceful coexistence and national cohesion in the contemporary Nigerian polity.

NOTES

1. Olufemi Vaughn, *Religion and the Making of Nigeria* (Durham, NC: Duke University Press, 2016); Olufemi Vaughn, "Sharia Politics, the 1999 Constitution, and the Politics of the Fourth Republic," in A. Carl Levan and Patrick Ukata (eds.), *The Oxford Handbook of Nigerian Politics* (Oxford: Oxford University Press, 2018)
2. David D. Laitin, *Hegemony and Culture: Politics, and Change among the Yoruba* (Chicago, IL: University of Chicago Press, 1986)
3. Vaughn, *Religion and the Making of Nigeria*, 2016.
4. John N. Paden, "Islam and Democratic Federalism in Nigeria," *Africa Notes: Center for Strategic and International Studies*, No. 8 (2002).
5. Joseph Kenny, "Sharia and Christianity in Nigeria: Islam and the 'Secular' State," *Journal of Religion in Africa*, Vol. 26, No. 4 (1996): 338–364; Vaughn, *Religion and the Making of Nigeria*, 2016.
6. Adrian Collet, "Recent Legislation and Reform Proposal for Customary and Area Courts in Nigeria," *Journal of African Law*, Vol. 22, No. 2 (1978): 161–187.
7. Akintunde Obilade, "Jurisdiction of Customary Law Matters in Nigeria: A Critical Examination," *Journal of African Law*, Vol. 17, No. 2 (1973): 227–240.

8. Kenny, "Sharia and Christianity in Nigeria: Islam and a 'Secular' State," 1996.

9. Laitin, *Hegemony and Culture: Politics and Change among the Yoruba*, 1996.

10. Richard Joseph, *Democracy and Prebendel Politics in Nigeria: The Rise and Fall of the Second Republic* (Cambridge, UK: Cambridge University Press, 1987); Tajudeen Abdulraheem, *Politics in Nigeria's Second Republic* (Oxford, UK: DPhil Thesis, University of Oxford, 1990).

11. David Williams, *President and Power in Nigeria: The Life of Shehu Shagari* (London: Frank Cass Publishers, 1982).

12. John Hunwick, "An African Case Study of Political Islam," *Annals of the American Academy of Political and Social Sciences*, Vol. 525 (November 1992): 143–155.

13. Joseph, *Democracy and Prebendel Politics In Nigeria: The Rise and Fall of the Second Republic*, 1987.

14. Paul Lubeck, "Islamic Protest under Semi-industrial Capitalism: Yan Tastine Explained," *Africa*, Vol. 55, No. 4 (1985): 369–389.

15. Henry Bienen, "Religion, Legitimacy, and Conflict in Nigeria," *Annals of American Political and Social Sciences*, Vol. 481, No. 1 (January 1986): 50–60.

16. Kenny, "Sharia and Christianity in Nigeria: Islam and a 'Secular' State, State," 1996.

17. Jan H. Boer, *Nigeria's Decades of Blood, 1980–2002: Studies in Christian-Muslim Relations, Vol. 1* (Belleville, ON, Essence: 2003).

18. Boer, *Nigeria's Decades of Blood, 1980–2002: Studies in Christian -Muslim Relations Vol. 1.*

19. Basir Isyaku, *The Kafanchan Carnage* (Zaria, Nigeria: Basir Isyaku Publication, 1991).

20. See Vaughn, *Religion and the Making of Nigeria*, chapter 2.

21. Matthew H. Kuka, *Religion, Politics, and Power in Northern Nigeria* (Ibadan, Nigeria: Spectrum Books, 1993), Chapter 6.

22. Kuka, *Religion, Politics, and Power in Northern Nigeria.*

23. Sheikh Abubakar Gumi and Ismaila Abubakar Tsiga, *Where I Stand* (Ibadan, Nigeria: Spectrum Books, 1992).

24. Roman Loimeier, *Islamic Reformism and Political Change in Northern Nigeria* (Evanston, IL: Northwestern University Press, 2011), 135.

25. Loimeier, *Islamic Reformism and Political Change in Northern Nigeria.*

26. John N. Paden, *Faith and Politics in Nigeria: Nigeria as a Pivotal State in the Muslim World* (Washington, DC: United States Institute Peace Press, 2008).

27. Gumi and Tsiga, *Where I Stand*, 108.

28. Gumi and Tsiga, *Where I Stand*, 189.

29. Ousman Kane, "Izala: The Rise of Muslim Reformism in Northern Nigeria," in Martin F. Marty and R. Scott Appleby (eds.), *Accounting for Fundamentalism: The Dynamic Character of Movement* (Chicago, IL: University of Chicago Press, 1994), 490–515.

30. Ricardo Rene Laremont, *Islamic Law and Politics in Northern Nigeria* (Trenton, NJ: Africa World Press, 2011), 159.

31. Laremont, *Islamic Law and Politics in Northern Nigeria*, 154–160.

32. Laremont, *Islamic Law and Politics in Northern Nigeria*, 154–160.

33. See *The Challenge Magazine*, No. 4 (1986).

34. See Babajimi O. Faseke, "Nigeria and the Organization of Islamic Cooperation: A Discourse in Identity, Faith and development, 1969–2016," *Religions* (MDPI, 2019) 4–5; Toyin Falola, *Violence in Nigeria: The Crisis of Religious Politics and Secular Ideologies* (New York: University of Rochester Press, 1998).

35. Francis A. Arinze (Cardinal), *Progress in Christian-Muslim Relations Worldwide* (Jos Plateau, Nigeria: Augustinian Publication, 1988).

36. Stan Anih, *The Cathedral, and the Mosque can they co-exist in Nigeria* (Enugu, Nigeria: SNAAP Publication, 1992), 44–45.

37. Anih, *The Cathedral, and the Mosque Can They co-exist in Nigeria*, 44–45.

38. Anih, *The Cathedral, and the Mosque Can They co-exist in Nigeria*, 44–45.

39. Paden, *Faith and Politics in Nigeria: Nigeria as a Pivotal State in the Muslim World*.

40. John Onaiyekan (Cardinal), *Religion: Peace and Justice in Nigeria* (Abuja, Nigeria: Breaking News Grounds, ND).

41. Onaiyekan (Cardinal), *Religion: Peace and Justice in Nigeria.*

42. Onaiyekan (Cardinal), *Religion, Peace and Justice in Nigeria.*

43. Onaiyekan (Cardinal), *Religion, Peace and Justice in Nigeria.*

Chapter 6

The Nigerian Police Highway Corrupt Practices

Strategies to Curb the Transgression

Bennett A. Odunsi

INTRODUCTION

The enduring culture of police corruption, payola, waywardness, and other ghostly activities on the Nigerian highways has not only disrupted peaceful coexistence but also irrevocably shattered the opportunity for improved police-public relationships in the foreseeable future. For the most part, the public are miffed, dismayed, down casted, and completely demoralized by the perverse culture of police corruption and government inaction in curbing the distasteful police misconducts. Despite the widespread public condemnation and growing demand for its containment, police recalcitrant practices grind on with impunity without the prospect of their abatement. Many attributed such pernicious practices to the nature of the internal organization structure that inspire immoral police practices. Scholars have linked the thriving culture of mendacity to two interrelated variables: (1) the mandatory "return practice" and (2) the lapses in oversight, which further stimulate unrestrained police behavior. This chapter examines the impacts of police corruption and its implication on police-citizens alliance. It concludes with suggestions on ways to restore harmonious relations that are critical for moving the country forward in the Fourth Republic

The pervasive culture of police corruption, impunity, extortionist tendencies, and other malpractices across the globe have significantly undermined the acclaimed police professional integrity, lowered police credibility, ruptured relations, weakened amicability and peaceful coexistence between the police and the public. Although many recognized and applauded police fundamental obligations as the guardian of society against miscreants, however, some have questioned police uprightness, ethical judgment, and competencies by virtue of their penchant for offending and jettisoning citizen rights with absolute impunity. Extant research suggests that police and law enforcement operational modalities, patterns of behavior, and mode of service to the public have generated deep-seated concerns and skepticisms across the globe.[1]

The Nigerian police, especially the Special Anti-Robbery Squad (SARS), has aroused intense public wrath due to its excessiveness and widespread misuse of power, gross misconduct, and degradation of citizen's rights. Appalled by wholesale corruption and long-standing extortionist tendencies in general, the police have become problematic in the republic. For example, the Human Right Watch group castigated the Nigerian police for overzealous criminality, questioned government ineptitude in quelling outrageous police practices, and cautioned that the unresolved police atrocities threaten the basic right of all Nigerians.[2]

This chapter explores the impact of the corrupt, corrosive, and lewd police rackets on public roads and highways in the country, its systemic impact on crime reduction, and police-public relations in Nigeria. It concludes with suggestions on the way forward in the Fourth Republic. The term Police/SARS unit will be used interchangeably to denote the entire police organization and its problematic operational modalities.

THE POLICE SOCIETAL ROLE

The global recognition of the police as the defender and protector of public interest has been the linchpin for the solemn and enduring enthusiastic public support for the organization. Unfortunately, public affection tends to wane when officers veered from avowed constitutional obligations to serve the citizens and protect human dignity.

Impelled by the vexing criminal activities and escalating violent crimes in the society, the Nigerian police SARS was established in 1992 as an effective antidote against the threatening and harrowing wave of criminality.[3] Deemed as an important unit of the Nigerian Police Force for covert operation, the original fifteen plain-clothes officers were charged with the arduous task of warding off criminal gang activities. It was hoped that SARS would root out heinous criminal operations within Lagos metropolis and southern Nigeria.[4] Accordingly, by 2002, SARS operational and investigative capacity had mushroomed by leaps and bounds with deep penetration into the country's thirty-six states and the Federal Capital Territory—Abuja—with substantial investigatory and prosecutorial authority. The new mandate offers police operatives tremendous leeway in the arrest and prosecution of armed robbers, kidnappers, including those suspected of malicious and criminal intents.[5] Contrary to public expectation, the Nigerian police SARS operatives have by and large rebuffed the avowed commitment to preservation of lives, and instead resorted to complete deprivation and retardation of citizen's human right entitlements.[6] Udeh's analysis of SARS performance in the polity echoed mass sentiments that police operatives paradoxically became major "terrorizer" of the public they were employed to defend and protect.[7] Anyamele's review of police practices revealed that "brutality and extra-judicial killings are the norms" and that SARS police unit has ultimately turned into "specialist torturers, oppressors, and covert killers."[8] The high level of police malpractices, inhumane and degrading treatment according to Udeh have become a profoundly routinized scheme within the Nigerian police to the chagrin of the public at large.[9] Commenting on the deplorable human condition at the police facility, the Amnesty International in its 2016 assessment categorized the SARS detention in Abuja as a disguised abettor where detainees waited in overcrowded poor living conditions amid harsh constant torture that included beatings, hangings, food deprivation, shootings, taunting, and jeering.[10]

Observers consider such police malpractice as the tip of the iceberg in comparison to other absurd police practices such as assault, rape, extra-judicial killings perpetrated against individuals, and the incomprehensible amount of illegally acquired cash carted away from police checkpoints on a daily basis. The Sahara Reporters analysis of police practices classified the Nigerian police "as some of the most brazenly corrupt in the world" that routinely setup "extortion roadblocks, torture, maimed and kill [citizens] for bribes and [still] remain in denial."[11]

Scholars unreservedly condemn the widespread corruption and dishonesty engendering a low level of public confidence in the police with the attendant lower rate of crime report and the subjective recourse to self-help in crime prevention. While scholars have offered varied and nebulous viewpoints on corruption, however, recent decades have witnessed scholarly convergence on what corruption entails. Some have equated police corruption with a wide range of illegal practices such as "bribery and extortion," while others have evoked "theft, fraud, racketeering, and tax evasions as a symbol of corruption."[12] Corruption within the Nigerian context covers a whole range of social behaviors in which various forms of morally questionable deception enable the achievement of "wealth, power, prestige, as well as much more [other] mundane ambitions."[13] It encompasses everything from "government bribery and graft, rigged elections and fraudulent" activities.[14]

Many perceived corruption as a universal phenomenon across the globe with slight variations but more profound in developing world. Bailey and Perito noted poignantly that "police corruption in developing countries is more pervasive than in developed countries."[15] Assessing the broad range of police corruption, scholars opine that corruption in the police department can be found in news reports of all countries from Kenya to Japan, from Mexico to Saudi Arabia, from the United States to UK. Corruption has entered society at all levels and in all professions, making police corruption as part of a whole range of corrupt practices carried out worldwide.[16]

Ivkovic has argued that police agencies across the globe are not immune from corruption allegations and that police officers such as "Blue Knights entrusted and empowered to enforce the law can become some of the most aggressive criminals themselves."[17] In recent years, research analysts have emphasized the global spread of police corruption. For example, a 1972 study of Chicago police indicated that "One of the three criminals is guilty of criminal act. The same applies to the Boston police where one in four was implicated in criminally related activities, compared with one in five officers in Washington, DC."[18] A 1973 Knapp Commission Report linked almost half of the New York police officers with corrupt exercises. Similarly, a 1994 report on Miami police discovered that 100 of the 1,046 officers either have been investigated or are currently under scrutiny for corruption-related allegations.[19]

In Nigeria, the growing public discourse on the enduring culture of corruption has to a large extent become a national "pastime," as stories abound on police affinity with bribery and public discontent that a resolution to this depraved cultural quagmire is difficult to find. There is a general awareness that operational modalities of the Nigerian police reflect the manifestation of a crude and uncanny global police custom. Scholarly research, newspaper reports, and public opinion survey echoed contemptuous testaments of endemic corruption and the belief that the police represent the "symbol of unfettered corruption."[20] Uppermost in the various corrupt police practices in Nigeria are extortion, bribery, wholesome embezzlement, burglary, brutality, and the perverse institutionalized systems of return requiring that rank and file pay up the chain of command percentages of monies extorted from the public.[21] According to Smith, "corruption has become the dominant discourse of complaint in the post-colonial world symbolizing people's disappointment with democracy and development, and their frustration with confirming social inequality."[22] The recently computed report by the Nigerian National Bureau of Statistics suggested that police officers are the public officials to whom bribe is most commonly paid to in Nigeria. The report suggests that the ethical norms expected of officers embedded in the police code of conduct are not followed. Indeed, the report further indicated that 46.4 percent of adults with direct contact with police officers in the twelve months prior to the survey made at least one bribe payment to an officer of the Nigerian Police Force.[23]

NATURE OF PUBLIC-POLICE DISAFFECTION

There is the general awareness that the uneasy coexistence and widespread public dissatisfaction with the police and law enforcement organizations are the result of unethical police practices and behavior particularly at the checkpoints on Nigerian highways. The public are for the most part mystified by the harrowing experiences and skewed occupational values displayed by officers manning the checkpoints on many roads and highways. Aside from the frequently exhibited macho image by police, citizens are extremely apprehensive, appalled by the pervasive human rights violations and the wrenching culture of corruption that officers exhibit. The public are equally enraged by police "insensitivity," incivility to the community, and the recurring perverse culture of impunity and the skewed police cultural and professional ethos contrary to its ethics. Scholarly researchers allude to mass disappointment over the modification and shift in the traditional police role as protector rather than the prevailing depiction of police as a menace to the public's wellbeing in the country.

In assessing the declining police-public matters, Okonkwo attributed the deterioration in relations to the "embedded" corrupt practices that have deeply penetrated the "brain and nerves of its members." He further opines on this matter that the Nigerian Police Force is the most unscrupulous organization that the public has totally lost confidence in and dissatisfied with.[24] The Glen Foundation in its 2006 national opinion poll result classified the Nigerian police as the most corrupt, ineffective, and inefficient public institution in the country.[25] In his narrative on police dishonesty, Akinlabi reverberated the prevailing public outcry of endemic corruption and the perverse assumption that the incorruptible are "societal deviants." He also acknowledges the reality that police-public relationship in Nigeria is perhaps "one of the most troublesome in sub-Saharan Africa—a pitiable situation attributable to the deviation from normative expectations and the outright disregard for procedural fairness."[26] Assessing public convictions on the level of police corruption and human rights violation, Festus Ogun observed that substantial number, if not all Nigerians, viewed the "police as their greatest enemy," and that majority of police officers are not fully committed or passionate about their positions but more interested in the benefits that accrue by virtue of their police status.[27]

The extensive public cynicism and disdain for police victimization spurred the expression that the police violate the rights of the citizens more than any other "person or body"; they are more inhumane, reckless, unapologetically disrespectful, maimed, injured, and dehumanize substantial number of Nigerian citizens with impunity.[28] Interestingly, the public resistance to predatory police practices has heightened mutual tension, hostility, distrust, and the conviction that the police are predators rather than protectors—especially of the poor and marginalized citizens. In a nutshell, pervasive skirmishes spurred by police repression, unending corruption, improper and objectionable behavior, and unethical practices have undoubtedly increased the politico-social divide between the public and the police.

POLICE CHECKPOINTS MENACE

The pervasive culture of extortion by some police officers at the various checkpoints on Nigeria's highways has generated inadvertently new demand for its closure. Consensus exists that the widespread police extortion rackets and ceaseless inhumane treatment of citizens at these facilities are indications of subtle support for such illicit operations by higher authority. The Human Rights Watch regarded the checkpoints as popular locations where motorists are hunted down, harassed, victimized, deprived of their earnings, and subjected to the crudest forms of punishment.[29] Generally, citizenries considered checkpoints as the most vulnerable epicenters for all forms of police illegalities where motorists are compelled to pay money or offer bribe, and those unyielding to illicit monetary request have "either been brutalized, maimed, sexually assaulted, or subjected to extra-judicial killings."[30]

Mostly affected by the police sinister activities are taxi and minibus drivers, motor cyclists, and private road users routinely subjected to varied forms of extortion on a regular basis "under threat" of "detention" and "physical harm." As one observer puts it, "these checkpoints have become a lucrative criminal enterprise for the police who normally demand bribes from drivers and passengers alike (enforcing) in some places a *de facto* standardized toll."[31] The severity of punishment inflicted on innocent citizens for noncompliance is adequately reflected in Inyang and Abraham's analysis with the lamentation that the checkpoint condition has "resulted in loss of lives on account of accidental discharge of bullet from police riffles, motorists who refused to pay the required toll fee have ended in their early graves."[32]

The recent interview of commercial drivers and passengers reveals frightening tales of dehumanization, deprivation, and forced dispossession of monetary assets amid threat of impoundment of vehicles and forceful detention.[33] The degree of public discontentment and vexation with deplorable carnage and human misery at the checkpoint is reflective in the expression that if "an armed robber and a police officer strayed into your compound and you have a riffle, it is safer to kill the police first and then go after the robber later."[34] Newspapers' report further reinforce unjustifiable police slaying and extra-judicial killings of those opposed to police request for hush money at the tollgates. For example, the October 16, 2011, shooting death of Emmanuel Victor in Yenagoa, Bayelsa State, for his objection to the illicit cash demanded of him by highway police officers was a typical case of police viciousness.[35]

The dreadful human casualties at checkpoints included the cold-blooded murder of a nine-year-old Timilehin Ebun on June 13, 2013, when police bullet aimed at a fleeing commercial driver sidestepping the required toll levy at the checkpoint ricocheted and killed the young innocent girl. In addition, the shooting of Saheed Aborisade within the vicinity of Police post in Oregun, Oyo State, for ignoring police solicitation for a hundred Naira bribery on July 12, 2004, was another act of police recklessness. The alarming mishaps with the police also included the shooting of a three-year-old Kasufura, Muritala by former police corporal Kechukwu Nwabueze in 2009 and the brutal slaying of Ugockukwu Ozuch less than a week after his wedding. Interestingly, the seeming inertia of police officials to act in stopping the vicious cycle of human deaths has galvanized public outburst and clamor for change.[36]

In his anatomy on the horrific human deprivation caused by the actions of bad cops, Isinula categorized the checkpoint as a horror den and a "death trap" where innocent Nigerians "driving to their offices or places of business were frequently harassed and often forcefully disposed of their hard-earned monies and valuables."[37]

Other hideous police action with human devastation at the checkpoints included the killings of a bus driver Kehinde Adeniji and a passenger Bolanle Bamidele between Ita-Odo and Aramoko area of Ekiti State, for rejecting the request for a N20 bribe solicitation by officers manning the checkpoint on June 3, 2014. Also, the killing of Fedelie Okoji, a father of five, by officer Blessing Igbinova in Lagos over a N20 levy further points to the brazen level of police misconduct and public dissension[38] that calls for swift policies to address this misconduct.

Unfortunately, the rift created by wicked police practices has aroused public outrage and displeasure over government passive response to incidents of police corruption and destruction of human life. Many are of the view that lukewarm government response to this malfeasance has undoubtedly shattered public enthusiasm for some form of relief against the police in the foreseeable future. Regrettably, police leadership indifference to police cruelty, malevolent, and illegal siege on innocent citizens without recourse has further diminished expectations for robust strategic plan by police officials to reform the system probably because they are benefactors.[39]

EFFECT OF CHECKPOINT EXTORTION ON CITIZENS/NATION

Scholars have pointed to dismal economic performance, political and social dislocation, and poor infrastructural and human resource development as some of the by-products of institutionalized corruption and called for its abatement.[40] Ironically, Nigerian political leaders disregarded the warnings and instead decided to preserve the existing police circumstance. Commenting on the thriving state of corruption and its ill effects on national development Okunriboye remarked that "corruption appears to be a never-ending national stigma read about on daily basis in our newspapers," and for all practical purposes, "has become firmly rooted in our scheme of operation."[41] In his narrative on the adverse implication of corruption, he linked the existing chaotic infrastructural development, dismal economic condition, and political and social disarray to corruption. As he puts it, "corruption corrodes the machinery of government and undermine the confidence of people in their leaders and the system in which they operate"[42] Finally, he attributed the gross dysfunction in government apparatuses in Nigeria to endemic corruption from epileptic electricity, poor running water, unpaid workers' salaries, to abandoned and incomplete projects.[43]

John Kerry, the former US secretary of state at the International Anti-corruption Forum in Washington, DC, categorizes corruption as an evil monster that should be completely eradicated given its adverse implication on nation-state. This is especially the case given the undue financial devastation, human rights dispossession, and socio-political and economic deprivation heaped on the country.[44] Addressing the World Economic forum in Davos on January 22, 2016, he denounced the pervasive global corruption and its subsequent threats to "global growth," "stability," and "global future."[45] In a demonstration of his anguish over the rising tide of global corruption, he cautioned the world communities of subsequent economic avalanches associated with the intensifications of such practice if left unchecked. Kerry viewed corruption as a form of social danger and a radicalizer with the capacity to delegitimize legal authority and stimulate unnecessary incursion of a predatory practice into government operation.[46]

Furthermore, corruption from Kerry's vantage point is an opportunity destroyer by virtue of the limitation imposed on credible investment opportunity and the unnecessary increases in business and government transactional costs.[47] Expressing his exasperation with the recurring vicious circle of checkpoints extortion and the difficulties associated with such cruel act, he called for a unified global effort to end such repulsive practices.[48]

Echoing his aversion for negative public opinion on police roguish tendencies for illegal wealth acquisition and the danger it portends, the Nigerian Inspector General of Police (IGP) Mohammad Abubakar "remorsefully" scolded the police in this manner: "justice has been perverted, peoples' right denied, innocent souls committed to prison, torture and extrajudicial killing perpetrated."[49] Perhaps, the IGP's most strident condemnation and disdain over outlandish police unethical practices and the loss of public confidence in the police became apparent when he quipped: "Illegalities thrive under your watchful eyes because you have compromised the very soul of our profession. Our respect is gone, and the Nigerian public has lost even the slightest confidence in the ability of the police to do any good things."[50]

Even so, assessing the financial loss to police extortionist practices in the Southeast geopolitical zone, Comrade Umeagbalasi and Justin Ijeoma contend that the police were able to squeeze ₦10,425 billion from that zone alone during an eighteen-month operation with 1,350 police checkpoints. An updated report offered detailed breakdowns of police illicit earnings within the five southeast geopolitical zone and the remaining five states throughout the country.[51]

The report further revealed other illegitimate tactics employed by police to carry out their unlawful corruption schemes. The most familiar and frequently used strategy includes extortion derived from mass arrest and enquiries into vehicular papers and so on. These methods are generally condemned by civil liberties and the Rule of Law advocates who see them as the easiest ploys for police corruption in Nigeria.[52]

In most cases police extortionists are usually accompanied by people in mufti that "offload" the loot in various denominations for "safe keeping pending the completion of the roadblock exercises. The looted funds are subsequently shared according to the prevailing distribution culture between the rank and file, police constables and the IGP."[53]

CONSEQUENCES OF CHECKPOINT EXTORTION

Academics have expressed grave concerns over the problematic socio-economic consequences placed on the Nigerian society by ubiquitous police highway checkpoints. Besides the unpleasant daily ordeal experienced by road users are the unwarranted delay, the extra cost associated with time spent at the checkpoints, and the transactional cost incurred from police extortion. Little wonder, then, that members of the informed public contend that the illegal practices tend to produce business hardship, reduce investment opportunities, and impose additional levy on consumer goods, as business owners are forced to impose extra levy on goods to defray the cost incurred from police extortions.[54] Moreover, they believe that this form of corruption mitigates the country's development project. This is the case because it promotes economic destabilization, reduces private investments, encourages social disunity and unrest, and other forms of abnormalities.[55]

Analyzing the financial trauma experienced by Nigeria through corrupt practices, the former EFCC chairman Nuhu Ribadu estimated that the country lost a whopping $380 billion between 1960 and 1992.[56] Generally, the political, economic, and social upheavals in the Fourth Republic are attributable to the nation's enduring legacy of corruption.[57] Smith's work captures the public sentiments on this issue when he asserts that

> when Nigerians talk about corruption, they refer not only to the abuse of State officers for private gain but also to a whole range of social behaviors in which various forms of morally questionable deception enable the achievement of wealth, power, or prestige as well as much more mundane ambition. Nigerian notions of corruption encompass everything from government bribery and graft, rigged elections, and fraudulent business deals to the diabolical abuse of occult powers.[58]

Current research on police preoccupation with checkpoint bribery and extortion rackets has undoubtedly reduced their effectiveness in crime abatement, diminished police physical condition for lack of adequate and proper exercise regimen which for all practical purposes are the "sine qua non" for effective policing.[59] Such an unorthodox behavior has intensified public clamor for some modification in police behavior. The Nigerian public, frequently, considers the police as uncharitable, mean-spirited, ruthless, incompetent, corrupt, resistant to change, unaccountable, ineffective, and criminal co-conspirators.[60] The level of public discontentment has reached a point where many literally avoid police help on criminal matters and instead resort to self-help or liaise with vigilante groups in resolving criminal matters.[61]

Other implicit ramifications of police checkpoint problems are social discomfort, economic retardation, and widespread logjams that generally impede free flow of traffic on the highways and side roads.[62] Observers expressed the view that the social and economic impediments associated with highway checkpoints are depressing, devastating, and include diminished investment opportunities, psychological stress induced by personal revulsion for being forced to stop against their will, traffic congestion, road surface damage, and fuel wastage.[63] Implicitly, corruption significantly weakens police confidence and professionalism, diminishes police effectiveness in crime detection, and alienates and breeds public-police animosity.[64] Corruption, in the words of Ackerman, promotes "inefficiency," "unfairness," and severely undermines the political legitimacy of the Fourth Republic.[65]

THE WAY OUT

The preceding pages have revealed the Nigerian police sleazy reputation for brutality, widespread exploitation, wholesale impunity, and the deep-seated institutionalized extortion rackets. The irony, as noted previously, on this matter is that the IGP, Abubakar, recognizes the disreputable character of the Nigerian police; yet not much is been done to effectively reform the police and the public image of the police force.

Regrettably, despite constitutional provisions against human rights violation, the various Nigerian governments have remained politically numb to public demand for checkmating police irascibility and contemptuous mode of operation and practices. However, the time is ripe for political leaders' bold action to end police harassments of civilians at highway checkpoints in the polity. In short, in the Fourth Republic, the police perverse mindset of we against them calculus reminiscent of the "old British consular policing arrangement" requires modification, realignment, and reformation to improve police-citizens relations.[66]

The lack of political will to amend or alleviate the horrific practice and assuage public discontentment has further polarized and widened the gulf between the public and the police. Scholars should join the crusade to eliminate this appalling institutionalized menace to the republic that is arguably condoned, embraced, and nurtured by some unscrupulous members of the Nigerian police organization and the political class.[67]

Many attributed police waywardness to multiple factors, the most notable are poor training, poor recruitment and screening practices, inadequate equipment, poor remuneration, low morale, lack of ethical standards, and the politicization of recruitment. Others believe that the preceding vices have turned the police force into an easy "dumping ground for bullies, miscreants, criminals, and misfits that are not good enough for other careers."[68]

The toxic range of emotions, boiling anger, and deep-seated animosity directed at young adults by the police are succinctly captured in Azuka's narrative that the police "was [and is] a lawless, uncouth, uncultured vicious group which acted like a terrorist group against the people it was [and is] meant to protect. Even though its name read anti-bribery, it paid scant attention to robbery and related issues. Its primary concern was young men who had dreadlocks and tattoos and wore trendy clothes or had expensive smart phones, laptops or good cars."[69]

The unyielding response to popular demand for the police to de-escalate tension, cleanse itself of illicit activities, restore confidence, and enhance mutual understanding must be heeded to tackle the politico-economic and socio-religious problems in the Fourth Republic. Indeed, the unrelenting siege on Nigerian youth exacerbated the massive call for the disbandment of the notorious police unit—SARS. To ameliorate relations, mitigate tension, and enhance police-citizens relations in the Fourth Republic, it is incumbent on the Nigerian government to correct existing institutional maladies and leadership issues. More importantly, it is critical for the regime to commit to complete transformation of virtually all government institutions including the "judiciary" that is "seemingly on life support."[70] There is also the recognition that lapses in oversight, clumsy leadership, and the lack of political fortitude toward police reformation must be altered and modified to enhance coordination and effectiveness in the Fourth Republic.[71] Extant laws must constrain police malpractices, prevent police sharp practices, outlaw extra-judicial killings, and establish adequate standards against prolonged detention beyond required time frame. In this regard, those in violation of set standards should be prosecuted as the nation tackles these conundrums in the Fourth Republic.

The relentless resistance by police organization against civilian review board must be halted and completely eradicated. Active participation of private citizens on police board ensures accountability, increases transparency, enhances democratic governance, and stimulates public involvement in decision-making. In as much as the police are public servant, paid from the national coffers, they should be made accountable to the public they serve. The idea of police decentralization and the establishment of state police must be the central focus of police reformation.

The traditional practice of having former police chief serve on police board is completely outdated, archaic, and should be discontinued. The long-standing tradition of illegal acquisition of wealth through illicit transaction by the police must be halted. Political leaders must also develop effective policy to prevent, detect, and investigate cases of police corruption, and punish those in violation of established policy.

In his commitment to obliterate illicit police practices, President Buhari promised to end corruption and ensure transparency in the recruiting process. Reiterating his earlier message, he demanded for transparency without any inklings of monetary gratification or extortion by police officials from enlisted applicants.[72] To this end, he promised to institutionalize the anti-corruption campaign through the codification of acceptable standards that focuses on retraining and reorientation of public service employees and the development of administrative and fiscal policies within established guidelines. He further warned that those who violate the new code of conduct will be subjected to prosecution irrespective of their positions or connection.

It is hoped that by the enforcement of appropriate and sanctioned Police Code of Conduct, the wrenching culture of corruption and dehumanization of Nigerian citizens, by some corrupt police officers at roadblocks and elsewhere, will come to a screeching halt. Such success which could come about through national support is likely to advance peaceful coexistence in the Fourth Republic.

NOTES

1. David Bayley and Robert Perito, "Police Corruption: What Past Scandals Teach about Current Challenges," *United States Institute of Peace* (November 2011), pp. 1–19.

2. See the CNN Wire Staff Report shines light on Nigerian Police Corruptions, August 18, 2010; See also Sara Simpson, Human Rights Watch Says Corruption Pervasive in Nigeria, in www.voanews.com/english/archives/2007-10/2007-10-09-voa72.cfm (Retrieved 11/04/20)

3. Maeti Udeh, "History of Nigeria Special Anti-Robbery Squad," *National African Student Association* (October 20, 2020).

4. Kimogelo Diamini, "Nigeria SARS: A Brief History of the Special Anti-Robbery Squad," *Aljazeera*, October 22, 2020.

5. Uche Anyamale, "End SARS Protest and Extra-Judicial Killings," *Punch Newspapers* (November 20, 2020).

6. Ibid. See also Annie Olaloku Teriba, "The Nigerian Protest Are about Much More Than Police Violence. SARS Abuse Reflects the Moral Bankruptcy of the System the Corrupt Nigerian Ruling Elite Has Put in Place," *Aljazeera*, October 20, 2020.

7. Udeh, "History of Nigeria Special Anti-Robbery Squad," op. cit.

8. Anyamele, "End SARS Protest and Extra-judicial Killings," op. cit.

9. Diamini, "Nigeria SARS: A Brief History of the Special Anti-Robbery Squad," op. cit. See Daniel Jordan Smith, "A Culture of Corruption, Everyday Deception in Nigeria," in http://press.princeton.edu/chaptersi8266.html (Retrieved 10/17/19)

10. Diamini, "Nigeria SARS: A Brief History of the Special Anti-Robbery Squad," op. cit.

11. See "Nigeria Police of Bribery and Corruption," *Sahara Report*, September 12, 2017. See also Chioma Gabriel, Corruption, Nigerian Police under Scrutiny, Special Report, *Vanguard Newspapers*, August 19, 2017, in https://www.vanguardngr.com/2017/08corruption-nigeria-police-scrutiny (Retrieved 10/20/20)

12. Smith, "A Culture of Corruption, Everyday Deception and Popular Discontent in Nigeria," op. cit.

13. Ibid.

14. Ibid.

15. See Lawan CPolice Cheri, "Corruption and People's Opinion on the Removal of Police Checkpoint in Yobe State," *Global Journal of Arts, Humanities and Social Sciences*, Vol. 3, No. 10 (October 2015), pp. 46–55.

16. Bailey and Perito, "Police Corruption: What Past Scandals Teach about Current Challenges," op. cit.

17. Sonya Kutnjak Ivkovic, "To Serve and Collect: Measuring Police Corruption," *Journal of Criminal Law and Criminology*, No. 2–3 (Winter 2003), pp. 593–649.

18. See Francis L. McCafferty and Margrett A. McCafferty, "Corruption in Law Enforcement: A Paradigm of Occupational Stress and Deviancy," *Journal of Academy of Psychiatry Law*, Vol. 26, No. 1 (1998), pp. 57–65.

19. Ibid.

20. Ibid. See also Hubert Williams, "Core Factors of Police Corruption Across the World," *Forum of Crime and Society*, Vol. 2, No. 1 (December 2002), pp. 85–99.

21. See the Clean Foundation Report, "Motions without Movement," Report of Presidential Committee on Police Reform in Nigeria, 2006. http://new.cleen.orgRepo rtofpresidentialcommitteeonPoliceReform.pdf (Retrieved 10/20/20).

22. Smith, "A Culture of Corruption: Everyday Deception and Popular Discontent in Nigeria," op. cit.

23. "Corruption: Nigeria: Police under Scrutiny," *Vanguard Newspaper*, August 19, 2017. See also Human Rights Watch, Despite Reforms, Police Routinely Practice Torture in https://www.alternatives.ca/article2016.html (Retrieved 7/7/21).

24. See Adaeze Okonkwo, "The Nigerian Police Force: A Threat or a Pride?" in http://www.gangi.com/article5000 (Retrieved 12/20/20).

25. See the Clean Foundation Report, "Motions without Movement," Report of Presidential Committee on Police Reform in Nigeria, 2006, op. cit.; Oluwagbenga M. Akinlabi, "Do the Police Really Protect and Serve the Public? Police Deviance and Public Cynicism towards the Law in Nigeria," *Journal of Criminology and Criminal Justice* (2016 online).

26. Festus Ogun, "Nigerian Police Force: Corruption and Human Rights Violations," *Justice*, June 9, 2016 in https://ogunfestus.files.wordpress.com/2016/06/npt.png (Retrieved 12/12/20).

27. Ibid.

28. See "The Nigerian Police and Corruption," in http://www.gietmania'com/talk/topics45266.ohtml (Retrieved 10/12/20)

29. Ibid.

30. See John D. Inyang and Ubong E. Abraham, "Corruption in the Police Force: A Study of Police Drivers Behavior along Highway in Southern Nigeria," *International Journal of Humanities and Social Services*, Vol. 3, No. 17 (September 2013), pp. 276–284.

31. Ibid.

32. Ibid.

33. Ibid.

34. Ibid.

35. Ibid.

36. Ibid. See Taiwo Kehinde, "Police Checkpoints in Nigeria; My Mind Always; Mitigating the Excess by Men in Black," September 2013, in http://taiwokehinde-mymind.blogspot.com/2013/09/policecheckpoints-in-nigeria-html (Retrieved 11/10/20).

37. Kamaye Isinula, "The New Police and FRSC Checkpoints," *P. M. News Nigeria*, July 11, 2013

38. D. Oyewale, "Facing their deadly Lust," *Tell Magazine*, No. 31 (August 2005).

39. Ibid.

40. Toyin Falola, *Corruption in the Nigerian Public Service* (Lewiston, NY: The Edwin Mellen Press, 1998), pp. 137–165.

41. Olu Okunriboye, "Corruption Trends in Nigeria," World African/Nigeria News Flash November 2017, in http://.nigeriabmasterweb.com/paperfrmes.html (Retrieved 12/10/20)

42. Ibid.
43. Ibid.
44. See John Kerry, "U.S. Department of State Diplomacy in Action: Press Statement on International Anti-corruption Day in Davos." in https://www.cfr.org/economic-development/remarks-secretary-kerry-world-economic-forum/2/1/217 (Retrieved 12/10/20).
45. Ibid.
46. Ibid.
47. Ibid.
48. Ibid.
49. Ibid.
50. "Nigeria Police Chief Says Own Officers are Corrupt," in http://www.reuters.com/artucle/ozalp-nigeria-policeidAFJOEIDO7220120214 (Retrieved 5/10/21).
51. Emeka Umeagbalasi and Justus Ijeoma, "Corruption in the Nigeria Police Force: Putting the Record Straight," *Sahara Reporters,* http://saharareporters.com/2020/08/27/corruption-nigeria-police-force-putting-records-straight (Retrieved 5/10/21). See also Emeka Umeagbalasi, "How Corrupt Nigerian Police Illegally Enriched the Force with Over N53.48 billion from Roadblock Extortion." A paper prepared and delivered at Media Forum, in Onitsha, Nigeria, December 11, 2011.
52. Ibid.
53. Ibid.
54. See V. E. Dike, "Corruption in Nigeria: A Paradigm for Effective Control, Africa Economic Analysis," in http://www.africaeconomicanalysis/gen/corruption-dike.html (Retrieved 8/20/21)
55. A. A. Ibrahim, "Police Corruption and the State Prevalence and Consequences," *Global Journal of Arts, Humanities and Social Sciences*, Vol. 3, No. 3 (March 2015), pp. 19–29.
56. Smith, "Culture of Corruption: Everyday Deception and Popular Discontent in Nigeria," op. cit.
57. Ibid.
58. Ibid.
59. Ibid.
60. Umeagbalasi, "How Corrupt Nigerian Police Illegally Enriched the Force with Over N53.48 billion from Roadblock Extortion," op. cit.
61. Ajayi Johnson Olusegun, "Public Perception of the Police and Crime Prevention in Nigeria," *International Journal of Criminology and Sociological Theory*, Vol. 7, No. 3 (December 2014), pp. 1–12.
62. Cheri, "Corruption and Peoples' Opinion on the Removal of Police Checkpoints in Yobe State," op. cit.
63. H. A. Ajie and O. E. Wokekoro, "The Impact of Corruption on Sustainable Economic Growth and Development in Nigeria," *International Journal of Economic Development Research and Investment*, Vol. 3, No. 1 (April 2012), pp. 91–109.
64. Susan Rose Ackerman, "The Political Economy of Corruption: Causes and Consequences," Institute for International Economics, 1995 in https://www.iie.com (Retrieved 8/21/21).
65. Williams, "Core Factors of Police Corruption Across the World," op. cit.

66. Bennett A. Odunsi, "Law Enforcement Issues and Strategies for Reformation," in E. Ike Udogu (ed.), *The Developing World: Critical Issues in Politics and Society* (Lanham, MD: Scarecrow Press, 2012), pp. 23–42.

67. Ibid.

68. See O. O. Karimu, "Effects of the Nigerian Police Force Personnel Welfare Condition on Performance," *European Journal of Research and Reflection in Arts and Humanities*, Vol. 3, No. 1 (2015), pp. 7–72.

69. Azuka Onwuka, "How many times will SARS be Scrapped?" *Punch Newspaper*, October 13, 2020.

70. Niran Adedokun, "Nigeria needs a revolution (Viewpoint)," *Punch Newspaper*, Thursday July 18, 2019; Toyin Falola, "SARS: Odours from a decaying system," *Punch Newspaper*, October 27, 2020; see also "End SARS: Rise and Fall of a Roque police Unit," *Punch Newspaper*, October 15, 2020.

71. Odunsi, "Law Enforcement Issues and Strategies for Reformation," op. cit.

72. Falola, "SARS: Odours from a decaying system," op. cit.

Chapter 7

Subaltern Voices and Implications for Nigerian Politics in the Fourth Republic

A Theoretical and Conceptual Analysis

Samuel Zalanga

INTRODUCTION

This chapter alludes to how the subalterns in the politics of Nigeria are exploited by political actors during political contestations and left to fend for themselves thereafter. Due to the peripheral political and economic role they play in the system, not much is written about their significance in the development of the polity. In truth, their voices are not heard. Yet, subalterns are essential citizens in the political and economic affairs of the country—especially with respect to political stability and peaceful coexistence as is the case in the current political climate. Indeed, they are frequently manipulated by political actors and religious leaders and serve in the frontline in political and religious battles. This chapter expresses the view that the political, economic, and social interests of the subalterns in Nigerian society should be taken seriously in discourses on how to advance national cohesion and to move the country forward in the Fourth Republic.

From a critical examination of the literature on subaltern studies, it is important to note from the onset that subalterns are a heterogenous group of people.[1] Even as individuals, their identity is characterized by intersectionality in the sense that they can be members of a class, an ethnic cleavage or "tribal" group, gender troupes, and religious collectivities. Each of these variables says something about their identity. It is in this respect that they are not a coherent group. Regarding interpretation, to be subaltern means being "subordinate in terms of class, caste, gender, and culture."[2] Traditionally, the concept was primarily applied to peasants who were treated as backward in the structure and process of colonial history. They were thought to be uncouth because of the way and manner the subalterns operated was outside the framework of the modern nation and class system. Their mode of behavior and interaction did not fit well with the conventional framework of analysis in Western historiography, which is essentially defined by modern rationality as a vision, worldview, and organizing principle.[3] This chapter does not assume that the subalterns today in Nigeria—whether in the form of people who are lower in rank in the modern social class system or as peasants—are not rational people. Indeed, even peasants have consciousness, and they did not only exist in the past, but they also continue to exist today in postcolonial Nigerian society, even though the structure, process, and dynamics of their existence are relatively different today when compared to the past. There are certain key observations about subaltern people in the literature that when critically assessed are relevant in understanding the situation of subalterns in Nigeria today.

First, it must be noted that because of the way history has unfolded, interregional relations of power mediated on how different groups of subalterns came to understand themselves, and this has played an important role in shaping how they have related to each other. In the case of Nigeria, for the great majority of people, the region where they are living and where they are born shapes how they see themselves and how they perceive people in another region of the country.[4] But more importantly, because most of the postcolonial elites live in the city and see the city at one point as playing a modernizing and civilizing role in history, they perceive people who live in rural areas to be a different region of the country, as a means for developing the urban centers. This happened when postcolonial elites used the marketing boards to tax rural people to extract surplus from the rural agricultural sector to develop urban centers—with limited or no input as to how their contributions are to be spent.[5]

Second, the identity of members of the subaltern group or people as suggested earlier developed in the form of "imagined community." Although, in the case of Nigeria, people in a particular region or ethnic group might perceive themselves as one and those outside the region as "others," the fact is that any social identity beyond the family is a socially constructed community. There is no ethnic or religious group that has no divisions and subdivisions of identities or variables that divide the group. That the people are willing to consider themselves as one is nothing natural, but a product of the ways and manner the people use their social agency, especially as shaped by social and political contingencies. It is in this respect that the failure to develop a strong national identity in Nigeria is a failure of leadership. There is nothing natural about being a Hausa, Fulani, Tiv, Yoruba, Igbo, Kanuri,

Ijaw, and Itsekiri to list a few ethnic groups. As forms of identities, they were socially constructed over time through the deliberate effort of political entrepreneurs—frequently to promote their interest.

Third, subaltern identity as it has played out in Nigeria and other societies was in its creation and evolution shaped by the project of modernity, which is unequal and uneven in its penetration of the state and society and its consequences for the life or history of the people. The northern part of Nigeria was historically much more highly influenced by the spread of Islam and Islamic culture from North Africa into the region dating back to the medieval period. This process of the spread of Islam deeply penetrated and shaped the culture of the region. On the other hand, Western modernity with all things that are peculiar to its colonization patterns or genres arrived and penetrated Nigeria from the coastal regions and impacted it in a different way compared to the way that Islam influenced the northern region.[6] Accordingly, even though today, there are subaltern citizens in all parts of Nigeria, the way they were incorporated into the modern world was uneven and different. This was the case partly because of the cultural and religious orientations. The consequences of such unequal and uneven penetration of modernity are still impacting the political alignments in the country and how each region is coping with access to and affordability of higher education and modern technology. Modern technologies are essential tools of information with which to promote good governance and national development which most subalterns lack.

COLONIAL NIGERIA: A BRIEF ANALYSIS

Colonial Nigeria was one in which the colonial overseers with a few Nigerians saw themselves as the elite and the rest of the population as subalterns. When the country gained its self-rule from Britain, a few Nigerian administrators not only stepped into the shoes of the departing imperialists but also assumed the position of the new elites because of their socialization. They governed like their former colonial bosses and saw to it that they controlled the modernization process and the social structure of the society.[7] Indeed, due to the theory of privilege, the elites never wanted their status as inheritors of the state to diminish.[8] Thus, when genuine development transforms the life (of some) of the people hitherto referred to as subalterns, the elites felt threatened. After all, there can be no rich folks without poor folks to admire them for their wealth. In short, if subalterns became drivers of their own history and autonomous people, they will no longer be subordinated or subservient to the elites. My argument or hypothesis is that if Nigeria is to move forward in the Fourth Republic in terms of development or modernization, attempts must be made to uplift the subalterns by providing them with the tools to do so—education and full participation in the political, economic, and social development.

The discourse in the literature on subaltern studies has highlighted an important insight that is relevant for understanding Nigeria's history on this matter. The relevant instinct is that the creation of the modern state did not assume the disappearance of the peasant. The modern state was, whether in the case of Europe, Africa, or Nigeria, superimposed on the peasant community with varied degrees of impact. The peasants became citizens while they also remained subjects in an "overdeveloped" postcolonial state that was adopted as a legacy of colonial rule.[9] What this development suggests in practice is that the culture of the subaltern troupe persisted even after colonial rule in a hybrid manner—because it was difficult to peel off their cultural values in one fell swoop. Thus, the subalterns exist even in the era of reason and the so-called enlightenment. This reality is not only true in the periphery of global capitalism and the non-Western world that they live in. In Nigeria and many African countries, the life of the peasant as a subaltern became complicated by being a partial seasonal modern worker, being one who is transitioning between rural and urban residences.

Arguably, Hegel and Marx made an important observation that remains an empirical question about the way subalterns in Nigeria might behave and conduct themselves given the problematic political nature of the state. The main question is whether the subalterns have a revolutionary aspiration for bringing about desirable and progressive social change.[10] Hegel and Marx were of the view that because peasants and slaves were in a subordinate and subaltern position, they were in a better position to develop critical consciousness about the antagonistic practice of their oppressors or masters. The primary desire of the masters was to maintain the status quo with all the privileges and perquisites that accompany their position and with all the means at their disposal. This case constitutes the denial of the full human dignity of the subaltern individual. On the part of the subalterns, however, the struggle for freedom is a super-priority issue in life and to achieve that they must develop critical consciousness about their situation, while deconstructing the social processes and mechanisms that are used to keep them down. The goal of doing all these is to develop ways that they can liberate themselves. To liberate themselves, it is not enough for them to understand their conditions, situations, and the strategies they can use to liberate themselves. In addition to that, subalterns also need to know how to accurately deconstruct the mindset of their oppressors whose desire is to keep them in perpetual bondage.[11]

Indisputably, given the political, economic, and social marginalization of the subalterns in Nigeria based on the preceding postulations, there is a constructive historical role that the subalterns are strategically positioned to play in furtherance of their interest. The empirical query, though, is whether the subalterns in Nigeria have really developed the appropriate critical consciousness and are prepared to do all that they need to do to liberate themselves while transforming the Nigerian society into a viable and successful country.

If the logic of Hegel and Marx's philosophy is that the pathway to a better and liberated future in Nigeria is in the hands and audacity of the subaltern citizens, then the need is to critically interrogate how the subalterns can accomplish these objectives without violence in the Fourth Republic. More importantly, due to different cultural and religious orientations of the subalterns throughout the country, it would be necessary to unite them. In short, it would be necessary to investigate how the subalterns in different regions of the country, different ethnic, religious, and gender troupes are operating to promote national unity and economic development. Regrettably, very much like other societies, evidence suggests that the subalterns do not speak with one voice. Indeed, for most of them their consciousness has not developed to a level where there is a deep sense of awareness of the shared humanity among all the subalterns in the republic. This is so partially due to primordial sentiments, powerful religious influence, patron-client system, and the fear of warlords and political god fathers who dominate local politics.

GOOD GOVERNANCE AND ITS IMPLICATIONS FOR THE SUBALTERNS: A CONCEPTUAL OVERVIEW

The following conceptual and theoretical synopsis is intended to situate the discourse on the efficacy, or presumed efficacy, of good governance on the subalterns—the silent majority in the polity. Indeed, good governance has been an issue of concern in practically every society from time immemorial. In ancient Greece, the work of Socrates and Plato documented genuine concerns about this view and philosophy. For example, Plato's Republic illustrates the complexities of the character of leaders that emerged at that epoch and the quality of governance in that Republic.[12]

Ostensibly, citizens whose psyche are dominated by appetitive desires or acquirements of wealth may become greedy and corrupt, and their reasoning capacity and rationality may become slaves to their rapacious desires that could in the process lead to great conflict in its wake. Notionally, too, Thucydides in his *On Justice, Power, and Human Nature: Selections from the History of the Peloponnesian War* documented what can be wrong in a society and the human consequences of bad governance.[13] In fact, it has been suggested that poor governance was one of the major contributors to the collapse of the Roman Empire. Bad governance has been a contributor to the rise and fall of the previous three republics in Nigeria and now threatens the Fourth

Republic.[14] Comparatively, the American and French Revolutions, plausibly, would have not happened if it were not for the lack of justice and fairness to all citizens, especially injustice toward the majority subaltern group. The centrality of the preceding illustrations is that the ruling class and the government that it controls in Nigeria must not, and should not, take the subalterns for granted in its governance in the Fourth Republic. The consequences of doing so for the polity could be disastrous as evident in the contemporary political, economic, and social malaise in the country today.

The foregoing suppositions notwithstanding, the contextual and historical concern about good governance in recent times was primarily brought about in Africa, and Nigeria in this case, by a neoliberal ideology wrapped up in a Structural Adjustment Program (SAP). SAP and its poignant accompanying body of practical guiding principles infused the formulation and implementation of public policy that have impacted the lives of the great majority of citizens in Nigeria and dealt a heavy blow on subaltern troupes in both rural and urban areas or settings of the republic.[15]

To fully comprehend the context for the emergence of neoliberalism, SAP, and their impact on the public, it is significant to concisely historicize and examine the genealogy of SAP. It emerged as an ideology and concrete attack on the post-war emergence of the welfare state in the Western world and the postcolonial decades of the 1960s and 1970s, which elevated if not idealized strong state intervention in the process of economic development and cultural change.[16]

During the postcolonial development decades, the general idea was that the market alone could not be relied upon to promote fair and equitable economic development. Consequently, the state was considered as an important institution that can improve the rougher edges of capitalist development.[17] But neoliberalism and SAP gave birth to a rejuvenation of the movement for good governance on grounds that state bureaucracies spearheading and managing development are inefficient and biased in favor of state officials and their political sponsors and allies, especially in the business sector. The state, controlled by selfish politicos, was construed as the enemy of the people while the market, and its laissez-faire characteristics, was the creator of a level-playing field for everyone to compete and succeed. The market was perceived as creating a more equitable society.[18] The state is still expected to play some role in promoting markets and ensuring their smooth functioning. However, this form of state intervention is a new approach to the management of public resources using the dogmas of market rationality for the efficient and productive allocation of scarce resources. Such a scheme would lead to the pursuit of good governance movement and a priori emphasis on democracy—that is, liberal democracy—as a strategy to diminish and eliminate the problem of poor or bad governance. The assumption was that bad governance has detrimental effects on the lives of many ordinary citizens—not least the subalterns.[19]

In theory, the emphasis on democracy is supposed to lead to a new approach to public management of resources through the involvement of community organizations and the empowerment of citizens. However, as it turned out, neoliberalism and structural adjustment in their "manifestations" paid lip service to democracy as the expansion of the market resulted in the colonization of other spheres of human life and social institutions by the ethics of the market. And the ethics of the market as dictated by the "law of self-interest" of the primary actors are, in the main, amoral.[20]

Under neoliberalism, the role of the state, to the chagrin of its guardians, shrank and was restricted and limited by the downsizing of the state bureaucracy and spheres of action that impacted the subalterns inordinately in terms of the economy. The state authority was also decentralized through the process of devolution of power. In the pursuit of this stratagem, efforts were made to cut the cost of governance and this was partially implemented by outsourcing of state activities to the private sector. What this meant in effect was that the provision of public services became, arguably, "result oriented" in terms of focus and efficacy. In some ways, government services became commodified and commercialized in the form of "cash and carry." This situation suggests that access to public services became mediated by the ability to pay and limited to those who had the effective purchasing power—that excluded most of the subalterns. In short, the logic underlying the operation of the government became market driven and not just market oriented.[21]

The anticipated benefit, all things being equal, of the shift to a result-oriented operational logic gives a higher emphasis on accountability, and more openness to transparency in the way and manner the government operates as against the hitherto corrupt custom in which it operated. With the new enterprise orientation and the decolonization of the process of governance, there was less emphasis on the rights of the citizens as such because the substantive conditions of people were ignored—in the quest for good governance.

Although development research policy and discourse in the 1980s was infused by a discussion on good governance, it is significant to highlight the fact that public advocacy for the recommended shift to good governance was primarily financed by banks in the private and public sector. This was the case with respect to multilateral financial agencies such as the World Bank and the International Monetary Fund (IMF)[22]—whose administrators were cognizant of some of the tomfooleries in the political governance in many developing nations.

As highlighted earlier, what also contributed to giving legitimacy to public advocacy in favor of good governance was the phenomenal disappointment with the state-dominated-cum socialist approach to development. This genre of governance which was corrupted in some cases by the leaders and their lackeys did not uplift the subalterns in the 1950s, 1960s, and 1970s.[23] The discourse on good governance was not initially embraced by developing countries; it was rather resisted in the Global South due in part to "the law of self-interest." This was the case during the era of the Cold War when some leaders in the developing countries capitalized on the East-West conflict—that is, Moscow and Washington mainly.

This development happened despite the widespread popularity among some economists of public choice theory and theoretical explications based on empirical studies illustrating how rent-seeking behavior results in dysfunctional governance. Public choice theory makes the strong argument that government officials and politicians are self-interested like all other people and so they will without hesitation run the public affairs of a country in a manner that primarily serves their interests and those of their allies.[24] For this reason, public choice theorists recommend the need for privatization of public services so that the market will regulate decisions about production and distribution of goods and services instead of "corrupt" government officials and politicians having total or centralized control over such decisions.

THE IMPACT OF THE COLD WAR ON POLITICAL AND ECONOMIC DEVELOPMENT

During the Cold War, leaders of many countries in the Global South resisted and pushed back on the campaign to eradicate bad governance partially because this system allowed leaders and their backers control over the state coffers and especially the subalterns. However, as noted previously, this stance by political bosses became a major concern for investors in such countries. In Africa, for example, the former Organization of African Unity and its chiefs became major obstacles with regard to the process of promoting good governance. As Deng and Lyons observed, "rather than promote good governance by awarding sovereign rights to those regimes that effectively or responsibly administered a given territory, African diplomatic principles, epitomized by the Organization of African Unity (OAU), accepted whatever regime occupied the presidential palace, regardless of who (or even whether) the regime governed [efficaciously]."[25]

What changed the trend in terms of the resistance of the OAU to the push for good governance was the collapse of the Berlin Wall and the emergence of Western leaders with immense global influence, such as the then British prime minister Margaret Thatcher, US president Ronald Reagan, German Chancellor Helmut Kohl, and Soviet Union president Mikhael Gorbachev.[26] The collapse of the former Soviet Union and Berlin Wall also meant there was no global ideological tension that leaders of the Global South countries could use as a buffer or an excuse to pushback against the effort of the global community to promote good governance and liberal democracy.

Through the influence that several Western nations exerted on the United Nations to push for and institutionalize the policy of good governance aimed at, inter alia, improving the condition of subalterns and good governance in the developing nations, the process was accepted on paper.[27] Nevertheless, in a critical assessment based on empirical studies, Amy Chua argues that it was difficult for many developing countries to simultaneously institutionalize democratic governance while also implementing neoliberal SAP.[28]

As the countries of the Global South—not least Nigeria—embraced democracy and democratization as part of the struggle to institutionalize good governance, there were certain realities that emerged that are worth noting. I shall explain later how they have become relevant for Nigeria. This was the case since Nigeria started to institutionalize democratic governance in 1999 marking the commencement of the Fourth Republic.

An important phenomenon that accompanied the process of developing democracy and good governance is the emergence of vocal non-state actors that started playing an active role in public governance. There were many powerful non-governmental organizations that emerged at both the national and international levels to do battle with bad policies promulgated by nation-states that violated citizens' rights. Human Rights Watch is an example. Moreover, the United Nations through its various agencies also became an active participant in promoting the rights of subalterns globally through some of its international human rights instruments. This is not to mention the activities of transnational corporations which with their financial clout do condemn bad policies in countries that they operate. Shell and City Bank are just two examples. What this development suggests is that compared to the past, governance in the areas of economic, social, and even political policy in a country is not the exclusive preserve of a nation or state government. This development was and is influenced, possibly, by the new globalization phenomenon.

A key observation to be made is that despite the different groups or actors that have become involved in governance, there is no reason to believe that the different groups agree on a coherent vision for what good governance is and the actors to promote its praxis. Paradoxically, in discourses on how to restructure the state and advance good governance, most of the population—the subalterns—are left out or excluded. Yet, their support and votes are sought after during electoral contestations. Additionally, given the interests of many non-state actors and their agendas, there is no reason to assume that their ultimate purpose in interacting with the state is to push for policies that could elevate the lives of the subalterns. The action of oil companies with regard to the subalterns in the Niger Delta is a good case in point.[29] Against this backdrop, one might ask, of what value is the campaign for good governance if it does not bring succor to the distressing concerns of the least advantaged subalterns and socially marginalized citizens in Nigeria and elsewhere?

Another issue that needs to be fleshed out with respect to the new dispensation of promoting democracy and good governance is that new concerns emerged that have to do with the right to self-determination. Moreover, concerns about people and how authority and social responsibility are executed as part of the way human beings—especially the subalterns—are publicly treated came to the fore.[30] The argument about the lack of coherence among different actors involved in the vision of promoting democracy and good governance can be sustained by citing empirical examples. The argument one could make about the tension between the different bodies and agencies is that they constitute a check on each other. In effect, what this situation suggests is that what people get as the benefit of democracy and good governance is the result of whatever the balancing of interests and forces produces. But the actors do not bring the same amount of weight and influence into the political mix and struggle.[31] For example, from the 1980s to the mid-1990s, the dominant voice when it came to the discourse on the strategy and implementation of democracy and good governance was the goals and vision of the Washington Consensus. The Consensus is represented by the World Bank and the IMF in the Global South.[32] Some of the key elements and concerns of the Washington Consensus were and are financial liberation (interest rates being determined by the market); privatization of state enterprises; trade liberalization (elimination or drastic reduction of tariffs and opening economies to foreign competition); eliminating barriers to foreign direct investment; management of exchange rates through the market; deregulation of labor markets; and finally, tax reform (cutting marginal tax rates and broadening tax base).[33]

Empirical evidence alludes that the implementation of key policy elements of the Washington Consensus was based on its interest and that it had a devastating effect on the quality of life of the ordinary citizens and subalterns—particularly in the way they visualized democracy and good governance.[34] The Washington Consensus Report appears to be more concerned about efficiency and results (in systems that are often dysfunctional) and not immediately or directly concerned about addressing human development and human factor of its actions on the subalterns. Frankly, it is in this respect that the role of the United Nations Development Report resonates well for those seeking to bridge the gap between the rich and poor in the Global South and Nigeria in particular.[35] This report emphasizes "on paper" the promotion not just of democracy but also of the kind of good governance that translates into concrete positive transformation of the lives of the ordinary people. In doing so, the report theoretically became a correction and reference source to the one-sided accentuation of market forces to allocate scarce resources as promoted by the Washington Consensus. Indeed, the Washington Consensus report diminished any explicit commitment to the human development of the least advantaged and socially marginalized people in society.

In all, in contrast to the World Bank and IMF's approach to good governance, the United Nations Development Program stressed and promoted local development and participation.[36] By choosing to emphasize public interest and the public good, the UN played the important role of both balancing and moderating the hegemony of the unpredictable market principles and their impact on marginalized citizens.

A major theme that can be drawn from the analysis of this chapter is the unfortunate economic and political reality that the subalterns who are the "silent majority" in Nigeria and at the receiving end of the failure of the postcolonial state do not speak with one voice. Moreover, the political elites in Nigeria treat the subalterns—whether farmers or members of the working class—as clients and are regularly marginalized in the politico-economic affairs of the state. For the Nigerian state to confront the contemporary political, economic, and social dilemmas, it would need to promote democracy and good governance with the inclusion of the "voices" of the silent majority—the subalterns.

CONCLUSION

Subaltern Voices in the Struggle for Good Governance in Nigeria: An Overview

The major thrust of this chapter is on a brief conceptual and theoretical discourse on the character of the state and how its governance structures do not impact the subalterns who are often seen but not heard. Therefore, their views and input on how to promote political stability, peaceful coexistence, and consequently good governance are seldom heard or irrelevant. Thus, the post-colonial atmosphere in the Nigerian public square and polity in the Fourth Republic is toxic and unstable in part because the reconstituted state and its custodians of power ignore the subalterns. They are mainly important for providing votes in electoral contestations to politicos, compensated during campaign season, and thereafter left to fend for themselves.

Comparatively, the fact is that this postcolonial state called Nigeria has also created a culture of brain drain. Not only are many Nigerians willing to leave the country and settle in other parts of the world but also even the educated ones that remain within the country constitute another form of brain drain. This is so in the sense that they use their education primarily for self-enrichment. They do not organize strategically to transform the country into a viable state because of the character of the state in which most Nigerians identify with their ethnic group and region rather than the nation-state. Moreover, in the Fourth Republic, Nigeria is confronted with a political situation in which the subalterns are treated by their political superintendents as meek clients and country's academics as perennial agitators. The preceding situations create political malaise and inertia among citizens in the republic.

In the past, there were serious critical and intellectual discussions on how to transform Nigeria. Today, by and large, the Nigerian intellectual, for the most part, has become a resource person who narrowly wants to use his or her human capital to pursue professional growth. In this drive, the intellectuals, with a few exceptions, are no longer interested in a broad commitment to social responsibility aimed at emancipating the subalterns.[37] There is no smoke without fire is a popular cliché that explains the current rationale for this nonchalant attitude of Nigerian intellectuals. For example, the state's archives are replete with reports and templates constructed by scholars, statesmen, and stateswomen intended to resolve the political, economic, and social quagmires in the republic that are gathering dust and atrophying because the custodians of power failed to implement them. A major reason for not implementing the efficacious recommendations in these reports is because politics trumps policy. In fact, if by implementing an effective policy, the president or governor could lose support from his/her financial backers at the next election, the highly constructive plan for the country or state will not see the light of day.

Problematically, too, agreements that are made and signed between the government and the university union on college-related issues are seldom honored by the regime. Given the state's track record on this matter, it might be difficult for the government to sign an agreement with the subalterns to empower them politically and expect the legislators to honor such an accord. In other words, if the government does not respect resolutions arrived at with the country's intelligentsia, it would be arduous for legislators to listen to the voices of the subalterns on public affairs.

Notwithstanding the inadequate funding of Nigerian universities, the tertiary institutions have produced men and women who have acquired the skills for boosting national development. However, the fact is that university employees, whether academic or non-academic, see their jobs today, driven by the "law of self-interest," as an opportunity for their personal growth. That they must take care of their families, friends, and relatives results in them ignoring, arguably, their "moral" responsibility with regard to emancipating the subalterns and advocating for uplifting their lives in a society in which they are the majority. This truism speaks to the contemporary character of the nation-state in which survival is at the forefront of daily life even for the educated. In fact, in many respects the subalterns are shortchanged, and it is done in a systematic and strategic process of extracting public resources and using it for the pursuit of the social and material interests of the few at the expense of the many.

An important theme to be drawn from an overview of this chapter is the gloomy reality that, as noted previously, the subalterns who are at the receiving end of the failure of the postcolonial state do not speak with one voice. The political elites see the subalterns as an entitlement because they "automatically" constitute their political and economic power base. This attribution or view of the subalterns is problematic. The paradox of the issue is that without the subalterns, the politico would have a hard time being elected; yet the subalterns who with their ballot papers handed power over to the legislator are frequently neglected by their representatives in terms of their participation in the economic and social development of the society. Undeniably, the granting of a greater voice to the subalterns in the Fourth Republic is imperative because their input—politically, economically, and socially—in Nigerian affairs could promote political stability.

Regrettably, political actors do make sure that their clients are not allowed a consciousness beyond their ethnic, religious, and regional factions; they effectively use their networks to keep this arrangement intact. A fact remains, though, that the subalterns could use their awareness of the workings of the political system to dethrone political elites. To fight back, however, the subaltern factions who dare to step out of their boundary are demonized, ridiculed, and isolated from their own people by political elites. The outcome of this action is that many subalterns "lower their voices" and end up not working collaboratively in pursuit of their shared and objective interests at the national level.

The irony of the matter is that the politicians that subalterns generally support are not actors who are politically committed to a progressive vision for their clients—the subalterns. The high level of poverty and the quotidian struggle for survival often worsened their situation and made–and still make–them subservient to their political bosses.

Moreover, the elites promote the concept of group worth to persuade subalterns in their ethnic and religious groups to feel that having a person from their group in a position of power and privilege should make them feel proud and enhance that group's worth.[38] This notion is emphasized irrespective of whether the elites are creating effective institutions and social processes that will ensure inclusive growth and development of the subalterns. Without a sustained and systematic deconstruction and debunking how religion and ethnicity are used to control and dominate the consciousness of the subaltern troupe, the future in terms of genuinely elevating their human development and dignity as citizens is bleak and the state's growth agenda may suffer as a result. Irrefutably, the contemporary state of socio-political and economic instability, in a country that has abundant natural resources and human capital, reflects the dilemma the country faces today for marginalizing its subalterns—the silent majority. Consequently, I argue that to tackle the political, economic, and social dilemmas in the Nigerian federation will require the participation of all Nigerians—not least the subalterns—in discourses on how to move the country forward in the Fourth Republic.

NOTES

1. R. Guha, *Selected Subaltern Studies: Selection of Essays from 5 Published Collections of Subaltern Studies Between 1982 and 1987* (Oxford, UK: Oxford University Press, 2011).
2. R. Peet and E. R. Hartwick, *Theories of Development: Contentions, Arguments, Alternatives* (New York: The Guilford Press, 2015), p. 236.
3. G. Pandey, The Subaltern as Subaltern Citizen, *Economic Weekly*, Vol. 41, No. 46 (2006), pp. 4735–4741.
4. E. Ike Udogu, *Politics and Society: An Anecdote on Culture and Environmental Determinism* (Charleston, SC: Palmetto Publishing, 2021).
5. R. Peet and E. R. Hartwick, *Theories of Development, Contentions, Arguments, Alternatives*, pp. 236–237,
6. A. A. Mazrui, *The Africans: A Triple Heritage* (BBC Publication, 1986).
7. E. Ike Udogu, "Democracy in Africa: Fiction of Fact in the 21st Century." Paper Presented at the 25th Meeting of the Global Awareness Society International, Budapest, Hungary, 2016, pp. 1–2. http://orgs.bloomu.edu2016_proceedings_pdsPDF (Retrieved 9/22/21).
8. Pita O. Agbese and E. Ike Udogu, "Taming of the Shrew: Civil-Military Politics in the Fourth Republic," in E. Ike Udogu (ed.), *Nigeria in the Twenty-First Century: Strategies for Political Stability and Peaceful Coexistence* (Trenton, NJ: Africa World Press, 2005), pp. 25–26.
9. M. Mamdani, *The Making of Citizen and Subject in Contemporary Africa* (Princeton, NJ: Princeton University Press, 1996.)
10. Karl Marx, *The Enlightened Brumaire of Louis Bonaparte, 1852* (New York: International Publishers, 1963).
11. W. E. Connolly, *Political Theory and Modernity* (Malden, MA: Basil Blackwell, 1991).
12. G. M. A. Grube and C. D. C. Reeve, *Plato: Republic* (Indianapolis, IN: Hackett Publishing Company, 1992).
13. P. Woodruff, *On Justice, Power, and Human Nature: Selections from the History of the Peloponnesian* War (Indianapolis, IN: Hackett Publishing Company, 1993).
14. See Toyin Falola and Julius O. Ihonvbere, *The Rise and Fall of the Second Republic* (London, UK: Zed Books, 1985); Richard A. Joseph, *Democracy and*

Prebendal Politics in Nigeria: The Rise and Fall of the Second Republic (Cambridge, UK: Cambridge University Press, 1987).

15. J. Miheve, *The Market Tells Them So: The World Bank and Economic Fundamentalism in Africa* (New York/London: Zed Books: 1996).

16. N. Wapshott, *Keynes, Hayek: The Clash that Defined the Modern Economics* (Royal Oaks, MI: Scribe Publications, 2014).

17. C. P. Oman and G. Wignaraja, *The Postwar Evolution of Development Thinking* (New York: Macmillan and OECD Development Center, 1991).

18. F. A. Hayek, *The Road to Serfdom* (London: Institute of Economic Affairs, 2004).

19. T. G. Weiss, "Governance, and Good Governance and Global Governance: Conceptual and the Actual Challenges," *Third World Quarterly*, Vol. 21, No. 5 (2000) pp. 795–814.

20. W. Brown, *In the Ruins of Neoliberalism: The Rise of Anti-democratic Politics in the West* (New York: Columbia University Press, 2019).

21. M. Friedman and R. D. Friedman, *Free to Choose: A Personal Statement* (St. Paul, MN: Paw Print, 2008).

22. J. A. Widner, *Economic Change and Political Liberalization in Sub-Saharan Africa* (Baltimore, MD: Johns Hopkins Press, 1994); T. Biebricher, *Political Theory of Neoliberalism* (Stanford, CA: Stanford University Press, 2019).

23. D. Seers, *The Meaning of Development* (Sussex, UK: University of Sussex Press, 1970).

24. M. S. Grindle and J. W. Thomas, *Public Choice and Public Change: The Political Economy of Reform in Developing Countries* (Baltimore, MD: Johns Hopkins University Press, 1994); J. M. Buchanan, "Social Choice, Democracy, and the Free Market," *Journal of Political Economy*, Vol. 62, No. 2 (1954), pp. 114–123; J. N. Bhagwati, "Directly Unproductive, Profiting Activities," *Journal of Political Economy*, Vol. 90, No. 5 (1982), pp. 988–1002.

25. Francis M. Deng and Terence Lyons, "Promoting Responsible Sovereignty in Africa," in Deng and Lyons (eds), *African Reckoning: A Quest for Good Governance* (Washington, DC: Brookings Institutions, 1998), p. 1.

26. T. G. Weiss, "Governance, Good Governance and Global Governance: Conceptual and Actual Challenges," *Third World Quarterly*, Vol. 21, No. 5 (2000), pp. 795–814.

27. D. Plchwe; B. Walpen and Gisela Neunhoffer, *Neoliberal Hegemony: A Global Critique* (London, UK: Routledge Publishers, 2007).

28. A. Chua, *World on Fire: How Exporting Free Market Democracy Breeds Ethnic Hatred and Global Instability* (New York, NY: Anchor Books, 2004).

29. T. Burgis, *The Looting Machine: Warlords, Oligarchies, Corporations, Smugglers, and the Theft of Africa's Wealth* (London, UK: HarperCollins Publishers, 2016).

30. T. G. Weiss, The Politics of Humanitarian Ideas, *Security Dialogue*, Vol. 31, No. 1 (2000), pp. 11–23.

31. Brendan Sweetman, *Crisis of Democratic Pluralism: The Loss of Confidence in reason and the Clash of Worldviews* (New York: Palgrave Macmillan, 2021);

J. S. Hacker, and P. Pierson, *Winner-take-All Politics: How Washington Made the Rich Richer, and Turned Its Back on the Middle Class* (New York, NY: Simon and Schuster, 2011).

32. M. Bratton and V. W. Nicholas, *Democratic Experiments in Africa: Regime Transitions in Comparative Perspective* (Cambridge, UK: Cambridge University Press, 2002).

33. D. Rodrick, Understanding Economic Policy Reform, *Journal of Economic Literature*, Vol. 34, No. 1 (1996), pp. 9–41.

34. J. Stiglitz, *Globalization, and Its Discontents* (London, UK: Penguin Books, 2017).

35. United Nations *Development Program, Human Development Report 1990* (New York: Oxford University Press, 1990).

36. World Bank, *World Development Report 1992, and World Development Report 1997* (New York: Oxford University Press, 1997/1992).

37. Y. B. Usman, *For the Liberation of Nigeria: Essays and Lectures 1963–1978* (London, UK: New Beacon, 1979); C. Ake, *Political Economy of Nigeria* (London, UK: Longman Press, 1985).

38. D. L. Horowitz, *Ethnic Groups in Conflict: With a New Preface* (Berkeley, CA: University of California Press, 2011).

Chapter 8

Human Rights Conundrums in the Fourth Republic

A Search for Solutions

E. Ike Udogu

INTRODUCTION

Human rights issues and challenges are *mondial.* They have moral, legal, social, and political undertones that problematize the governance system in many African states. The irony is, despite the ostensible interest shown by lawmakers toward addressing the dilemmas of rights infractions in the continent, not all citizens enjoy equivalent rights in most African polities.[1] Even so, constitutionally and doctrinally (in religious teaching) individuals are expected to enjoy equivalent human rights. This is the case because they are enshrined and guaranteed in majority of national constitutions, in the Universal Declaration of Human Rights, and other human rights instruments. Moreover, human rights canons are set out in most theological texts. Regrettably, however, because of the unsatisfactory implementation of human rights precepts in a polity, the call for the respect of citizens' rights by the United Nations, Amnesty International, Human Rights Watch, and various national rights activists continues.[2]

In Nigeria, the violations of the human rights of citizens are rampant partially because of the country's political and economic instability. The despotic rule of the various military juntas that governed this multi-lingual and multi-ethnic republic made more severe human rights infractions in the society. Yet, the respect for the human rights of citizens is critical for the advancement of political stability, economic revitalization, and promotion of democratic consolidation in the society.[3] Probably, it was the realization of the ubiquity of human rights infringements in the republic that prompted a government agency to draft an inspiring document on human rights—a human rights instrument aimed at tackling rights breaches in the country. The title of this stirring and unique text is National Action Plan for the Promotion and Protection of Human Rights in Nigeria (NAPPPHRN), 2006.[4] I will apply NAPPPHRN interchangeably with its abbreviated acronym NAP in this chapter. The NAPPPHRN text was the outcome of a Vienna Declaration and Program of Action World Conference on Human Rights. The meeting was held in Vienna, Austria, in 1993. Nigeria implemented NAP in 2006 after thirteen years of careful deliberations on the vexing human rights condition in Nigeria. Indeed, this manifesto was and is intended to solve the human rights quagmires in the federal republic.[5]

Because of its comprehensiveness and allure, NAP will serve as the template for my analysis on the human rights challenges in the Fourth Republic. NAP covers five broad areas of human rights discourses. These are (1) Civil and Political Rights; (2) Economic, Social, and Cultural Rights; (3) the Right to Sustainable Development, Peace, and a Protected Environment; (4) the Rights of Women; and (5) the Rights of Children and Young Persons.[6] For the purpose of this disquisition, however, I shall take on the following:

(1) Examine concisely the issues raised in three specific areas—Civil and Political Rights; Economic, Social, and Cultural Rights; and the Rights of Women in the NAPPPHRN's template.
(2) Evaluate the extent to which the government, its agents and agencies lived up to or not of the human rights precepts contained in the preceding three explicit areas.
(3) Suggest possible ways that the superintendents of the state can assuage the difficulties in implementing the human rights themes raised in the well-crafted NAPPPHRN text intended to promote political stability and peaceful coexistence in Nigeria's Fourth Republic.

CIVIL AND POLITICAL RIGHTS

The Right to Life

Article 33 of the 1999 Constitution states, "Every person has the right to life, and no one shall be deprived intentionally of his [or her] life."[7] Despite this provision in the constitution, the actions of agents of the government have proven otherwise in the Fourth Republic. The infraction of this right happens in the forms of torture and extra-judicial killings by government security agents. The paradox is that wanton killings of civilians are happening during the advent of civilian rule. Even so, the military epochs, which witnessed the application of force in the technique of governance, were a harbinger for rights violations in the civilian regimes. Accordingly, the mimicry of the governance method of the military by the civilian regimes left much to be desired on human rights issues in the republic. Moreover, the participation of former military officers in the democratic process, with their authoritarian streak, made human rights praxis difficult in the Fourth Republic. For example, President Olusegun Obasanjo was a former army general before he became a politician and "born-again" democrat. Little wonder, then, that his administrative genre, as a civilian president, aped that of a military genus. Indeed, he oversaw the infamous Odi massacre and its human rights abuses in the country.

Anecdotally, on November 20, 1999, following reports that ethnic militiamen killed twelve police officers in the city of Odi, Bayelsa State, in the Niger Delta, government authorities ordered soldiers and mobile police officers to invade the city. During the incursion, agents of the government killed as many as 2,000–2,500 unarmed civilians. The purpose of the mission was to teach citizens of this region a lesson for provoking the regime and to persuade other groups not to attempt it. More importantly, it was to put a stop to their harassment of the oil companies exploiting oil that sustains the national economy. These are the same oil companies responsible for environmental degradation—a human rights issue—that was and is destroying and putting civilian lives at risk in the Niger Delta.[8]

Additionally, the regime sent the military to a city of Zaki Biam in Benue State in October 2001 where it killed 100 civilians from the Tiv ethnic group for allegedly kidnapping and killing nineteen soldiers. The rights violation happened when the government sent soldiers to quell a community uprising between the Tivs and Jukuns in the state. In May 2016, the nation's ferocious security forces were alleged to have killed about forty members of the Indigenous people of Biafra—an outspoken secessionist group agitating for the Sovereign State of Biafra.[9]

Commonly, government response to peaceful protests is violence aimed at discouraging other citizens from emulating similar rallies in the republic. This was the case when seventeen civilians died during a protest in Kaduna in April 2011. Additionally, there was the killing of over 700 civilians in Bauchi, Maiduguri, and Damaturu following Boko Haram's carnage on innocent citizens.[10] Historicizing the actions of this Islamic renegade, Human Rights Watch reported that Boko Haram conflict in the northeast entered its tenth year in 2019. Regrettably, the "renewed fighting between security forces and Boko Haram [in 2019 claimed] 640 civilians. An estimated 27,000 people, including 37 aid workers, have been killed since the onset of the conflict in 2009, according to the United Nations Office for Coordination of Humanitarian Affairs (UNOCHA)."[11]

Little wonder, then, that in a somber summary on the violation of the right to life episodes in the republic, Emmanuel O. Ojo noted with disquiet that

> [during the Fourth Republic] confrontations between increasingly militant youths, oil companies, and government authorities continued and reportedly 28 Delta youths were killed in such conflicts over protests or suspected vandalism near oil flow stations. . . . Police killed two people in Abuja and injured hundreds of persons who were involved in a 5-day petrol increase strike. [In addition], the Federal Government instructed the police to use deadly force in conflict in Lagos State with the Oodua People's Congress (OPC). [Furthermore], the police in Lagos reportedly killed 509-armed robbers and injured 113, [while] making 3,166 arrests![12]

Notwithstanding the foregoing accounts, relating to the violation of the right to life precept enshrined in the constitution, on paper NAP states that the republic's commitment to adhere to the right to life flows from international human rights instruments. For example, Article 3 of the Universal Declaration of Human Rights states: Everyone has the right to life, liberty, and security of person.[13] Article 6 of the International Covenant on Civil and Political Rights affirms: Every human being has the inherent right to life. Law shall protect this right. No one shall be arbitrary deprived of his life.[14] Article 4 of the African Charter on Human and Peoples' rights asserts: Human beings are inviolable. "Every human being shall be entitled to respect for his life and the integrity of his person." No one may be arbitrarily deprived of this right.[15]

On the matter of right to life, NAPPPHRN affirms that the official role of the state is to "curtail the power of private people to kill one another; acknowledge the duty of the state to protect human life; make it unlawful to take life intentionally without due process; and provide sanctions for those that breach the law."[16] On paper, the response of the 2006 NAPPPHRN to the right to life issue is spot on. However, the implementation of NAP's human rights provisions in the country is difficult as illustrated in the preceding expositions.

Right to Dignity of Human Person

The Constitution states in Article 34: "Every individual is entitled to respect for the dignity of his person, and accordingly (a) no person shall be subject to torture or to inhuman or degrading treatment."[17] The NAPPPHRN embellishes this constitutional obligation with the following proclamation: "Everyone has the right not to: Be threatened or punished in a cruel, inhuman or degrading way; be held in slavery or servitude; perform forced or compulsory labor."[18] Nevertheless, the irony of this principle of human rights is that the Nigerian police which should be in a position of protecting this right is culpable in the violation of the right to life and dignity of the human person.[19]

Right to Private and Family Life

The 1999 Constitution asserts the right to citizens' privacy in Article 37 as follows: "The privacy of citizens, their homes, correspondence, telephone conversations and telegraphic communications is hereby guaranteed." Despite the regime's claims that legal restrictions were in force to allow state institutions to apply necessary instrument for observing citizen's privacy, the facts on the ground have proven otherwise. For instant, despite the government's effort to flush out Nigerian supporters of corruption in the society, law enforcement agencies have undertaken searches and arrested suspects without official warrants.

Furthermore, the state and local government officials use politicians and powerful state actors to evict residents from their domiciliary and in some cases demolished homes without prior, and sometimes inadequate, notice. In some of these cases, displaced residents did not receive compensation, even when the courts ordered remuneration for displaced persons. Furthermore, given the regime's antagonism and frustrations toward the terrorist group, Boko Haram, and the state's inability to subdue the rebellious gang, government's activities toward this troupe and suspected collaborators do violate human rights. Indeed, reports in 2018 stated that the army was guilty for burning family homes of alleged supporters of the insurgents in villages where the terrorist faction had been operating.[20] This regime's action violates Article 12 of the Universal Declaration of Human Rights that affirms: "No one shall be subjected to arbitrary interference with his privacy, family, home or correspondence, nor to attacks upon his [or her] honor and reputation." Everyone has the right to the protection of the law against such interference or attacks.[21] Indeed, Article 17 (1&2) of UN Convention against Torture and Other Cruel, Inhuman or Degrading Treatment or Punishment provides protection against these rights.[22]

Right to Freedom of Thought, Conscience, and Religion

Article 38 of the Constitution alludes to these rights thus: "Every person shall be entitled to freedom of thought, conscience or belief and freedom, including freedom to change his religion or belief." The purported policy in NAPPPHRN for achieving the foregoing human rights provision are as follows: (1) promoting and protecting the religious rights of all people in Nigeria, (2) prohibiting discrimination on the basis of religion, (3) protecting all religions in Nigeria, and (4) promoting the culture of religious tolerance.[23]

Despite the foregoing declarations of the regime's desire to quell sectarian conflicts in the country, inter-religious and intra-religious clashes continue to fester. A report states that more than 1,000 cases of conflicts between Muslims and Christians happened in Nigeria between 2001 and 2008 notwithstanding constitutional and policy provisions intended to curb such acts.[24] It is striking that the recurrence of inter-religious conflicts increases when there exists economic downturn. This was and is often the case when some overzealous clerics manipulate religion to further their interests and not necessarily those of the members of their congregation. Regrettably, the government's attempts to resolve sectarian conflicts tend to inflame the situation because of the lethal force that hyper security agents employ.

For example, the Nigeria 2019 International Religious Freedom Report declared that

> the constitution bars the federal and state governments from adopting a state religion, prohibits religious discrimination, and provides for individuals' freedom to choose, practice, propagate, or change their religion. Throughout the year, Shia Muslims, under the auspices of the Islamic Movement of Nigeria (IMN), conducted a series of demonstrations—including several in July against the ongoing detention of IMN leader Sheikh Ibrahim El-Zakzaky—resulting in violent confrontations between protesters and security forces, which left as many as 30 dead, including protesters and police. . . . Following the violence, the government banned the IMN and declared the group a terrorist organization. . . . The government's ban of the IMN [was criticized] as a threat to religious freedom for all believers. [Even so], the government continued its detention of El-Zakzaky despite a December 2016 court ruling that ordered his release by January 2017.[25]

Nigeria, a signatory to several international human rights instruments, is encouraged to promote freedom of thought, conscience, and religion. To give weight to the preceding provision, Article 18 of the UN Convention against Torture and Other Cruel, Inhuman or Degrading Treatment or Punishment states: "Everyone shall have the right to freedom of thought, conscience, and religion. This right shall include freedom to have or to adopt a religion or belief of his [or her] choice."[26] Ditto the same plea in Article 18 of the UN International Covenant on Civil and Political Right.[27] Although the Nigerian government professes to adhere to this provision of human rights, it is obvious that its security agents frequently failed to live up to the principles stated in the constitution and human rights documents. To be sure, some law enforcement agents violate citizens' human rights at the behest of powerful political entrepreneurs, and not the government, to further their interests.

Right to Freedom of Expression and Press

In Article 39 of the Constitution, the right to freedom of expression and the press is noted. The role of the press in exposing rights violations in political systems that lack transparency and accountability is invaluable. Thus, it is refreshing that the government-sponsored NAPPPHRN model states that its prerogative and policy on freedom of expression and press are the following: (1) support the process of democratization [by allowing a free flow of information], (2) enhance transparency, (3) redress inequalities regarding access to information, (4) redress inequalities regarding access to the means of disseminating information, (5) issue regulations to ensure the responsible use of freedom of expression so that vulnerable people are not harmed, and (6) build an information backbone capable of giving all citizens access to the Internet.[28]

Paradoxically, the government's proclamations and praxis on the freedom of the press and expression are hollow in the republic.[29] Suffice it to say that the activities of the press in Nigeria are still relatively robust. That notwithstanding, the security forces are determined to checkmate journalists and other media reporters if they do not fancy their press reports. In fact, Human Rights Watch reported that in January 2019 "armed soldiers stormed offices of *Daily Trust* newspaper briefly holding staff for purportedly publishing classified military information. In June of the same year, the Nigerian Broadcasting Commission (NBC) postponed the licenses of the African Independent Television (AIT) and Raypower Radio Station for supposedly airing provocative and inflaming programs against the regime."[30] Soon, thereafter, the aggressive and intimidating Department of State Security (DSS) proclaimed a crackdown on social media users for daring to post repugnant materials described as threatening to the republic's peace and stability.

Moreover, in August, the DSS arrested Omoyele Sowore, a 2019 presidential candidate, the publisher of Nigeria news website, Sahara Reporter. Sowore, it was alleged, was planning an insurrection aimed at toppling the government by calling for a nationwide protest with the rallying cry "Revolution Now." When the court eventually ordered him released, the DSS simply ignored the court order.[31] By this act, the DSS ignored the rule of law and violated Sowore's human rights.

Overall, in 2019, security officers detained and harassed many journalists. Consequently, these journalists lost their liberty as called for in the constitution. Some of the journalists detained included, but not limited to, Abubakar Idris, Stephen Kefas, Jones Abiri, and Agba Jalingo. Given the government's crackdown and violation of their rights, many journalists had to practice self-censorship to mitigate the frequency of their arrests.[32] However, several human rights instruments guarantee citizens and news correspondents their rights to freedom of opinion and expression. For example, Article 19 of the Universal Declaration of Human Rights declares: "Everyone has the right to freedom of opinion and expression; this right includes freedom to hold opinions without interference and to seek, receive and impart information and ideas through any media and regardless of frontiers."[33] Identical rights are enshrined in Articles 19 and 20 of the International Covenant on Civil and Political Rights.[34]

Right to Peaceful Assembly and Association

Article 40 of the Constitution states: "Every person shall be entitled to assemble freely and associate with other persons, and in particular, he [she] may form or belong to any political party, trade union or any other association for the protection of his [her] interest."[35] These rights to peaceful assembly and association are enshrined in Article 20 (1&2) of the Universal Declaration of Human Rights.[36] Also, Articles 10 and 11 of the African Charter on Human and Peoples' Rights sanction these rights.[37]

Notwithstanding the tenet of Article 40 of the Constitution and other human rights declarations in support of peaceful assembly and association, the federal government and its federating units oppose such rights deemed to be offensive to the state or a threat to the regime. For example, Kaduna State proscribed the Islamic group, Islamic Movement of Nigeria, a Shia-Muslim sect, from peaceful association and assembly. The state government and its political aficionados alleged that the group represented a menace to public order and peace.[38]

In Nigeria, the month of October 2020 will always be marked with indignation and infamy in the republic's history. This was the month that Nigeria's security agents descended on its youths peacefully demonstrating against the notorious activities of the Special Anti-Robbery Squad (SARS). At the rally, law enforcement agents killed at least twelve peaceful protesters on October 20, 2020. Security officers shot compatriots at the Lekki tollgate in Lagos after ostensibly switching off the streetlights and cutting phone networks. An irony in this human rights infraction against unarmed citizens was that the actions of the protestors were festive and patriotic—with marchers waving the national flag and, declaring their allegiance to the state, by singing the national anthem.

In truth, the precursor to this carnage at Lekki followed nationwide protests against police brutality rampant in the republic. This demonstration started on October 8, 2020, when a video surfaced showing aggressive police officers, of the infamous SARS, shooting and killing a young man in Delta State. The Nigerian authorities at first denied the reports. Nevertheless, given SARS' bad reputation in the country, the Lekki incident was the last straw that broke the camel's back for many Nigerians who have confronted SARS in the past. Consequently, protests flared up across the country calling for the disbandment of this unit of the country's law enforcement agency with the rallying cry #endSARS.[39] Regrettably, no major reform to the activities of this security force is noticeable—a reformation that is critical for assuaging citizens' concerns of the human rights infractions of this force and moving the country forward in the Fourth Republic.

Right to Freedom from Discrimination

Article 42 of the Constitution states: "A citizen of Nigeria of particular community, ethnic group, place of origin, sex, religion or political opinion shall not, by reason only that he [or she] is such a person [be subjected to discrimination]." NAPPPHRN embroidered this provision by spotlighting and underscoring the state's commitment to eliminate any form of inequality, focusing on ethnic group, gender, and economic status.[40] However, in Nigeria, the issue of ethnic discrimination, despite the state's public condemnation, is alive and problematic. Its sensitivity makes the discussion as to how to eradicate the human rights impact in the body politic of the country difficult. Indeed, ethnicity becomes a problem in the society when it is politicized and applied shrewdly to gain electoral, economic, and social advantage.[41] Undeniably, one of the reasons for the recurring discourses on restructuring the country has ethnic overtone. The truth is that some groups—especially ethnic minority collectivities—are marginalized in the sharing of, what is referred to in Nigerian parlance as, the national cake.[42] This development problematizes the nation's politics because it denies minorities equivalent rights with citizens of the majorities in the polity, especially the big three—Hausa-Fulani, Yoruba, and Igbo. The encouragement of inter-ethnic marriages expressed in the constitution to promote national cohesion was a strategy intended in part to combat the centrifugal vices of ethnic discrimination in Nigerian politics.

ECONOMIC, SOCIAL, AND CULTURAL RIGHTS

The NAPPPHRN's template addressed the preceding rights within the context of the following: right to employment, right to housing and shelter, right to health, right to food, right to water, and right to education.[43] These rights' guidelines, like a political platform, are splendid in theory. Section 17(3) of the Constitution provides that "the government of Nigeria shall direct its policy towards ensuring that all Nigerians have the opportunity of securing adequate means of livelihood, as well as adequate opportunity to secure suitable employment."[44]

Ironically, these rights provisions intended for improving the quality of life for all citizens have been elusive. This is not because the country lacks the wherewithal to provide the economic environment necessary to do so. It has not fulfilled its pledges to citizens partially because of mismanagement of the country's vast natural resources and corruption. For example, take the right to education that is critical for producing adequate human capital, improving the economic welfare of citizens, social mobility, and boosting the country's development project.

Right to Education

Given the centrality of education in the quest to develop and improve the living standard of all citizens, it is worth noting that Section 18 of the Constitution states as follows: (1) Government shall direct its policy toward ensuring that there are equal and adequate education opportunities at all levels. (2) Government shall promote science and technology. (3) Government shall strive to eradicate illiteracy; to this end, government shall as and when practical provide

a. Free Compulsory, Universal Primary Education.
b. Free Secondary Education.
c. Free University Education.
d. Free Adult Literacy Program.[45]

As noted earlier, the ability of Nigeria to develop depends on providing adequate education essential for producing ample human capital. These well-trained professionals will provide the skill that could catapult the country to greater heights developmentally. Lamentably, however, many internal factors work against the cherished spirit of Section 18 of the Constitution. These dimensions include, but are not limited to, corruption, bribery, political ethnicity, nepotism, and the issue of citizenship. For example, it is a given that some state-owned universities discriminate against students from out of state in their admission standard.[46] There are Nigerians not hired to teach or serve at the administrative level at tertiary institutions outside their state of origin. Such prejudicial practices smack at the issue of citizenship and human rights in the republic. For instance, expressing his opinion on the issue of bigotry and, indeed, of his human rights infraction, Ikenna Onyido recounted his experience at a state university accordingly:

> When I was called out to Makurdi [in Benue state], we worked ourselves virtually to death trying to establish a varsity. Then I became the DVC [Deputy Vice Chancellor], where you will leave your house around 8am not knowing when you will come back. I hail from Okija [in Anambra state], and Makurdi became my home. [However], when the issue of becoming a VC came up, the hostility I saw and experienced, together with my family and some people around me were unprecedented. I had eight court cases to keep my job. Eventually, when a native Vice Chancellor was hired, he wanted us thrown

> out of the place. I think that was my greatest disappointment in the Nigerian system. People told it to your face that you do not belong to this place, go home there is a federal university in your place. Well, you could say those were Tiv People. [Ironically], what happened when I was hired as VC of University of Agriculture, Umudike [in Abia state]? . . . The Abia State House of Assembly passed a motion rejecting the appointment. They insisted I must not come, that there is Nnamdi Azikiwe University in Awka [in Anambra state]. At the state varsity, the challenge is which local government are you coming from? Those were my greatest disappointments [with prejudice and the issue of citizenship in the republic].[47]

This political development in Nigeria brings to the fore the question of citizenship and how it should be defined and acted upon. It is disconcerting that at the university level such bias in hiring and retaining administrators and academics should happen. What is equally disquieting to rights observers and activists is that such human rights breach is not unique at the university level; indeed, bigotry on political and economic issues in the nation-state is a dilemma. Nevertheless, on the question of education and rights matters, Article 26(2) of the Universal Declaration of Human Rights avows: "Education shall be directed to the full development of the human personality and to the strengthening of respect for human rights and fundamental freedoms." Nigeria is a signatory to this human rights contrivance.

THE RIGHTS OF WOMEN

Discrimination against women in Nigeria is commonplace, especially in the rustic areas of the country. Undeniably, religion and patriarchy play major roles in fostering bigotry and the infringement on women's human rights in the developing world—not least in Nigeria and Africa.[48] The activities of Boko Haram in the North and its anti-Western education crusade bear the foregoing thesis out.

Protocols contained in the UN Convention on the Elimination of All Forms of Discrimination against Women (CEDAW) are especially poignant in the condemnation of discrimination against women globally. Article 2 of CEDAW enjoins states to condemn discrimination against women in all its forms. This clause, among other things, calls upon states:

a. To embody the principle of the equality of men and women in the national constitutions or other appropriate legislation if not yet incorporated therein and to ensure, through law and other appropriate means, the practical realization of this principle.

b. To adopt appropriate legislative and other measures, including sanctions where appropriate, prohibiting all discrimination against women.
c. To establish legal protection of the rights of women on an equal basis with men and to ensure through competent national tribunals and other public institutions the effective protection of women against any act of discrimination.
d. To refrain from engaging in any act or practice of discrimination against women and to ensure that public authorities and institutions shall act in conformity with this obligation.
e. To take all appropriate measures to eliminate discrimination against women by any person, organization, or enterprise.
f. To take all appropriate measures, including legislation, to modify or abolish existing laws, regulations, customs, and practices, which constitute discrimination against women.
g. To repeal all national penal provisions which constitute discrimination against women.[49]

Moreover, articles in international human rights instruments contraptions denounce discrimination be they racial, ethnic, gender, sexual, disabilities, and in other forms.[50] For example, Article 2 of the International Convention on Civil and Political Rights states: "Each State Party to the present Covenant undertakes to respect and to ensure to all individuals within its territory and subject to its jurisdiction the rights recognized in the present Covenant, without distinction of any kind."[51] Ditto this precept in Article 2 of the Universal Declaration of Human Rights[52] and Article 2 of the African Charter on Human and Peoples' Rights.[53] Fortunately, Nigeria is a signatory to these human rights instruments and therefore under obligation to respect them in order to advance political stability and peaceful coexistence in the Fourth Republic.

Accordingly, NAPPPHRN's template underscores the constitutional commitment to promoting men's rights in the republic. NAP affirms that the rights of women are hallowed in the principle that "everyone in Nigeria, male and female, is protected against any discrimination be it direct or indirect by the state or any person on grounds including, gender, sex or any other attribute."[54] The respect for the dignity of the human person and equality before the law are outlined in Sections 17 and 34 of the Constitution. The policy framework for the rights of women in the country flows from the comprehensive CEDAW, among other international documents relating to the respect of women's rights. Some of these are the African Charter on Human and Peoples' Rights, International Covenant on Civil and Political Rights, Beijing Platform of Action of 1995, among others.[55]

Despite the foregoing public commitments to promote women's rights in Nigeria, the response of the state and its agencies in the country prove otherwise. The Violence against Persons Prohibition (VAPP) Act of 2015 tackles the issues of sexual violence, physical violence, psychological violence, and socio-economic violence on women. Further, VAPP alludes to the problems of "forceful ejection from home, harmful widowhood practices, female genital cutting, and other harmful traditional practices."[56] For instance, the National Crime Victimization and Safety Survey for 2013 reported that 30 percent of male and female respondents in the country claimed to have been victims of domestic violence.[57]

Additionally, the nation's penal code permits husbands to use physical means to discipline or punish their wives as long as it does not result in "grievous harm," which is defined as loss of sight, hearing, speech, facial disfigurement, or life-threatening injuries.[58] Unfortunately, law enforcement agents frequently refuse to intervene in domestic disputes. Likewise, in rural areas, courts and police seldom intervene to protect women who dare to accuse their husbands of abuse if the alleged abuse did not exceed local, religious, patriarchal, or customary norms.[59]

The issue of equal pay for equal work for men and women is problematic globally. In Africa and Nigeria, the cultural role of women is that of a homemaker. This function, especially in rural Nigeria, tends to devalue women and their worth in the society. Women, also, are marginalized and discriminated against economically, particularly in the private sector. They suffer from bigotry in the areas of employment, promotion to higher professional position as bosses, and frequently denied parity and equity in salary allocation with men.[60] Even so, Article 15 of the African Charter on Human and Peoples' Rights advocates equal pay for equal work for men and women.[61] Article 23(2) of the Universal Declaration of Human Rights states: "Everyone without any discrimination has the right to equal pay for equal work."[62] The government, despite its international human rights obligations, is culpable of not adhering fully to the foregoing human rights principles.

Tables 1 and 2 in Amnesty International Nigeria 2019 report are major illustrations of the republic's obligations to international human rights treaties.[63] Nigeria's signatories to the documents listed in the tables signify her commitment to be a major partner with the rest of the world in the promotion of human rights. Another important dimension of these tables is that human rights campaigners could reference them in their struggles against the government and its law enforcement agencies when they flout and violate the human rights of Nigerian citizens. For example, Amnesty International, Human Rights Watch, and other national human rights organizations could use these sources to argue their cases on behalf of human rights victims in courts and elsewhere.

Nigeria's 1999 constitutional provisions on human rights, the NAPPPHRN 2006, and her obligations to uphold international and African human rights contraptions are impressive. Nevertheless, the preceding critiques on human rights infractions in the republic suggest that it is one thing to proclaim and approve human rights regimes, and quite another to implement them. Thus, given Nigeria's weak record on implementing human rights are there possible solutions that might help ameliorate and mitigate her performance? If so, what might they be to advance peaceful coexistence in the Fourth Republic? Against the background of the foregoing quarries, I would advocate the adoption of the principle of good governance, and the grooming and mentoring of transformational leaders in the Fourth Republic.

GOOD GOVERNANCE

Notionally, there exists a symbiotic or reciprocal relationship between the practice of good governance and respect for human rights. A [supplementary] second hypothesis is that the practice of good governance will promote the "good political life," facilitate political stability in the society,[64] and further peaceful coexistence in the Fourth Republic. Consequently, I shall in the proceeding analyses attempt the following: (1) expatiate tersely on the concept good governance and (2) expound briefly on why its praxis could mollify human rights infractions in the polity and a priori further political stability in the Fourth Republic.

Generally, good governance is both a goal and a process. Rajesh Tandon and Kumi Naidoo explained that the practice of good governance, among other things, subsumes the following features and attributes:

1. Universal protection of human rights
2. Laws that are implemented in a non-discriminatory manner
3. An efficient, impartial, and quick judicial system
4. Transparent public agencies
5. Accountability for decisions made about public issues and resources
6. Devolution of resources and decision-making power to [communities] in rural and urban areas, and
7. Participation and inclusion of all citizens in debating public policies and choices.[65]

Additionally, Maurice A. Coker and Ugumanim B. Obo affirm that "good governance implies governing on the basis of equity, and social justice, and an end to corruption, nepotism and political manipulation of public institutions."[66] M. I. Obadan alludes to the following attributes as critical for advancing good governance: (1) accountability, (2) transparency, (3) predictability in government behavior, (4) openness in government transactions, and (5) observance of the rule of law.[67] Ditto the foregoing views on good governance by the United Nations Economic and Social Commission for Asia and the Pacific.[68]

The preceding summaries of the definitions and explications of good governance are not comprehensive or absolute. However, they provide sufficient superstructure from which to continue with the discourses on why good governance is necessary for Nigeria and how its practice should improve the regime's ability to tackle human rights abuses in the republic. The debate is not on whether the implementation of good governance principles is good for the polity. Most members of the informed public concur with the notion that its praxis is significant for the society. The problem, however, is that the application of the values of good governance regimes for the promotion of human rights in Nigeria has been elusive in part because of the political character of its superintendents and custodians of power.

Indeed, several conferences have been held in Nigeria to discuss how to wrestle with the problems of bad governance and how to superimpose it with the philosophies and perspectives of good governance. Frequently, the discourses produced excellent outcomes and models for solving the conundrum produced by dreadful governance. Regrettably, however, the templates produced for good governance ostensibly clash with the political, ideological, economic, and social interests of the major political actors and the subordinate administrators of the government.[69]

The converse of good governance is bad governance that tends to trigger injustice, abuse of human rights, and incitation of political instability that has been the bane of the Fourth Republic. Indeed, P. N. Nkwi provides the following as the traits of bad governance: (1) excessive personalization of power evidenced by a personality cult, tendency toward building up ethnocratic or family power, consideration of public property as a personal estate; (2) denial of fundamental human rights, limitation of press freedom, freedom of speech, and freedom of association; (3) predominance of illegitimate governments without accountability to anybody; (4) generalized corruption engineered by the elite with an excessive appetite to grab wealth at all cost.[70]

If good governance, as contended earlier, is quintessential for promoting human rights in Nigeria, what are its key rudiments that political actors should imbibe and apply in the Fourth Republic? The Economic and Social Commission for Asia and the Pacific recommends some basic attributes that might further the good governance project and a priori further human rights practice in Nigeria. These are political participation, rule of law, transparency, responsiveness, equity, inclusiveness, among others.[71]

The preceding suppositions are useful in the exposition of ways for promoting good governance and human rights in Nigeria. For this disquisition and chapter, however, I will briefly discuss three essential aspects of the good governance model, as they relate to improving human rights practices and promoting political stability and peaceful coexistence in the Fourth Republic. These are the rule of law, transparency, and accountability. My essential argument is that it is urgent for the guardians of the state to examine these areas and exhortations because they have the propensity to advance the practice of good governance and human rights.

Rule of Law

Generally, the rule of law provides a legal framework that accentuates the supremacy of the law and restricts the discretionary power of the state's political pillars. Additionally, it stresses the protection of individual (as well as group) rights from the arbitrary interference of government aficionados and its agencies. Moreover, it requires the full protection of human rights, especially those of marginalized citizens and minorities.[72] In Nigeria, the discourse on the rule of law is hegemonic within civil society, among human rights academics and practitioners. Even so, the result of the pressure brought to bear on the superintendents of power to live up to the objectives of the nation's constitution on human rights has been limited; and, indeed, it leaves much to be desired. The government's failures to observe the rule of law with enthusiasm obstruct the good governance process and project.[73] The regime's defaults on the rule of law also impede efforts to implement the inspiring canons on human rights contained in the inspiring and comprehensive NAPPPHRN, 2006.

If Nigeria is to succeed in promoting the principles of good governance in the federation, an efficacious enforcement of the rule of law is a necessity. This is so because it strengthens the exercise of human rights and furthers the system's legitimacy so critical in the Fourth Republic. The application of the rule of law represents one of the areas under consideration for promoting the good governance project and human rights in the republic. What about transparency and accountability in the discourse on good governance, and how their execution could mitigate human rights infractions in Nigeria?

Transparency and Accountability

Generally, transparency implies that official government policies that affect citizens should be accessible to the public. Furthermore, the acquirement of information on public policies made and passed by the government is possible through a Freedom of Information Act or by other legal and practical means. Accountability and transparency are symbiotic.

Accordingly, I collapsed both concepts in my critique. In short, accountability flows from transparency and vice versa. Transparency makes it possible for governments, private institutions, civil society organizations, and so on to be accountable to the public on activities that affect their lives and society, as for example, national security issues. The outcome of the policy of transparency and accountability furthers good governance, respect for human rights, and public support for the regime. This is so because overall citizens, and especially pertinent civil society groups, can freely check on the efficacy of the administration's policies. They can also demand corrective measures in cases of malfeasance and human rights infractions.[74] Conversely, the absence of transparency and accountability opens the system for inefficient policies and other vices that could stultify good governance and respect for human rights.

Regrettably, the principles of bad governance have characterized Nigeria's political system since it gained home rule in 1960 from Britain. Inefficient governance practice was problematized by the periodic incursions of military juntas. The country has also had ineffective and despotic leaders who in their governance techniques never practiced transparency and accountability. Little wonder, then, that to address the foregoing issues, General Muhammadu Buhari—now the current president—once expressed his frustration at the lack of transparency and accountability in the republic. In a lecture he delivered at the Arewa House Conference Hall in Kaduna, over two decades ago, he affirmed:

> It is an understatement to say that there has been a clear lack of accountability in the conduct of public affairs in the country. The public service, as the executive agency of the government of the day at the various levels–at federal, state and local levels–wield enormous powers. . . . [However], the public has virtually no knowledge or control over what they do in a regime when the public has no representatives in a legislature because a legislative assembly does not exist. With such ignorance and in the absence of legislative monitoring, control of public officers and ensuring accountability become impossible tasks for the public. . . . The last time the annual financial account of the Federal Government was prepared and submitted for audit was, I understand, in 1980. [In addition], at the 1984 Conference of Auditor-General of the Federation and State Directors of Audit, [the accountants] revealed to the astonishment of no one that eleven states last submitted their annual account for audit in 1967.[75]

The preceding accounts on the issues of transparency and accountability suggest that the path to developing good governance principles and the exercise of the respect for human rights are complex but necessary to move the country forward in the Fourth Republic. It is, however, reassuring that the instrumentalities for achieving this objective already exist. These are the national constitution, the NAPPPHRN, and her obligations and signatories to international human rights instruments. What remains is for leadership to develop the political pluck to practice transparency, accountability, and the execution of human rights canons.

The enforcement of human rights in the society will happen if the federation produces transformational leaders—another recommended solution on how to move the republic forward in the Fourth Republic. This is possible because transformational leaders are more disposed to collaborating with civil society groups to promote the praxis of good governance and human rights in Nigeria. This is the case because civil society organizations have traditionally been in the forefront in agitating for a political system capable of providing all Nigerian citizens with sufficient enablement for their daily survival. Civil society groups are, therefore, more open to working with transformational leaders. What, then, are the attributes of transformational and effective leaders in Nigeria and Africa?

TRANSFORMATIONAL AND EFFECTIVE LEADERSHIP

To paraphrase an argument made elsewhere, Nigeria—as well as the rest of Africa—does not lack well-articulated templates for solving Nigeria's political and developmental problems. It is lamentable, however, that her leaders lack the political will to implement the frameworks effectively.[76] For example, Nigeria needs transformational chiefs at the national, state, and local levels of government if the country is to exculpate itself from its current political, economic, and social quagmires. These transformational leaders are expected to imbue the characteristics of transformational leaders portrayed in the superbly crafted Mombasa Declaration and the Code of African Leadership. The Mombasa Manifesto, which I have liberally reproduced because the Code's guidelines are spot on, declares:

> Good leaders globally guide governments of nation-states to perform effectively for their citizens. They deliver high security for the state and the person; a functional rule of law; education; health; and a framework conducive to economic growth. They ensure effective arteries of commerce and enshrine personal and human freedoms. They empower civil society and protect the environmental commons. Crucially, good leaders also provide their citizens with a sense of belonging to a national enterprise of which everyone can be proud. They knit rather than unravel their nations and seek to be remembered for how they have bettered the real lives of the governed rather than the fortunes of the few.[77]

If the foregoing attributes are essential elements that a transformational leader in Nigeria should imbibe, what then are some negative leadership qualities of poor leaders that Nigerian leaders should eschew? The Mombasa Manifesto declared, among other things, the following:

> Less benevolent, even malevolent, leaders deliver far less by way of performance. Under their stewardship, roads fall into disrepair, currencies depreciate and real prices inflate, health services weaken, life expectancies slump, people go hungry, schooling standard fall, civil society becomes more beleaguered, the quest for personal and national prosperity slows, crime rates accelerate, and overall security becomes more tenuous. Corruption grows. Funds flow out of the country into hidden bank accounts. Discrimination against minorities (and occasionally majorities) becomes prevalent.[78]

Transformational leaders, critical for preparing Nigeria for her renaissance in the Fourth Republic, need a thorough education on the dogmas of the Code of African Leadership. Indeed, the Code affirms that "[Nigerian] leaders serve their peoples and nations best when they offer true vision of national growth and advance justice and dignity for all; encourage wider participation that includes minorities and majorities; promote professionalism and deep respect for national constitution that includes abiding by term limits; demonstrate leadership by example; advance transparency and accountability in their governance technique; show their belief in the rule of law; implement policies aimed at vanquishing poverty and promoting respect for human rights and civil liberties; and support for peaceful transfer of power."[79]

In sum, in the Fourth Republic, the leadership cadres that Nigeria needs are transformational and effective leaders. These leaders are those who have absorbed the leadership characteristics and values enshrined in the outstanding Mombasa Declaration and Code of African Leadership template. Imbued with patriotism and self-confidence, having imbibed the preceding leadership etiquettes, Nigeria's political trailblazers would adhere to the principles of good governance. Accordingly, these nationalists, with political courage, can implement human rights dogmas with enthusiasm. These are human rights doctrines outlined in the national constitution; the splendidly crafted NAPPPHRN, and international human rights contrivances, essential for Nigeria's political, economic, and social rebirth in the Fourth Republic.

NOTES

1. E. Ike Udogu, "Human Rights and Minorities in Africa: A Theoretical and Conceptual Overview," *Journal of Third World Studies*, Vol. XVIII, No. 1 (Spring 2001), p. 89.

2. Sambuddha Ghatak and E. Ike Udogu, "Human Rights Issues of Minorities in Contemporary India: A Concise Analysis," *Journal of Third World Studies*, Vol. 29, No. 1 (Spring 2012), p. 204.

3. Udogu, "Human Rights and Minorities in Africa: A Theoretical and Conceptual Overview," p. 97.

4. *National Action Plan for the Promotion and Protection of Human Rights in Nigeria* (Abuja, Nigeria: Federal Republic of Nigeria, 2006), p. 4.

5. *National Action Plan for the Promotion & Protection of Human Right*, 2006, p. 4.

6. *National Action Plan for the Promotion & Protection of Human Rights*, 2006, p. 8.

7. Ifeanyi I. Onwuazombe, "Human Rights Abuse and Violations in Nigeria: A Case Study of the Oil-producing Communities in the Niger Delta Region," *Annual Survey of International and Comparative Law*, Vol. 22, No. 1 (2017), pp. 119–120.

8. Onwuazombe, "Human Rights Abuse and Violence in Nigeria: A Case Study of the Oil-producing Communities in the Niger Delta Region," pp. 121–122 and 126–128; Adetoro R. Adenrele and Omiyefa M. Olugbenga, "Challenges of Human Rights Abuses in Nigerian Democratic Governance – Which Way Forward?" *Journal of Social Economic Research*, Vol. 1, No. 5 (2014), p. 89; Anthony O. Osuji, George N. Duru, and Anselem C. Okechukwu, "The Impasse of Democracy and Human Rights Abuse in Nigeria 1999–2019," *Global Journal of Applied Management and Social Sciences*, Vol. 17 (August 2019), pp. 96 & 102.

9. Ikechukwu B. Ozoigbo, "Democracy and Human Rights in Nigeria: A Critical Inquiry," *Global Journal of Arts, Humanities and Social Sciences*, Vol. 5, No. 5 (June 2017), p. 29.

10. Adenrele and Olugbenga, "Challenges of Human Rights Abuses in Nigerian Democratic Governance: Which Way Forward?" p. 89.

11. Human Rights Watch World Report, Nigeria: Events of 2019, p. 1. http://www.hrw.org/world-report/2020/country-chapters/nigeria (Retrieved 11/12/20).

12. Emmanuel O. Ojo, "Human Right and Sustainable Democracy in Nigeria 1999–2003," *Journal of Social Sciences*, Vol. 13, No. 1 (2006), p. 23.

13. *Universal Declaration of Human Rights, 1948*. https://www.un.org/en/universal-declaration-human-rights/index.html (Retrieved 11/14/20).

14. *United Nations Human Rights: Office of the High Commissioner, International Covenant on Civil and Political Rights*, 1976. https://www.ohchr.org/EN/ProfessionalInterest/Pages/CCPR.aspx (Retrieved 11/14/20).

15. *African Charter on Human and Peoples' Rights*, 1986. https://www.achpr.org/legalinstruments/detail?id=49 (Retrieved 11/12/20).

16. *National Action Plan for the Promotion & Protection of Human Rights in Nigeria*, p. 12.

17. E. Ike Udogu, *Examining Human Rights Issues and the Democracy Project in Sub-Saharan Africa: A Theoretical and Prospects for Progress in the Millennium* (Lanham, MD: Lexington Books, 2018), pp. 151–152.

18. *National Action Plan for the Promotion and Protection of Human Rights in Nigeria*, p. 14.

19. Ndubuisi J. Madubuike-Ekwe and Olumide K. Obayemi, "Assessment of the Role of the Nigerian Police Force in the Promotion and Protection of Human Rights in Nigeria," *Annual Survey of International & Comparative Law*, Vol. 23, No. 1, Article 3 (2019), pp. 19–20.

20. *United States Department of State, Bureau of Democracy, Human Rights and Labor*, Nigeria 2019 Human Rights Report, p. 16. www.state.gov/wp-content/uploads/2020/02/NIGERIA-2019-HUMAN-RIGHTS-REPORT.PDF (Retrieved 11/12/20)

21. *Universal Declaration of Human Rights*. http://www.un.org/en/universal-declaration-human-rights-/index.htm (Retrieved 11/14/20).

22. *United Nations Convention against Torture and Other Cruel, Inhuman or Degrading Treatment or Punishment*. https://unhcr.org/en-us/protection/migration/49e479d10/convention-against-torture-other-cruel-inhuman-degrading-treatment-punishment.html (retrieved 11/14/20).

23. *National Action Plan for the Promotion and Protection of Human Rights in Nigeria*, p. 26.

24. Adenrele and Olugbenga, "Challenges of Human Rights Abuses in Nigerian Democratic Governance: Which Way Forward?" p. 90.

25. *Nigeria 2019 International Religious Freedom Report*. www.State.gov/wp-content/uploads/2020/05/NIGERIA-2019-INTERNATIONAL-RELIGIOUS-FREEDOM-REPORT.pdf (Retrieved 11/13/2020).

26. *UN Convention against Torture and Other Cruel, Inhuman or Degrading Treatment or Punishment*.

27. *United Nations Human Rights Office of the High Commissioner, International Covenant on Civil and Political Rights*.

28. *National Action Plan for the Promotion and Protection of Human Rights in Nigeria*, p. 28.

29. Udogu, *Examining Human Rights Issues and the Democracy Project in Sub-Saharan Africa: A Theoretical Critique and Prospects for Progress in the Millennium*, pp. 159–160.

30. *Human Rights Watch World Report: Events of 2019*.

31. *Human Rights Watch World Report: Events of 2019*.

32. *United States Department of State, Bureau of Democracy, Human Rights and Labor*, Nigeria 2019 Human Rights Report, pp. 20–21.

33. *Universal Declaration of Human Rights, 1948*.

34. *International Covenant on Civil and Political Rights, 1966 and 1986*, https://ohchr.org/en/professional/interest/pages/ccpr.aspx (Retrieved 11/12/20).

35. Udogu, *Examining Human Rights Issues and the Democracy Project in Sub-Saharan Africa: A Theoretical Critique and Prospects for Progress in the Millennium*, p. 152.

36. *Universal Declaration of Human Rights*, 1948.

37. *African Charter on Human and Peoples' Rights, 1981 and 1986*, https://achpr.org/legalinstruments/detail?id=49 (Retrieved 11/12/20).

38. United States Department of State, Bureau of Democracy, Human Rights and Labor, Nigeria 2019 Human Rights Reports, pp. 22–23; Udogu, *Examining Human*

Rights Issues and the Democracy Project in Sub-Saharan Africa: A Theoretical Critique and Prospects for Progress in the Millennium, pp. 160–161.

39. *Time*, "The Nigerian Army Shot Dead at Least 12 Peaceful Protesters in Lagos, Rights Group Says." https://www.Time.com/5902112/Nigeria-3ndsars-protest-shortings (Retrieved 11/15/20); "CNN stands by its report on Lekki shooting documentary." https://www.bodedolu.com/cnn-stands-by-its-report-on-the-lekki-shooting-documentary/ (Retrieved 11/20/20); See "Nigerian army admits to having live rounds at Lekki Toll Gate protests, despite previous denials." https://www.cnn.com/2020/11/21/africa/nigeria-shooting-lekki-toll-gate-intl/index.html (Retrieved 11/22/20).

40. *National Action Plan for the Promotion and Protection of Human Rights in Nigeria*, p. 38.

41. E. Ike Udogu, "The Allurement of Ethnonationalism in Nigerian Politics: The Contemporary Debate," *Journal of Asian and African Studies*, Vol. XXIX, Nos. 3–4 (July–October 1994), pp. 159–160.

42. Udogu, "The Allurement of Ethnonational in Nigerian Politics: The Contemporary Debate," pp. 165–166.

43. *National Action Plan for the Promotion & Protection of Human Rights in Nigeria*, pp. 40–52.

44. *National Action Plan for the Promotion and Protection of Human Rights in Nigeria*, p. 40.

45. *National Action Plan for the Promotion and Protection of Human Rights in Nigeria*, p. 54.

46. Adenrele and Olugbenga, "Challenges of Human Rights Abuses in Nigerian Democratic Governance – Which Way Forward?" p. 91.

47. Ikenna Onyido, "Nation-building and the Nigerian University" USA/Africa Dialogue Series November 8, 2020.

48. E. Ike Udogu, "Religion, Patriarchy and Feminist Epistemology on Women's Human Rights in the Developing World: The Contemporary Discourse." A Paper Presented at the 28th Conference of the Global Awareness Society International, Marrakech, Morocco in May 2019, pp. 1–14.

49. *UN Convention on the Elimination of All Forms of Discrimination Against Women*. https://www.ohchr.org/en/professionalinterest/pages/cedaw.aspx (Retrieved 11/16/20).

50. *United States Department of State, Bureau of Democracy, Human Rights and Labor*, Nigeria 2019 Human Rights Report, pp. 37–40.

51. *International Covenant on Civil and Political Rights*. https://www.ohchr.org/en/professionalinterest/pages/ccpr.aspx (Retrieved 11/1/20).

52. *Universal Declaration of Human Rights, 1948.*

53. *African Charter on Human and Peoples' Rights, 1981 and 1986.*

54. *National Action Plan for the Promotion and Protection of Human Rights in Nigeria*, p. 65.

55. *National Action Plan for the Promotion and Protection of Human Rights in Nigeria*, p. 65.

56. *United States Department of States, Bureau of Democracy, Human Rights and Labor*, Nigeria 2019 Human Rights Report, p. 29; Violence Against Persons

(Prohibition) Act, 2015, pp. 1–33. https://ilo.org/dyn/natlex/docs/ELECTRONICS/104156/126946/f-1224509348/NGA104156.pdf (Retrieved 11/2/20).

57. *United States Department of State, Bureau of Democracy, Human Rights and Labor*, Nigeria 2019 Human Rights Report, pp. 30–31.

58. Udogu, *Examining Human Rights Issues and the Democracy Project in Sub-Saharan Africa: A Theoretical Critique and Prospects for Progress in the Millennium*, p. 163.

59. *United States Department of State, Bureau of Democracy, Human Rights and Labor*, Nigeria 2019 Human Rights Report, p. 31; Udogu, "Religion, Patriarchy and Feminist Epistemology on Women's Human Rights in the Developing World: The Contemporary Discourse," pp. 18–22.

60. Udogu, *Examining Human Rights Issues and the Democracy Project in Sub-Saharan Africa: A Theoretical Critique and Prospects for Progress in the Millennium*, p. 163; E. Ike Udogu, "National Constitution and Human Rights Issues in Africa," *African and Asian Studies*, Vol. 2, No. 2 (2003), pp. 101–123.

61. *African Charter on Human and Peoples' Rights, 1981 and 1986.*

62. *Universal Declaration of Human Rights, 1948.*

63. See Nigeria: Human Rights Agenda, Amnesty International, May 31, 2019, pp. 5–7. https://www.amnesty.org/en/documents/afr44/0431/2019/en/ (Retrieved 10/25/21)

64. E. Ike Udogu, "Reviving Democracy and Good Governance in Nigeria's Current Politics: A Conceptual Analysis," *Africa Quarterly*, Vol. 44, No. 2 (August 2004), p. 76.

65. Rajesh Tandon and Kumi Naidoo, "What is Good Governance? NGOs in the Field and Beyond," 1994. https://www.oneword.org.org/ecpdm/pubs/govahk.htm (Retrieved 11/21/20)

66. Maurice A. Coker and Ugumanim B. Obo, "Crisis of governance and the violations of human rights: The Nigerian Experience, 1999 to 2007," *African Journal of Political Science and International Relations*, Vol. 6, No. 3 (March 2012), p. 64.

67. M. I. Obadan, *The State, Leadership, Governance and Economic Development* (Ibadan: The National Centre for Economic Management and Administration, 1998), pp. 24–25.

68. Coker and Obo, "Crisis of governance and the violations of human rights: The Nigerian Experience, 1999 to 2007," p. 65.

69. P. N. Nkwi, "Democracy and Good Governance," *International Centre for Applied Social Research and Training*, (1999), pp. 1–3. https://www.unesco.org/most/p95nkwi.html (Retrieved 11/22/20)

70. Nkwi, "Democracy and Good Governance," p. 3.

71. *Economic and Social Commission for Asia and the Pacific*, "What is Good Governance?" https://www.unescap.org/huset/gg/governance.htm (Retrieved 11/22/20).

72. Joseph Takougang, "The Future of Human Rights in Sub-Saharan Africa," in John M. Mbaku (ed.), *Preparing Africa* for the Twenty-First Century: Strategies for Peaceful Coexistence and Sustainable Development (Aldershot, UK: Ashgate Publishing Limited, 1999), pp. 177–197.

73. Udogu, "Reviving Democracy and Good Governance in Nigeria's Current Politics: A Concise Analysis," p. 80.

74. E. Ike Udogu, "The Struggle for Stability in Nigeria's Contemporary Politics (1990–1999) and Lessons for the Fourth Republic," in John M. Mbaku and E. E. Saxena (eds.), *Africa at the Crossroads: Between Regionalism an Globalization* (Westport, CT: Greenwood Publishing Group Inc., 2004), pp. 372–373.

75. A. Madugba, "Buhari Regrets Ousting Shagari Government," *The News*, May 18, 1998; Udogu, "Reviving Democracy and Good Governance in Nigeria's Current Politics: A Concise Analysis," p. 83.

76. E. Ike Udogu, "Rethinking Development Strategies in Africa: The Triple Partnership as an Alternative Approach: A Case of Uganda," *Africa Today*, Vol. 58, No. 4 (2012), p. 142.

77. Robert I. Rotberg, *Africa: Progress and Problems of Governance and Leadership in Africa* (Philadelphia, PA: Mason Crest Publishers, 2007), p. 34; E. Ike Udogu, "The Issue of Political Leadership in the Third World: What is to be done?" *Journal of Third World Studies*, Vol. XXV, No. 1 (2008), p. 18; K. Morrell and J. Hartley, "A Model of Political Leadership," *Human Relations*, Vol. 59, No. 4 (2006), pp. 483–504.

78. Rotberg, *Africa: Progress and Problems of Governance and Leadership in Africa*, p. 34; Udogu, "The Issue of Political Leadership in the Third World: What is to be done?" p. 18.

79. Udogu, "The Issue of Political Leadership in the Third World: What is to be done?" p. 19; Code of African Leadership, Mombasa, 20 March 2004. https://www.worldpeacefoundation.org/ALC.code%20of%African%leadership (Retrieved 1/16/21)

Bibliography

Abang, Mercy. "Nigeria's Medical Brain Drain: Healthcare Woes as Doctors Flee." *Al Jazeera News*, April 8, 2019.

Abayomi, Tunde. "Non-Governmental Organizations in the Protection and Promotion of Human Rights in Africa: Critique of Approach and Methods." In Awa U. Kalu and Yemi Osinbajo (eds), *Perspectives on Human Rights* (Lagos, Nigeria: Federal Ministry of Justice, 1992).

Abdulkarim, A. A., R. M. Ibrahim, A. O. Fawi, O. A. Adebayo, and A. W. B. R. Johnson. "Vaccine and Immunization, the Past, Present and Future in Nigeria." *Nigerian Journal of Pediatrics*, Vol. 38, No. 4 (2011), pp. 186–194.

Abonsade, O., and R. J. Mundt. *Politics in Nigeria* (New York: Longman Publishers, 2020).

Achebe, C. *The Trouble With Nigeria* (London, UK: Heinemann Press, 1983).

Adebayo, Angela. "Fake Medicine in Nigeria—When Drugs Don't Work." *Inventa International*, February 21, 2017.

Adebisi, Yusuff Adebayo, Joshua Ottah Umah, Omotayo Carolyn Olaoye, Aishat Jumoke Alaran, and Ayomide Busayo Sina-Odunsi. "Assessment of Health Budgetary Allocation and Expenditure Toward Achieving Universal Health Coverage in Nigeria." *International Journal of Health Life Science*, Vol. 6, No. 2 (2020). https://sites.kowsarpub.com/ijhls/articles/102552.

Adenrele, Adetoro, and Omiyefa M. Olugbenga. "Challenges of Human Rights Abuses in Nigerian Democratic Governance—Which Way Forward?" *Journal of Social Economic Research*, Vol. 1, No. 5 (2014), pp. 87–96.

Adepoju, Paul. "A Breakdown of Nigeria's 2020 Budget for Health." *HealthNews. NG*, January2, 2020. http://www.researchgate.net/publication/a-break-down-of-nigerias-2020-budget-for-health.

Agbese, Pita O., and E. Ike Udogu. "Taming of the Shrew: Civil-Military Politics in the Fourth Republic." In E. Ike Udogu (ed.), *Nigeria in the Twenty-First Century: Strategies for Political Stability and Peaceful Coexistence* (Trenton, NJ: Africa World Press, 2005).

Agbese, Pita O., E. Ike Udogu, and Georgia K. Kieh, Jr. (eds). *Reconstructing the Authoritarian State in Africa* (Melton Park, UK: Routledge Publishers, 2018).

———. "Sanitizing Democracy in Nigeria." *TransAfrica Forum*, Vol. 9, No. 1 (1992), pp. 41–45.

———. "The Impending Political Demise of Nigeria's Forthcoming Third Republic." *Africa Today*, Vol. 37, No. 3 (1990), pp. 23–44.

———. *The State in Africa: Beyond False Starts* (Chicago, IL: Third World Publishers, 2014).

Aidoo, Akwasi. "Africa: Democracy Without Human Rights?" *Human Rights Quarterly*, Vol. 15 (1993), pp. 703–715.

Ajimotokan, Adeteju. "Korea Jostles for Slice of Nigeria's $1B Medical Tourism Spending." *This Day*, March 21, 2019. https://www.thisdaylive.com/index.php/2019/03/21/korea-jostles-for-slice-of-nigerias-1b-medical-tourism-spending/.

Aka, Philip C. *Genetic Counseling and Preventive Medicine in Post-Bosnia* (London, UK: Palgrave Macmillan Publishers, 2020).

———. *Human Rights in Nigeria's External Relations: Building the Record of Moral Superpower* (Lanham, MD: Lexington Books, 2016).

———. "The Dividend of Democracy: Analyzing U.S. Support for Nigerian Democratization." *Boston College Third World Law Journal*, Vol. 22, No. 2 (2002), pp. 225–279.

———. "The Need for an Effective Policy of Ethnic Reconciliation." In E. Ike Udogu (ed.), *Nigeria in the Twenty-First Century: Strategies for Political Stability and Peaceful Coexistence* (Trenton, NJ: Africa World Press, 2005).

Akamere, F. A. A. *Issues and Concepts in Government and Politics of Nigeria* (Lagos, Nigeria: Olu-Abbey Modern Press, 2001).

Ake, Claude. *Democracy and Development in Africa* (Washington, DC: Brookings Institution, 1996).

———. "Rethinking African Democracy." *Journal of Democracy*, Vol. 2, No. 1 (1991), pp. 32–44.

Alston, Philip. "Revitalizing United Nations Development." *Melbourne University Law Review*, Vol. 18 (1991), pp. 216–257.

———. "The UN's Human Rights Record: From San Francisco to Vienna and Beyond." *Human Rights Quarterly*, Vol. 16 (1994), pp. 375–390.

Alubo, Ogoh, and Vitalis Hunduh. "Medical Dominance and Resistance in Nigeria's Healthcare System." *International Journal of Health Services*, Vol. 47, No. 4 (2017), pp. 778–794.

Alubo, S. O. "Human Rights and Militarism in Nigeria." In George W. Shepherd, Jr., and Mark O. C. Anikpo (eds), *Emerging Human Rights: The African Political Economy Context* (Westport, CT: Greenwood Press, 1990).

Aluko, Alajide. "The Organization of African Unity and Human Rights." *Round Table*, Vol. 283 (July 1981), pp. 234–242.

Ambrose, B. P. *Democratization and the Protection of Human Rights in Africa: Problems and Prospects* (Westport, CT: Praeger, 1995).

Aminzade, R. *Race, Nation, and Citizenship in Postcolonial Africa: The Case of Tanzania* (Cambridge, UK: Cambridge University Press, 2015).

Amman, B. "Nigeria's Rocky Road to a Third Republic." *Swiss Review of World Affairs*, Vol. 39, No. 2 (1989), pp. 28–39.

Amoah, Philip. "The African Charter on Human Rights and Peoples' Rights." *African Journal of International and Comparative Law*, Vol. 4, No. 1 (March 1992), pp. 226–240.

An-Naim, Abdullahi Ahmed (ed.). *Human Rights in Cross-Cultural Perspectives: A Quest for Consensus* (Philadelphia, PA: University of Pennsylvania Press, 1992).

Aregbeshola, Bolaji S. "A Tax-Based, Noncontributory, Health Financing System Can Accelerate Progress Toward Universal Health Coverage in Nigeria." *MEDIC Review*, Vol. 20, No. 4 (2018), pp. 40–45.

Aregbeshola, Bolaji S., and Samina M. Khan. "Predictors of Enrolment in the National Health Insurance Scheme Among Women of Reproductive Age in Nigeria." *International Journal of Health Policy Management*, Vol. 7, No. 11 (2018), pp. 1015–1023.

Asante, S. K. B. "Nation Building and Human Rights in Emergent African Nations." *Cornell International Law Journal*, Vol. 2 (Spring 1967), pp. 72–107.

Awolowo, Obafemi. *Path to Nigerian Freedom* (London, UK: Faber and Faber, 1947).

Ayida, A. *The Rise and Fall of Nigeria* (London, UK: Malthouse House Press, 1990).

Badawi El-Sheikh, Ibrahim. "African Commission on Human and Peoples' Rights and Prospects and Problems." *Netherland Quarterly*, Vol. 7 (1992), pp. 120–134.

Balogun, Joseph A. *Health Professions in Nigeria: An Interdisciplinary Analysis* (London, UK: Palgrave Macmillan Publishers, 2021).

———. *Healthcare Education in Nigeria: Evaluation and Emerging Paradigms* (Milton Park, UK: Routledge Publishers, 2020).

———. *Nigerian Healthcare System: Roadmap to Universal and High Quality Healthcare* (New York: Springer Nature, 2021).

Bamidele, O. *Nigeria's Third Republic* (Huntington, NY: Nova Science Publishers, 1999).

Bassey, C. "Retrospect and Prospects of Political Stability in Nigeria." *African Studies Review*, Vol. 32, No. 1 (1989), pp. 97–113.

Beckman, B., and H. Jega. "Scholars and Democratic Politics in Nigeria." *Review of African Political Economy*, Vol. 22, No. 64 (1995), pp. 167–181.

Bello, Emmanuel G. "Human Rights: The Rule of Law in Africa." *International and Comparative Law Quarterly*, Vol. 30 (July 1981), pp. 628–637.

Benedek, Wolfgang. "The African Charter and Commission on Human and Peoples' Rights: How to Make it More Effective." *Netherland Quarterly Journal of Human Rights*, Vol. 11, No. 1 (1993), pp. 25–40.

Biebricher, T. *Political Theory of Neoliberalism* (Stanford, CA: Stanford University Press, 2019).

Bondzie-Simon, E. "A Critique of African Charter on Human Rights and Peoples' Rights." *Harvard Law Journal*, Vol. 31 (1988), pp. 407–430.

Bratton, M., and V. W. Nicolas. *Democratic Experiments in Africa: Regime Transitions in Comparative Perspective* (Cambridge, UK: Cambridge University Press, 2002).

Bunch, C. "Women's Rights as Human's Rights." *Human Rights Quarterly*, Vol. 12 (1990), pp. 486–498.

Butts, K. H., and S. Metz. *Armies and Democracy in the New Africa: Lessons From Nigeria and South Africa* (Carlisle, PA: US Army War College, 1996).

Campbell, I. *Nigeria's Continuing Crisis: The Quest for Democratic Order* (London, UK: Research Institute for the Study of Conflict and Terrorism, 1995).

Carlsson, Ingvar, and Anne-Marie Lindgren. *What is Social Democracy?* (Stockholm: Arbetarrorelsen Tankosmedja, 2007).

Carothers, Thomas. *Critical Mission: Essays on Democracy Promotion* (Washington, DC: Carnegie Endowment for International Peace, 2004).

Chambers, Simone. "Democracy, Popular Sovereignty and Constitutional Legitimacy." *Constellation*, Vol. 11, No. 2 (June 2004), pp. 163–173.

Chua, A. *World on Fire: How Exporting Free Market Democracy Breeds Ethnic Hatred and Global Instability* (New York, NY: Anchor Books, 2004).

Cohen, J. "Minimalism About Human Rights: The Most We Most We Can Hope For?" *Journal of Political Philosophy*, Vol. 12 (2004), pp. 190–213.

Cohen, Ribin, Goran Hyden, and Winston P. Nagan (eds). *Human Rights and Governance in Africa* (Gainesville, FL: University Press of Florida, 1993).

Conteh-Morgan, E. *Democratization in Africa: The Theory and Dynamics of Political Transition* (Westport, NJ: Praeger Publishers, 1997).

Dada, J. Abiodun. "The Significance and Limits of NGOs in Human Rights Protection in Nigeria." *Journal of Law, Policy and Globalization*, Vol. 19 (2013), pp. 82–92.

Deng, Francis M., and Lyons Terrence. "Promoting Responsible Sovereignty in Africa." In F. M. Deng and T. Lyons (eds), *African Reckoning: A Quest for Good Governance* (Washington, DC: Brookings Institution, 1998).

Diamond, L., A. Kirk-Greene, and O. Oyediran (eds). *Developing Democracy: Toward Consolidation* (Baltimore, MD: The Johns Hopkins Press, 1999).

———. "Nigeria in Search of Democracy." *Foreign Affairs*, Vol. 62 (1984), pp. 914–921.

———. "The Global State of Democracy." *Current History*, Vol. 99, No. 641 (2000), pp. 413–418.

———. "The Quality of Democracy: An Overview." *Journal of Democracy*, Vol. 15, No. 4 (2004), pp. 20–31.

———. *Transition Without End: Nigerian Politics and Civil Society Under Babangida* (Boulder, CO: Lynne Rienner, 1997).

Diamond, Larry. "Beyond Authoritarianism and Totalitarianism: Strategies for Democratization." *The Washington Quarterly*, Vol. 12, No. 1 (1989), pp. 141–163.

Dicker, Richard. "Monitoring Human Rights in Africa." *Journal of Modern African Studies*, Vol. 29 (1991), pp. 505–510.

Dlamini, C. R. M. "The Violation of Human Rights in Africa: A Lesson for South Africa?" *South African Journal of Human Rights*, Vol. 7 (1991), pp. 291–303.

———. "Towards Regional Protection of Human Rights in Africa: The African Charter on Human and Peoples' Rights." *Comparative and International Law Journal of Southern Africa*, Vol. 24 (1991), pp. 189–203.

Donnelly, Jack. "Human Rights and Human Dignity: An Analytical Critique of Non-Western Conceptions of Human Rights." *American Political Science Review*, Vol. 76, No. 2 (June 1982), pp. 303–316.

Ejobowah, John. *Competing Claims to Recognition in the Nigerian Public Sphere: A Liberal Argument About Justice in Plural Societies* (Lanham, MD: Lexington Books, 2008).

———. "Constitutional Design and Conflict Management in Nigeria." *Journal of Third World Studies*, Vol. 18, No. 2 (2001), pp. 143–160.

Ekechi, F. K. "Perceiving Women as Catalyst." *Africa Today*, Vol. 43, No. 3 (1996), pp. 235–249.

Elaigwu, J. I. *The Shadow of Religion on Nigerian Federalism, 1960–93* (Abuja, Nigeria: NCIR Monograph Series No. 3, 1993).

Elu, J. "Human Development in sub-Saharan Africa: Analysis and Prospects for the Future." *Journal of Third World Studies*, Vol. XVII, No. 2 (2000), pp. 53–71.

Enahoro, P. *The Complete Nigeria* (Lagos, Nigeria: Malthouse Press, 1992).

Enwerem, I. M. *A Dangerous Awakening: The Politicization of Religion in Nigeria* (Ibadan, Nigeria: IFRA Publishers, 1995).

Etannibi, A. "Policy and Perception of Police in Nigeria." *Police Studies*, Vol. 11, No. 4 (1988), pp. 205–206.

Eyoh, D. "African Perspectives on Democracy and the Dilemmas of Post-Colonial Intellectuals." *Africa Today*, Vol. 45, Nos. 3–4 (1998), pp. 281–306.

Falola, T., and M. M. Heaton. *A History of Nigeria* (Cambridge, UK: Cambridge University Press, 2008).

——— (ed.). *Nigeria in the Twentieth Century* (Durham, NC: Carolina Academic Press, 2002).

———. *The History of Nigeria* (Westport, CT: Greenwood Press, 1999).

———. "The Nigerian Condition: Which Way Out (4), USA/Africa Dialogue Series." https://www.newtimes.com.ng/2021/08/01/9790-the-nigerian-condition-the-way-out/.

———. *Violence in Nigeria: The Crisis of Religious Politics and Secular Ideology* (Rochester, NY: University of Rochester Press, 1998).

Fanon, F. *Black Skin, White Masks* (London: Penguin Classics, 2021).

Fatton, Robert, Jr. "Liberal Democracy in Africa." *Political Science Quarterly*, Vol. 105, No. 3 (1990), pp. 455–473.

Forrest, T. *Politics and Economic Development in Nigeria* (Boulder, CO: Westview Press, 1995).

Frank, Thomas M. *Human Rights in Third World Perspective* (Dobbs Ferry, NY: Oceana Publications, 1982).

Friedman, M., and R. D. Friedman. *Free to Choose: A Personal Statement* (St. Paul, MN: Paw Prints, 2008).

Gill, Simone V., Misha Vessali, Jacob A. Pratt, Samantha Watts, Janey S. Pratt, Preeti Raghavan, and Jeremy M. DeSilva. "The Importance of Interdisciplinary Research Training and Community Dissemination." *Clinical Translational Science*, Vol. 8, No. 5 (2015), pp. 611–614.

Graf, W. "Issues and Substance in the Prescription of Liberal Democratic Forms of Nigeria's Third Republic." *African Affairs*, Vol. 88, No. 350 (1989), pp. 91–100.

Grindle, M. S., and J. W. Thomas. *Public Choices and Policy Change: The Political Economy of Reform in Developing Countries* (Baltimore, MD: Johns Hopkins Press, 1994).

Hayek, F. A. *The Road to Serfdom* (London: Institute of Economic Affairs, 2004).

Herbst, J. "Political Liberalization in Africa After Ten Years." *Comparative Politics*, Vol. 33, No. 3 (2001), pp. 357–375.

———. *States and Power in Africa: Comparative Lessons in Authority and Control* (Princeton, NJ: Princeton University Press, 2000).

Horowitz, D. L. *Ethnic Groups in Conflict* (Berkeley, CA: University of California Press, 2011).

Howard, Rhoda. "The Dilemma of Human Rights in Sub-Saharan Africa." *International Journal*, Vol. 35, No. 4 (Autumn 1980), pp. 724–747.

Huntington, S. P. *The Third Wave: Democratization in the Late Twentieth Century* (Normal, OK: University of Oklahoma Press, 1993).

Hyden, G. *African Politics in Comparative Perspective* (New York: Cambridge University Press, 2013).

Ibelema, M. "Nigeria: The Politics of Marginalization." *Current History*, Vol. 99, No. 211 (2000), pp. 211–214.

Ighobor, Kingsley. "Diagnosing Africa's Medical Brain Drain: Higher Wages and Modern Facilities are Magnets for Africa's Health Workers." *African Renewal*, December 2016–March 2017.

Igiebor, G. Osariyekemwen. "Political Corruption in Nigeria: Implications for Economic Development in the Fourth Republic December 16, 2019." https://doi.org/10.11777/0169796X19890745.

Iheduru, O. M. *The Politics of Economic Restructuring and Democracy in Africa* (Westport, CT: Greenwood Press, 1999).

Ihonvbere, Julius O. "A Balance Sheet of Africa's Transition to Democratic Governance." In John M. Mbaku and Julius O. Ihonvbere (eds), *The Transition to Democratic Governance in Africa: The Continuing Struggle* (Westport, CT: Praeger, 2003), pp. 33–55.

———. *Africa and the New World Order* (New York: Peter Lang, 1999).

———. *Dismantling the Leviathan: Constitutionalism and the National Question in Nigeria* (Lagos, Nigeria: Lagos State University, 2001).

———. "The State of Human Rights in Africa." *Contribution in Economics and Economic History*, No. 219 (2001), pp. 101–120.

Ikein, A. A. *The Impact of Oil on Developing Country: The Case of Nigeria* (New York: Praeger Press, 1990).

Ikime, O. (ed.). *Groundwork of Nigerian History* (Ibadan, Nigeria: University of Ibadan Press, 1980).

Ilesanmi, S. O. "Constitutional Treatment of Religious and the Politics of Human Rights in Nigeria." *African Affairs*, Vol. 100, No. 40 (2001), pp. 529–540.

Jega, Attahiru M. "Civil Society and the Sustainability of Democracy in Nigeria: Challenges of 2003 Election." http://www.gamji.com/NEWS2219.htm.

———. "Restructuring the Nigerian Federation: Challenges and Prospects." A Presentation Delivered as the No, 4 in the Public Lecture Series of Nasarawa State University, Kefi, on Wednesday August 4, 2021.

Joseph, Richard A. *Democracy and Prebendal Politics in Nigeria: The Rise and Fall of the Second Republic* (Cambridge: Cambridge University Press, 1987).

Kalu, Kelechi A., Nwabufo O. Uzodike, David Kraybill, and John S. Moolakkatu. *Economic Development and Nigerian Foreign Policy* (Lewiston, NY: Edwin Mellen Press, 2000).

———. *Peacebuilding in Africa: The Post-Conflict State and its Multidimensional Crisis* (Lanham, MD: Lexington Books, 2021).

———. "Political Economy in Nigeria: The Military, Ethnic Politics and Development." *International Journal of Politics, Culture and Society*, Vol. 10, No. 2 (1996), pp. 387–404.

———. *Territoriality, Citizenship, and Peacebuilding: Perspective on Challenges to Peace in Africa* (London, UK: Adonis and Abbey Publishers Ltd, 2013).

Khan, S. A. *Nigeria: The Political Economy of Oil* (Oxford: Oxford University Press, 1994).

Kieh, George K., Jr. *Beyond State Failure and Collapse: Making the State Relevant in Africa* (Lanham, MD: Lexington Books, 2007).

———. "Democratization and Peace in Africa." *Journal of Asian and African Studies*, Vol. 31, Nos. 1–2 (1996), pp. 99–111.

———. "Liberal Democratization and Democracy." In E. Ike Udogu (ed.), *The Developing World: Critical Issues in Politics and Society* (Lanham, MD: Scarecrow Press, 2012), pp. 1–22.

———. "The Travails of Democratization in Africa." In George K. Kieh, Jr. (ed.), *Africa and the Third Millennium* (Trenton, NJ: Africa World Press, 2008).

Koehn, P. "Comparative Transition to Civilian Rule: Nigeria's First and Second Experiments." *Journal of Modern African Studies*, Vol. 27, No. 2 (1989), pp. 33–43.

Kukah, M. H., and T. Falola. *Religious Militancy and Self Assertion: Islam and Politics in Nigeria* (Aldershot, UK: Avery Press, 1996).

Lewis, P. "Endgame in Nigeria? The Politics of Failed Democratic Transition." *African Affairs*, Vol. 93, No. 372 (1994), pp. 323–340.

Lewis, P. M., P. T. Robinson, and B. R. Rubin. *Stabilizing Nigeria: Sanctions, Incentives, and Support for Civil Society* (New York: Council on Foreign Relations and the Century Foundation, 1998).

Lindberg, Staffan I. *Elections and Democracy in Africa* (Baltimore, MD: Johns Hopkins University Press, 2006).

Madubuike-Ekwe, Ndubisi J., and Olumide K. Obayemi. "Assessment of the Role of Nigerian Police Force in the Promotion and Protection of Human Rights in Nigeria." *Annual Survey of International & Comparative Law*, Vol. 23, Issue 1, Article 3 (2019), pp. 19–48.

Magnarella, Paul J. "Preventing Interethnic Conflict and Promoting Human Rights Through More Effective Legal, Political, and Aid Structure: Focus on Africa." *Georgia Journal of International and Comparative Law*, Vol. 23 (1993), pp. 327–345.

Mahmud, S. "The Failed Transition to Democratic Rule in Nigeria: Its Implication for Democracy and Human Rights." *Africa Today*, Vol. 40, No. 4 (1993), pp. 87–95.

Mahmud, S. S. "The State and Human Rights in Africa in the 1990s: Perspectives and Prospects." *Human Rights Quarterly*, Vol. 15 (1993), pp. 485–498.

Maier, K. *This House Has Fallen: Nigeria in Crisis* (London: Penguin Books, 2002).

Makoba, J. *Rethinking Development Strategies in Africa: The Triple Partnership as an Alternative Approach: The Case of Uganda* (New York: Peter Lang, 2012).

Mama, A. "Feminism or Femocracy? State Feminism and Democratization in Nigeria." *African Development*, Vol. 20, No. 1 (1995), pp. 35–58.

Mamdani, M. *The Making of Citizen and Subject in Contemporary Africa* (Princeton, NJ: Princeton University Press, 1996).

Manias, Elizabeth. "Effects of Interdisciplinary Collaboration in Hospitals on Medication Errors: An Integrative Review." *Expert Opinion Drug Safety*, Vol. 17, No. 3 (2018), pp. 259–275.

Marenin, O. "Policing Nigeria: Control and Autonomy in the Exercise of Coercion." *Journal of African History*, Vol. 28, No. 1 (1985), pp. 73–93.

Martin, Anne B., Micah Hartman, Benjamin Washington, Aaron Catlin, and National Health Expenditure Accounts Team. "National Healthcare Spending in 2017: Growth Slows to Post-Great Recession Rates: Share of GDP Stabilizes." *Health Affairs*, Vol. 38, No. 1 (2018), pp. 10–1377.

Matthew, K. "The OAU and Political Economy of Human Rights in Africa: An Analysis of the African Charter on Human and Peoples' Rights." *Africa Today*, Vol. 34 (1987), pp. 85–104.

Mbachu, O. "Capitalism, Socialism, and Democracy: A Nigerian Perspective." *Coexistence: A Review of East-West and Development Issues*, Vol. 27 (1990), pp. 187–197.

Mbaku, John M. "Constitutionalism and the Transition to Democratic Governance in Africa." In John M. Mbaku and Julius O. Ihonvbere (eds), *The Transition to Democratic Governance in Africa: The Continuing Struggle* (Westport, CT: Praeger, 2003).

———. *Multiparty Democracy and Political Change: Constraints to Democratization in Africa* (Trenton, NJ: Africa World Press, 2006).

Mbanaso, Michael U., and Chima J. Korieh (eds). *Minorities and the State in Africa* (Amherst, NY: Cambria Press, 2010).

McDougall, Gay J. "International Law, Human Rights, and Namibian Independence." *Human Rights Quarterly*, Vol. 8 (1986), pp. 443–470.

Meribole, Emmanuel C., Olusesan Ayodeji Makinde, Akin Oyemakinde, Kolawole Azeez Oyediran, Akinyemi Atobatele, Fadeke A. Fadeyibi, Aderemi Azeez, et al. "The Nigerian Health Information System Policy Review of 2014: The Need, Content, Expectations, and Progress." *Health Information and Libraries Journal*, Vol. 35, No. 4 (December 2018), pp. 285–297.

Merkel, Wolfgang. *Social Democracy in Power: The Capacity to Perform* (London: Taylor and Francis, 2008).

Millar, Abi. "The Rise of Fake Medicine in Africa." *Journalist Portfolio*, December 28, 2019. https://abimillar.com/2019/12/28/the-rise-of-fake-medecine-in-africa/.

Mojekwu, Chris C. "International Human Rights: The African Perspective." In Jack L. Nelson and Vera M. Green (eds), *International Human Rights: Comparative Issues* (Stanfordville, NY: Human Rights Group, 1980), pp. 85–95.

Motala, Ziyad. "Human Rights in Africa: A Cultural, Ideological and Legal Examination." *Hastings International and Comparative Law Review*, Vol. 12 (1989), pp. 373–410.

Mower, A. Glenn, Jr. "Human Rights in Black Africa: A Double Standard?" *Human Rights Journal*, Vol. 9, No. 1 (1976), pp. 39–70.

Muanya, Chukwuma. "Why 15% Budget Allocation to Health is Tall Order, FG." *The Guardian Lagos*, October 26, 2020.

Muhammad, Faisal, Jamil Hassan Abdulkareem, and A. B. M. Alauddin Chowdhury. "Major Public Health Problems in Nigeria: A Review." *South East Asia Journal of Public Health*, Vol. 7, No. 1 (2017), pp. 6–11.

Ndegwa, S. N. "A Decade of Democracy in Africa." *Journal of Asian and African Studies*, Vol. 36, No. 1 (2000), pp. 1–16.

Nkwankwo, Clement. "The OAU and Human Rights." *Journal of Democracy*, Vol. 4 (1992), pp. 50–54.

Nnoli, O. *Ethnicity and Development in Nigeria* (Aldershot, UK: Ashgate Publishing Company, 1995).

Nolushungu, N. C. "Fragments of Democracy: Reflections on Class and Politics in Nigeria." *Third World Quarterly*, Vol. 12, No. 1 (1990), pp. 86–115.

Nore, P., and T. Turner (eds). *Oil and Class Struggle* (London, UK: Zed Press, 1980).

Nwabueze, B. O. *Nigeria: Political Crisis and Solutions* (Ibadan, Nigeria: Spectrum Books, 1994).

Nwankwo, C. C., D. Mbachu, and B. Ugochuku. *Human Rights Practices in Nigerian Police* (Lagos, Nigeria: Constitutional Rights Project, 1993).

Nwokedi, E. "Nigeria's Democratic Transition: Explaining the Annulled 1993 Presidential Election." *Round Table*, No. 330 (1994), pp. 189–204.

Nwosu, O. *The African Woman: Nigerian Perspective* (Lagos, Nigeria: Bima Publications, 1999).

Obansa, S. A. J., and Akinnagbe Orimisan. "Healthcare Financing in Nigeria: Prospects and Challenges." *Mediterranean Journal of Social Sciences*, Vol. 4, No. 1 (January 2013), pp. 221–236.

Obembe, Taiwo A., Ademola T. Olajide, and Michael C. Asuzu. "Managerial Dynamics Influencing Doctor-Nurse Conflicts in Two Nigerian Hospitals." *Journal of Family Medicine and Primary Care*, Vol. 7, No. 4 (2018), pp. 684–692.

Odeyemi, Isaac A. O., and John Nixon. "Assessing Equity in Health Care Through the National Health Insurance Schemes of Nigeria and Ghana: A Review-Based Comparative Analysis." *International Journal of Equity Health*, Vol. 22 (2013).

Odunsi, Bennett A. "Law Enforcement Issues and Strategies for Reformation." In E. Ike Udogu (ed.), *The Developing World: Critical Issues in Politics and Society* (Lanham, MD: Scarecrow Press, 2012).

———. "Police and Human Rights Infractions: The Need for Reform." In E. Ike Udogu (ed.), *Nigeria in the Twenty-First Century: Strategies for Political Development and Peaceful Coexistence* (Trenton, NJ: Africa World Press, 2005).

———. "The Impact of Leadership Instability on Democratic Process in Nigeria." *Journal of Asian and African Studies*, Vol. 31, Nos. 1–2 (1996), pp. 66–81.

———. *The Role of Ombudsman in Nigeria: Redress of Grievance* (Lewiston, NY: Edwin Mellen Press, 2007).

Ogundipe, Sola, Chioma Obinna, and Gabriel Olawale. "Shortage of Medical Personnel: Tougher Times Ahead for Nigerians (1)." *Vanguard Newspaper, Lagos*, January 27, 2015.

Ojo, Emmanuel O. "Human Rights and Sustainable Democracy in Nigeria 1999–2003." *Journal of Social Sciences*, Vol. 13, No. 1 (2006), pp. 15–29.

Ojo, Olusola, and Amadu Sesay. "The OAU and Human Rights: Prospects for the 1980s and Beyond." *Human Rights Quarterly*, Vol. 8 (1986), pp. 89–103.

Ojo, Temitope O., and Adebowale F. Akinwumi. "Doctors as Managers of Healthcare Resources in Nigeria: Evolving Roles and Current Challenges." *Nigeria Medical Journal*, Vol. 56, No. 6 (2015), pp. 375–380.

Okafor, Victor O. *Nigeria's Stumbling Democracy, and its Implications for Africa's Movements* (Westport, CT: Praeger Security International, 2008).

Okebukola, Peter O., and William R. Brieger. "Providing Universal Health Insurance Coverage in Nigeria." *International Quarterly of Community Health Education* (2016), pp. 1–6.

Okeke, O. *Hausa-Fulani Hegemony: The Dominance of the Muslim North in Contemporary Nigerian Politics* (Enugu, Nigeria: Acena Publishers, 1992).

Okere, B. Obinna. "The Protection of Human Rights in Africa and the African Charter on Human and Peoples' Rights: A Comparative Analysis With the European and American Systems." *Human Rights Quarterly*, Vol. 6 (1984), pp. 141–159.

Okereke, C. "Police Power and Law Enforcement Tactics: The Case of Nigeria." *Police Studies*, Vol. 15, No. 3 (1992), pp. 107–117.

Okome, M. O. "Women, the State, and the Travails of Decentralizing the Nigerian Federation." *West Africa Review*, Vol. 2, No. 1 (2000), pp. 1–19.

Okunola, Akindare. "Five Facts Every Nigerian Should Know About Our Healthcare." *Global Citizen*, September 9, 2020.

Olagunju, T., A. Jinadu, and S. Oyovbare. *Transition to Democracy in Nigeria 1985–1993* (Ibadan, Nigeria: Spectrum Press, 1993).

Olajide, Ademola T., Michael C. Asuzu, and Taiwo A. Obembe. "Doctor-Nurse Conflict in Nigerian Hospitals: Causes and Modes of Expression." *British Journal of Medicine & Medical Research*, Vols. 9, 10 (2015), pp. 1–12.

Olaopa, Tunji. "Opinion: Ibrahim Badamasi Babangida (IBB) in the Eye of History." http://www.newstimes.com.ng/2021/08/13/10275-ibrahim-badamasi-babangida-ibb-in-the-eye-of-history/.

Oleribe, Obinna O., Iheaka Paul Ezieme, Olabisi Oladipo, Ezinne Patience Akinola, Deborah Udofia, and Simon D. Taylor-Robinson. "Industrial Action by HCWs in Nigeria in 2013–2015: An Inquiry into Causes, Consequences and Control—A Cross-Sectional Descriptive Study." *Human Resource Health*, Vol. 14, No. 1 (2016), p. 46.

Olupona, J. K., and T. Falola (eds). *Religion and Society in Nigeria Historical and Sociological Perspective* (Ibadan, Nigeria: Spectrum Press, 1991).

Onadipe, A. "Nigeria's Trouble Years." *Contemporary Review*, Vol. 267, No. 3 (1995), pp. 230–236.

Onasanya, Adeola A. "Increasing Health Insurance Enrolment in the Informal Economic Sector." *Journal of Global Health*, Vol. 10, No. 1 (June 2020).

Onigbinde, Oluseum, et al. "Nigeria Health Budget Analysis, Policy Brief in First Quarter (2018)." https://yourbudgit.com/wp-content/uploads/2018/04/Nigeria-Health-Analysis.pdf.

Onwuazombe, Ifeanyi I. "Human Rights Abuse and Violations in Nigeria: A Case Study of the Oil-Producing Communities in the Niger Delta Region." *Annual Survey of International and Comparative Law*, Vol. 22, No. 1 (2017), pp. 115–160.

Onyeji, Ebuka. "Analysis: Why Nigeria's Vision 20: 2020 Was Bound to Fail." *Premium Times*, January 19, 2020.

Onyemaechi, N. O. C., and Uchenna R. Ofoma. "The Public Health Threat of Road Traffic Accidents in Nigeria: A Call for Action." *Annals of Medical and Health Sciences Research*, Vol. 6, No. 4 (2016), pp. 199–204.

Ophori, Endurance A., Musa Y. Tula, Azuka V. Azih, Rachel Okojie, and Precious E. Ikpo. "Current Trends in Immunization in Nigeria: Prospects and Challenges." *Tropical Medicine & Health*, Vol. 42, No. 2 (June 2014), pp. 67–75.

Osaghae, Eghosa O. *Crippled Giant: Nigeria Since Independence* (London, UK: C. Hurst & Co. Publishers, 1998).

———. "Ethnic Minority and Federalism in Nigeria." *African Affairs*, Vol. 90, No. 359 (1991), pp. 237–258.

———. "Human Rights and Ethnic Conflict Management: The Case of Nigeria." *Journal of Peace Research*, Vol. 33, No. 2 (1996), pp. 171–181.

———. "The Ogoni Uprising: Oil Politics, Minority Agitation and the Future of Nigerian States." *African Affairs*, Vol. 94, No. 376 (July 1995), pp. 325–344.

Osia, K. "Leadership and Followership: Nigeria's Problems of Governance." *Scandinavian Journal of Development Alternatives*, Vol. 11, Nos. 2–3 (1992), pp. 175–194.

Osoba, S. O. "Corruption in Nigeria: Historical Perspective." *Review of African Political Economy*, Vol. 23, No. 29 (1996), pp. 371–386.

Osuji, Anthony O., George N. Duru, and Anselem C. Okechukwu. "The Impasse of Democracy and Human Rights Abuse in Nigeria 1999–2019." *Global Journal of Applied Management and Social Sciences*, Vol. 17 (August 2019).

Ottaway, M. *Africa's New Leaders: Democracy of State Reconstruction*? (Washington, DC: Carnegie Endowment for International Peace, 1999).

———. "Democratization in Collapse States." In W. I. Zartman (ed.), *Collapsed State: The Disintegration and Restoration of Legitimate Authority* (Boulder, CO: Lynne Rienner, 1995).

——— (ed.). *Democracy in Africa: The Hard Road Ahead* (Boulder, CO: Lynne Rienner, 1997).

Oyovbaire, S. E. *Federalism in Nigeria: A Study of the Development of the Nigerian State* (London: Macmillan Press, 1985).

Ozoigbo, Ikechukwu B. "Democracy and Human Rights in Nigeria: A Critical Inquiry." *Global Journal of Arts, Humanities and Social Sciences*, Vol. 5, No. 5 (June 2017), pp. 25–31.

Paden, J. N. *Nigerian Muslim Perspectives on Religion, Society, and Communication With the Western World* (Washington, DC: Office of Research U.S. Information Agency, 1990).

Palmberg, M. *National Identity and Democracy in Africa* (Pretoria, SA: Human Science Research Council, 2000).

Pandey, G. "The Subaltern as Subaltern Citizens." *Economic and Political Weekly*, Vol. 4, No. 46 (2006), pp. 4735–4741.

Parpart, Jane L. (ed.). "Women's Rights and the Lagos Plan of Action." *Human Rights Quarterly*, Vol. 8 (1986), pp. 180–196.

Paul James C. N. "Participatory Approaches to Human Rights in Sub-Saharan Africa." In Abdullahi A. An-Na'im and Francis N. Deng (eds), *Human Rights in Africa: Cross-Cultural Perspectives* (Washington, DC: Brookings Institution, 1990), pp. 213–239.

———. "Rural Development, Human Rights, and Constitutional Order in Sub-Saharan Africa." *Third World Legal Studies* (1989), pp. 57–84.

Peet, R., and E. Harwick. *Theories of Development: Contentions, Arguments, Alternatives* (New York: The Guilford Press, 2015).

Rahim, I. M. Abdel, Aze Abdeen, B. A. Faki, A. E. Mustafa, and S. Nalder. "Introducing Training in Primary Healthcare Program Management into the Curriculum." *Medical Education*, Vol. 21, No. 4 (1978), pp. 288–292.

Rembe, N. Selasini. *Africa and Regional Protection of Human Rights: A Study of the African Charter on Human and Peoples' Rights: Its Effectiveness and Impact on the African States* (Roma, Lesotho: Center for International Juridical Cooperation, 1985).

———. *The System of Protection of Human Rights under the African Charter on Human and Peoples' Rights: Problems and Prospects* (Roma, Lesotho: Institute of Southern African Studies, National University of Lesotho, 1991).

Rivara, Frederick. "The Effects of Violence on Health." *Health Affairs*, Vol. 38, No. 10 (October 2019), pp. 1622–1629.

Rodrik, D. "Understanding Economic Policy Reform." *Journal of Economic Literature*, Vol. 34, No. 1 (1996), pp. 9–41.

Samuel, H. U. *Public Policy Coordination in Nigeria* (National Kuru, Nigeria: Institute for Policy and Strategic Studies, 1992).

Sanusi, H. U. *Public Policy Coordination in Nigeria* (National Kuru, Nigeria: Institute for Policy and Strategic Studies, 1992).

Schaffer, Frederick C. *Democracy in Transition* (Ithaca, NY: Cornell University Press, 1998).

Shettima, K. H. "Engendering Nigeria's Third Republic." *African Studies Review*, Vol. 38, No. 3 (1995), pp. 61–98.

Sklar, R. L., and C. S. Whitaker. *Nigeria: Rivers of Oil, Trails of Blood, Prospects for Unity and Democracy* (Washington, DC: Center for Strategic and International Studies, 1996).

Sorensen, G. *Democracy and Democratization* (Boulder, CO: Westview Press, 1993).

Soyinka, W. *The Open Sore of a Continent: A Personal Narrative of the Nigeria Crisis* (New York: Oxford University Press, 1996).

Soyinka-Airewele, P. "Civil Society and Universities in the Democratization and Development Enterprise." In E. Ike Udogu (ed.), *Nigeria in the Twenty-First Century: Strategies for Political Stability and Peaceful Coexistence* (Trenton, NJ: Africa World Press, 2005).

———. "When Neutrality is Taboo: Navigating Institutional Identity in Protracted Conflict Settings—The Nigerian Ife/Modakeke Case." *African and Asian Studies*, Vol. 2, No. 3 (2003), pp. 259–305.

Stiglitz, J. *Globalization and its Discontent* (London: Penguin Books, 2017).

Suberu, R. T. "Can Nigeria's New Democracy Survive?" *Current History*, Vol. 100, No. 646 (2001), pp. 207–212.

———. *Federalism and Ethnic Conflict in Nigeria* (Washington, DC: United States Institute of Peace Press, 2001).

———. "The Democratic Recession in Nigeria." *Current History*, Vol. 93 (1994), pp. 213–218.

Sweetman, B. *Crisis of Democratic Pluralism: The Loss of Confidence in Reason and the Clash of Worldviews* (New York: Palgrave Macmillan Press, 2021).

Tignor, Robert L. "Political Corruption in Nigeria Before Independence." *Journal of Modern African Studies*, Vol. 31, No. 2 (June 1993), pp. 175–202.

Trevors, J. T., Gerald H. Pollack, Milton H. Saier, and Luke Masson. "Transformative Research: Definitions, Approaches and Consequences." *Theory Biosciences*, Vol. 131, No. 2 (2012), pp. 117–123.

Tripp, A. M. "Women and Democracy: The New Political Activism in Africa." *Journal of Democracy*, Vol. 12, No. 3 (2001), pp. 141–155.

Udogu, E. Ike. "A Concise Discourse on Human Rights Practices in Africa: The Case of Peripheral Population." *Southwestern Journal of International Studies*, Vol. 3, No. 1 (Spring 2009), pp. 103–124.

———. "An Examination of Minority Groups and Human Rights Issues in Europe and Africa." *Journal of Political Science*, Vol. 28 (2000), pp. 21–43.

———. "Ethnicity and Democracy in Sub-Saharan Africa." In John M. Mbaku (ed.), *Preparing Africa for the Twenty-First Century: Strategies for Peaceful Coexistence and Sustainable Development* (Aldershot, UK: Ashgate Publishing Company, 2001).

———. "Ethnicity, the State and the Issue of Nation-Building in Nigeria's Forthcoming Republic." *Scandinavian Journal of Development Alternatives and Area Studies*, Vol. 18, No. 4 (1999), pp. 5–22.

———. *Examining Human Rights Issues and the Democracy Project in Sub-Saharan Africa: A Theoretical Critique and Prospects for Progress in the Millennium* (Lanham, MD: Lexington Books, 2014).

———. "Human Rights and Minorities: A Theoretical Overview." In Paul T. Zeleza and Philip J. McConnaughay (eds), *Human Rights, the Rule of Law, and Development in Africa* (Philadelphia, PA: University of Pennsylvania Press, 2004).

———. "Human Rights Constraints: Analysis and Potential Solutions." In E. Ike Udogu (ed.), *The Developing World: Critical Issues in Politics and Society* (Lanham: MD: Scarecrow Press, 2012).

———. "Human Rights of Minorities in Africa: A Theoretical and Conceptual Overview." *Journal of Third World Studies*, Vol. 18, No. 1 (2001), pp. 87–104.

———. *Leadership and the Problem of Electoral Democracy in Africa: Case Studies and Theoretical Solutions* (Newcastle Upon Tyne, UK: Cambridge Scholars Publishing, 2016).

———. "Liberal Democracy and Federalism in Contemporary Politics." In Toyin Falola (ed.), *Nigeria in the Twentieth Century* (Durham, NC: Carolina Academic Press, 2002).

———. "National Constitutions and Human Rights Issues in Africa." *African and Asian Studies*, Vol. 2, No. 2 (2003), pp. 101–123.

———. "Political Leadership and Governance in Democratic Nigeria." *Africa Quarterly*, Vol. 40, No. 3 (2000), pp. 109–131.

———. "The Allurement of Ethnonationalism in Nigerian Politics: The Contemporary Debate." *Journal of Asian and African Studies*, Vol. XXIX, Nos. 3–4 (1994), pp. 160–171.

———. "Theoretical and Analytical Discourses on the Human Rights of Indigenous Peoples of Africa." In E. Ike Udogu (ed.), *Human Rights Dilemmas in the Developing World: The Case of Marginalized Populations at Risk* (Lanham, MD: Lexington Books, 2018).

Uwadibie, N. O. *Decentralization and Economic Development in Nigeria: Agricultural Policies and Implementation* (Lanham, MD: University Press of America, 2000).

———. "Oil and Microeconomic Policies in the Twenty-First Century." In E. Ike Udogu (ed.), *Nigeria in the Twenty-First Century: Strategies for Political Stability and Peaceful Coexistence* (Trenton, NJ: Africa World Press, 2005).

Uwadibie, N. O., and A. E. Luma. "Decentralization and Agricultural Policy: The Case of Nigeria, 1976–1993." *The Journal of African Policy Studies*, Vol. 3, No. 1 (1997), pp. 19–38.

Uwazurike, C. "Confronting Potential Breakdown: The Nigerian Re-Democratization Process in Critical Perspectives." *The Journal of Modern African Studies*, Vol. 31, Nos. 1–2 (1994), pp. 21–38.

Uya, E. (ed.). *Contemporary Nigeria: Essays in Society, Politics, and Economy* (Buenos Aires, Argentina: Edipublishers, 1992).

Uzochukwu, B. S. C., M. D. Ughasoro, E. Etiaba, C. Okwuosa, E. Envuladu, and O. E. Onwujekwe. "Healthcare Financing in Nigeria: Implication for Achieving Universal Health Coverage." *Nigerian Journal of Clinical Practice*, Vol. 18, No. 4 (July–August 2015), pp. 437–444.

Vaughan, Olufemi. "Assessing Grassroots Politics and Community Development in Nigeria." *African Affairs*, Vol. 94, No. 377 (1995), pp. 501–518.

———. *Chiefs, Power, and Social Change: Chiefships and Modern Politics in Botswana, 1880s–1990s* (Trenton, NJ: Africa World Press, 2003).

———. *Nigerian Chiefs, Traditional Power in Modern Politics* (Rochester, NY: University of Rochester Press, 2006).

———. "Religion and State Formation." In E. Ike Udogu (ed.), *Nigeria in the Twenty-First Century: Strategies for Political Stability and Peaceful Coexistence* (Trenton, NJ: Africa World Press, 2005).

———. *Religion and the Making of Nigeria* (Durham, NC: Duke University Press, 2016).

Wapshott, N. *Keynes Hayek: The Clash That Defined Modern Economics* (Royal Oaks, MI: Scribe Publications, 2014).

Weiss, T. G. "Governance, Good Governance and Global Governance: Conceptual and Actual Challenge." *International Organization*, Vol. 21, No. 5 (2017), pp. 389–408.

———. "The Politics of Humanitarian Ideas." *Security Dialogue*, Vol. 31, No. 1 (2000), pp. 11–23.

Welch, Claude E., Jr. "Human Rights and African Women: A Comparison of Protection Under Two Major Treaties." *Human Rights Quarterly*, Vol. 15 (1993), pp. 549–574.

——— (ed.). *NGOs and Human Rights: Promise and Performance* (Philadelphia, PA: University of Pennsylvania Press, 2001).

———. *Protecting Human Rights in Africa: Roles and Strategies of Non-Governmental Organization* (Philadelphia, PA: University of Pennsylvania Press, 1995).

———. "The OAU and Human Rights: Towards a New Definition." *Journal of Modern African Studies*, Vol. 19, No. 3 (September 1981), pp. 401–421.

———. "The Organization of African Unity and the Promotion of Human Rights." *Journal of Modern African Studies*, Vol. 29, No. 4 (1991), pp. 535–555.

Welch, Claude E., Jr., and Ronald I. Meltzer (eds). *Human Rights and Development in Africa* (Buffalo, NY: University of Buffalo Press, 1984).

Welcome, Menizibeya O. "The Nigerian Healthcare System: Need for Integrating Adequate Medical Intelligence and Surveillance Systems." *Journal of Pharmacy and Bio-Allied Sciences*, Vol. 3, No. 4 (2011), pp. 470–478.

Widner, J. A. *Economic Change and Political Liberation in Sub-Saharan Africa* (Baltimore, MD: Johns Hopkins Press, 1994).

William, D. C. "Assessing Future Democratic Accountability in Nigeria: Investigative Tribunals and Nigerian Political Culture." *Scandinavian Journal of Development Alternatives and Area Studies*, Vol. 11, Nos. 2–3 (1992), pp. 51–65.

Wiseberg, Laurie S. "Human Rights in Africa: Toward a Definition of the Problem of a Double Standard." *Issue*, Vol. 6 (1976), pp. 3–13.

World Health Organization. *Global Health Observatory (GHO) Data World Health Statistics 2016: Monitoring Health for the SDGs* (Geneva, Switzerland: World Health Organization, 2016).

Index

Page numbers followed by n indicate notes.

About the Contributors

Philip C. Aka is professor and former dean of the Faculty of Law at the International University of Sarajevo in Bosnia and Herzegovina. In Spring 2020, he was a visiting professor at the Southern Illinois University School of Law at Carbondale, Illinois. Dr. Aka is the author of *Genetic Counseling and Preventive Medicine in Post-War Bosnia* (Palgrave Macmillan, 2020) and of the award-winning book *Human Rights in Nigeria's External Relations: Building the Record of a Moral Superpower* (Lexington Books, 2017). He is a corresponding editor of *International Legal Materials*, published by Cambridge University Press and an associate editor of *Humanities and Social Sciences Communications*, an open-access online journal. Aka holds a PhD degree in political science from Howard University in Washington, DC, a JD degree from Temple University Beasley School of Law in Philadelphia, as well as LLM (summa cum laude) and SJD degrees from the Indiana University Robert H. McKinney School of Law at Indianapolis. He is a member of the Illinois State Bar.

Joseph A. Balogun, PhD, FAS, is a distinguished professor in the College of Health Sciences at Chicago State University, Chicago, USA; Emeritus Professor of Physiotherapy, and associate director of Research Development and Innovation at the University of Medical Sciences, Ondo State, Nigeria; and a visiting professor/program consultant at the Center for Excellence in Reproductive Health Innovation, University of Benin, Edo State, Nigeria. Professor Balogun is the deputy editor of the *African Journal of Reproductive Health* and serves on the Editorial Board of the *International Journal of Physiotherapy Theory and Practice*, *Journal of the Nigeria Society of Physiotherapy*, and *International University of Sarajevo Law Journal (IUS).*

Kelechi A. Kalu is vice provost for International Affairs and professor of Political Science, University of California, Riverside, California, and former provost for Global Strategies and International Affairs, Ohio State University, Ohio. Professor Kalu is the author of several books, book chapters, and articles. He is the author of *Agenda Setting and Public Policy in Africa*; *Economic Development and Nigerian Foreign Policy*; *Peacebuilding in Africa: The Post-Conflict State and Its Multidimensional Crisis*; *Socio-Political Scaffolding and the Construction of Change: Constitutionalism and Democratic Governance in Africa*; and *United States-Africa Security Relations*, to list a few.

George Klay Kieh, Jr., is dean of the Barbara Jordan-Mickey Leland School of Public Affairs and professor of Political Science at Texas Southern University, Houston, Texas. He was a former dean of the College of Arts and Sciences, University of West Georgia, Carrollton, Georgia, and professor of Political Science. He was also former dean of International Affairs; professor of Political Science and African and African American Studies at Grand Valley State University, Michigan; and former chair of the Department of Political Science and International Studies at Morehouse College, Atlanta, Georgia. Dr. Kieh, Jr., is the author of *Beyond State Failure and Collapse: Making the State Relevant in Africa*; *Africa and the New Globalization*; *The State in Africa: Issues and Perspectives*, and others. He has published several book chapters and articles, too. Dr. Kieh, Jr., is the current president of the African Studies and Research Forum (ASRF).

Bennett A. Odunsi is professor of Public Policy and Administration at Jackson State University, Jackson, Mississippi. His research interests are in public policy, justice studies, and ombudsman systems in the developing nations. He is the author of *The Role of the Ombudsman in Nigeria: Redress of Grievances*. He has also published articles in the *Journal of Third World Studies*, *Journal of Asian and African Studies*, and several book chapters. Dr. Odunsi has received several awards and recognitions for his service and scholarship including, but not limited to, Top's African-Centered Scholars of the Decade.

E. Ike Udogu is faculty fellow and professor of African, Comparative and International Politics at Appalachian State University, Boone, North Carolina. Dr. Udogu was a recipient of the Albert Nelson Marquis Lifetime Achievement Award and 2000 Outstanding Scholars of the 21st Century Honor. Dr. Udogu is the author of *Nigeria and the Politics of Survival as a Nation-State* (1997) and editor of *Nigeria in the Twenty-first Century: Strategies for Political Stability and Peaceful Coexistence* (2005). Dr. Udogu is also the author of *Examining Human Rights Issues and the Democracy Project in Sub-Saharan Africa: A theoretical Critique and Prospects for Progress in the Millennium*; *Human Rights in Islamic North Africa: Clashes between Constitutional Laws and Penal Codes*; and editor of *Human Rights Dilemmas in the Developing World: The Case of Marginalized Populations at Risk*, among others. He is the author of several book chapters and articles on Nigeria and Africa, and a former president of the Association of Third World Studies. He was a former director of Research and Publication, ASRF, during which time he received the Distinguished Leadership and Scholarship Award and African Excellence in Scholarship Honor, to list a few.

Olufemi Vaughan received his DPhil at Oxford University and is currently an endowed professor and professor of African Studies at Amherst College, New York. He has published several books including *Nigerian Chiefs—Traditional Power in Modern Politics, 1890s–1990s* (2000); *Tradition and Politics*: *Indigenous Political Structures in Africa*, inter alia. He is a recipient of the Distinguished Scholar's Award, Association of Global Studies; and he is a Woodrow Wilson Global Scholar.

Samuel Zalanga is a professor and chair of the Department of Sociology at Bethel University, St. Paul, Minnesota. He was the former editor of *Journal of Third World Studies* and currently the director of Research and Publication, ASRF. He was a recipient of the US Fulbright Fellowship for Teaching and Private Research, Nnamdi Azikiwe University, Awka, Anambra State, Nigeria. Professor Zalanga was a participant in the book project, *An Interdisciplinary Primer in African Studies*, and author of several articles and book chapters.

www.ingramcontent.com/pod-product-compliance
Ingram Content Group UK Ltd.
Pitfield, Milton Keynes, MK11 3LW, UK
UKHW042044051026
476324UK00002BA/179

9 781666 900491